Do Over Dogs

Give Your Dog a Second Chance for a First Class Life

Pat Miller, CPDT-KA, CDBC

Wenatchee, WA

Do Over Dogs
Give Your Dog a Second Chance for a First Class Life
Pat Miller

Dogwise Publishing
A Division of Direct Book Service, Inc.
403 South Mission Street, Wenatchee, Washington 98801
1-509-663-9115, 1-800-776-2665
www.dogwisepublishing.com / info@dogwisepublishing.com

Graphic design: Lindsay Peternell
Cover photograph: David Childs, www.DavidChildsPhotography.com
Interior photographs: Pat Miller, Lisa Waggoner, Cold Nose College; Barbara Davis, BADDogs, Inc.; Jessica Westermann/Jessica Rooney; Laura Dorfman, Kona's Touch; Mardi Richmond/Melanee Barash; MJ and Dale Williams; Nancy Fitzgerald; Sybil Schiffman; Humane Society of Washington County (MD); San Antonio (TX) Animal Control, Paul Miller, and Kristi Falteisek.

ISBN 978-1-929242-69-6

Library of Congress Cataloging-in-Publication Data
Miller, Pat, 1951 Oct. 14-
Do-over dogs : give your dog a second chance for a first-class life / by Pat Miller.
p. cm.
ISBN 978-1-929242-69-6
1. Dog adoption. 2. Dog rescue. 3. Dogs--Behavior. 4. Dogs--Training. I. Title.
SF427.M586 2010
636.7'0832--dc22
2010014585

Printed in the U.S.A.

Dedication

To all the Do-Over dogs in the world—and to the humans who know how to love them enough.

And to my wonderful husband, who brings home—and lets me bring home—our own personal Do-Over Dogs. And cats. And horses. And pigs.

Sturgis, the latest rescue in the Miller household.

Table of Contents

INTRODUCTION

This is a promising time for dogs in our culture. While some trainers and authors claim that we love our dogs too much in this country, treat them like humans, and spoil them, I think we are just beginning to love them enough. The number of dogs in shelters has decreased significantly in the last thirty-plus years, which means many fewer dogs die of homelessness each year. When I started working in animal protection in 1976, some 18-20 million "surplus" dogs and cats were euthanized each year. Today, in 2010, that number is three to four million. Still far too many, but certainly far fewer.

If it offends you to hear our beloved animal companions referred to as "surplus," rest assured that it offends me too. Yet that's exactly how they've been regarded—and treated—for much of the time I've worked with animals professionally. Not because those who work at animal shelters are callous, or don't care, but because they've had no choice. Shelter workers are often blamed when animals are euthanized—but the animal protection professionals I've worked with are among the most compassionate, caring people I know. It hurts their hearts every time they are compelled to euthanize healthy animals simply because there aren't enough homes.

And there aren't. Despite the claims of those who would argue that if shelters just tried harder they wouldn't have to euthanize any animals, the truth is that we aren't yet at the point where every animal can find the lifelong loving home that he or she deserves.

The "no-kill" movement has raised public awareness of the pet-overpopulation tragedy, but the solutions they offer are simplistic—a bright promise for a future time, but not yet a reality. While shelter workers try their hearts out to save the lives of the animals they care for, the simple truth is that until fewer puppies are born, and until more humans learn how to communicate with, and understand, and make a lifetime commitment to the dogs they adopt, our canine companions will continue to die at animal shelters for lack of homes.

So what does this have to do with Do-Over Dogs? There was a time when the animal protection profession believed that if we could just spay and neuter enough animals, the killing would stop. Indeed, turning off the faucet, or at least turning it down to a relative dribble, has greatly reduced the puppy population in many shelters around the country. But shelter kennels are still well-populated with adolescent and adult dogs who somehow failed to make the connection with the humans in their homes that would ensure a lifetime of love and care. Animal protection and rescue professionals have come to realize that the next important piece of the puzzle, if we are ever to have hope of resolving the tragedy of unwanted pets, is behavior—of both dogs and humans.

No one gets a dog with the intention of giving it up. But even the best of intentions may falter when the realities of responsible dog ownership hit home. Sometimes the human has unrealistic expectations of the dog. "She chews up everything in the house," one woman complains as she hands off the leash of her 16-week-old Shih-Tzu. "Oh, and she pees on the oriental carpet." Shelter workers bite their tongues to avoid responding with, "Well duh, she's a puppy—what did you expect? Did you even try to housetrain her?"

With leisure time at a premium in our society, some people just don't realize that they can't crate a dog routinely for ten hours a day while they're at work without suffering behavioral consequences. Tired from a hard day at the office, they come home to a soiled crate and a Border Collie who is bouncing off the walls with pent-up energy and poo-covered paws, insistent on playing with his humans. The humans just want a calm dog who will lie at their feet and gaze lovingly at them while they eat dinner and watch television. "Too hyper," they sigh as they surrender the eight-month-old dog dancing at the end of the leash.

Sometimes the behaviors that lead a dog to a shelter are more serious. A young couple tearfully gives up their five-year-old German Shepherd mix because he's growling at the new baby. For five years, Fritz was their "only child" and none of their friends had children, so Fritz was never socialized with small humans. They can't risk the safety of their human child, so Fritz must go.

Petunia, a striking brindle-and-white American Pit Bull Terrier, was picked up as a stray and given her name by shelter staff. Petunia is afraid of her own shadow. No one knows why, since she was a stray, but she trembles in the back of her kennel and avoids eye contact with all humans.

These are Do-Over Dogs. The shelter is now faced with trying to find permanent homes for a puppy who has learned that the entire house is her chew toy and that carpeting is to pee on; a high-energy herding dog who has had no training and who has been taught to soil his den; a large dog who has a history of being aggressive with children; and a poorly socialized dog who, in many circles, already has two strikes against her just by virtue of her breed.

The best shelters and rescues—those that recognize the important role that behavior plays in creating a permanent relationship and have the funding to do something about it—have behavior departments that work with dogs such as these to repair the damage done by unaware, unthinking or uncaring humans. The best rescue groups commit resources to behavior modification for the dogs who are in their kennels and foster homes. The best owners commit to sharing their hearts and homes with their dogs for life, and do whatever it takes to manage or modify their dogs' problematic behaviors.

As overall numbers of homeless dogs slowly decrease, more and more resources are available to help Do-Over Dogs—the ones who need and deserve—a second chance for a first class life. This book is intended to help that happen. As a culture, we don't yet love them too much. We just need to love them enough.

Chapter 1

Why Some Dogs Need a Do-Over

Some people adopt their new canine family member with no intention of taking on a project—but get one anyway. Others open their hearts and homes to a dog they know is damaged, hoping to give them a second chance at a first class life. There are numerous reasons why your own dog might need a Do-Over. He may have been abused or neglected before he joined your family. Perhaps you adopted your dog from a shelter or rescue group that saved him from a puppy mill or a hoarder environment. He might have been a stray, found running loose on the streets without his human. Maybe you've had him since he was a pup, but you realize now that you coulda-shoulda done things differently, and that you've inadvertently ended up with a canine family member who's not quite what you thought you ordered.

Whatever his history, somehow he ended up being under-socialized, reactive, aggressive, fearful, destructive, vocal, touch sensitive, or host to one of many other problematic behaviors.

Your choices now are:

- To live with and love your dog despite his undesirable behaviors.
- To try to rehome him—often a Herculean task for a dog with significant behavioral issues; you *love* him and are thinking of giving him up—why would someone who has no emotional connection to him want to take on your problem?
- To surrender or return him to a shelter or rescue group, at which time you must be honest about his behavior, knowing there's a good chance the organization will euthanize him.
- To take him to your own veterinarian for euthanasia.
- *Or* to make a serious commitment to work with him to manage and modify his behavior.

For your dog's sake—and yours—I hope you choose the last option, or barring that, the first one. While there are certainly some dogs who are beyond their peoples' ability or willingness to manage or modify unwanted behaviors, in the majority of cases there are things that can be done to improve the quality of life for dogs and their committed humans. Take Scooter, for example…

The dog with the unknown past

As I type, Scooter is curled up sleeping on a plaid blanket at my feet, peacefully unaware that one month ago he was less than 24 hours away from being euthanized at the shelter here in Washington County, Maryland, where my husband, Paul, happens to be the executive director. Scooter is a nine-pound Pomeranian. He failed the resource-guarding part of the shelter's behavior assessment.

The little dog was picked up as a stray in Hagerstown four months earlier, frightened and hungry, his golden coat matted to the skin. Overwhelmed by the chaos of the shelter environment, he huddled in the back of his kennel throughout his five-day stray holding period, avoiding eye contact with anyone who walked past.

On his third day I was at the shelter in my capacity as a volunteer, conducting behavioral assessments. Having had the good fortune of sharing my life at one time with an exceptional Pom, I'm drawn to the breed. When I saw Scooter I felt compelled to make his acquaintance. Entering his kennel slowly to avoid scaring him further, I sat on the floor and talked to him. Soon he crawled up on my lap and sat, looking into my eyes. I had high hopes that he'd come around.

And he did. Since the shelter was experiencing a winter low-population period, staff kept the little dog far beyond his minimum holding time, working with him to help him gain confidence in the stressful shelter environment. They nursed him through a bout of canine upper respiratory infection, shaved his mats, bathed him, and finally felt it was time for him to be assessed.

Although he had become considerably more comfortable in the difficult shelter environment, he was still very stressed. He was tense with most of the handling, and downright ferocious about guarding his valued resources such as food and toys. Staff felt he was not a suitable candidate for adoption.

He spent another week parked in his kennel while staff urged the local Pomeranian Rescue group to come get him. They said they were full. Finally, knowing I had an interest in the little guy, Shelter Manager Debbie McClain e-mailed me and asked me if I wanted to rescue him.

We already had four dogs at home. We'd had five before, but weren't really looking to do it again. I e-mailed my husband and said, "What do you think?" He didn't answer back and so I put the little dog out of my mind.

When Paul arrived home that evening he walked into the kitchen and said, "Have you seen the huge dust bunny in the laundry room?" Since he's not one to pay much attention or object to dust bunnies, small *or* large (thank goodness!), I was surprised by his comment, but shrugged it off. When he urged me to go see it, I humored him and opened the door to the laundry room. There was Scooter looking lost and pathetic—huddled on the floor, shaved to the skin, clearly frightened and confused about yet another change to his frighteningly unpredictable world. I cried.

Scooter in his early Do-Over days: shaved, confused and pathetic.

Because he was found as a stray, we knew nothing about him. We could only guess about his history. Heavy tarter on his teeth and a slightly graying muzzle suggested that he was middle-aged—perhaps somewhere between five and seven. His matted coat made it clear he hadn't been receiving proper care and attention for some time, although it's doubtful he was roaming the streets for long—Hagerstown is a community that quickly takes in stray dogs.

Scooter was a perfect fit for the category of "the dog with the unknown past." We could only speculate that he was a casualty of the recession: homeless due to foreclosure; perhaps the companion of a senior citizen who could no longer care for him; or an owner who grew tired of him—we'll never know.

We discovered a list of additional behavior challenges as he settled in. This is common when you take in a dog with an unknown history. As you explore your relationship with him you discover new things you do that are worrisome to him, and new things he does that are worrisome to you.

In addition to his resource guarding, which ultimately was the least of our worries, Scooter displayed a significant amount of touch sensitivity. He would often growl when picked up. His first night with us, we attempted to crate him but he barked frantically, so we put him on our bed. He gave a huge sigh and curled up at the foot of the bed—clearly indicating he was accustomed to sleeping *with* his humans. All was well until I was awakened in the middle of the night by his incessant licking. When I reached up and pressed the side of his face to distract him from licking, he snarled angrily, snapped, and bit my hand three times. Luckily for me he had good bite inhibition—despite his startling aggressive display, I didn't feel *any* pressure of his teeth on my skin.

The list continued to grow in the days that followed. He peed a lot—both inside and out. He even peed on the bed the first night—fortunately at the foot of the bed. On my side. He barked a lot (not so surprising for a Pom), but especially off-putting was the ferocious display of barking and snarling when Paul would kiss me good-bye in the morning as he left for work—a display that continued after the kiss was over, as Scooter followed Paul to the door. He would also wander off if he was able to slip out an open door, completely oblivious to attempts to call him back.

I hadn't intended to adopt a Do-Over Dog, but I got one. It happens that way a lot.

Socializing your Do-Over Dog

Earlier, I briefly mentioned the importance of socialization and the problem of under-socialization. If you are lucky, your Do-Over Dog has had at least some socialization at his previous home or at a shelter. But if he has missed out on important socialization lessons, regardless of his age, you'll want to undertake a remedial behavior modification program when you bring him home. Because you've missed the most critical socialization period—between two weeks to four months of age, he may never recover fully from his lack of early socialization, but you *can* help him become more comfortable in his new world.

Socialization means giving your pup *positive* exposures to the world while he's young enough to be forming his world view. The "world" in this case includes a variety of people, other dogs, places, sights and sounds. Such a socialization process is your best immunization against fear-related behaviors. Socialization ideally takes place from the age of two weeks to four months. The longer you wait, the faster the window of opportunity closes. If you adopt an under-socialized older Do-Over Dog, you'll want to begin behavior modification to help him overcome his early social deprivation. Ongoing socialization is important throughout a dog's life, even for those who *were* well-socialized.

The fearful dog

Many Do-Over Dogs are fearful, a significant challenge for shelter workers and new owners. While dogs from a variety of backgrounds can be fearful, the most common cause among Do-Over Dogs is undersocialization. Lexie, a two-year-old Maltese purchased from a breeder at eight weeks, was fearful because her owner hadn't understood the critical importance of early socialization during her early months, and didn't take her out to meet new people, places and things. Daisy, a two-year-old Yorkshire Terrier adopted from a rescue group, was fearful because she was under-socialized—she grew up as a breeder in a puppy mill, with little exposure to the real world. Duke, a four-year-old German Shepherd/Labrador Retriever mix, was fearful because, in addition to being under-socialized, he was physically punished by his previous owner.

Many dogs are selectively fearful. Scooter was afraid of many things in the chaotic shelter environment, but out in the real world primarily appears to be afraid of sharp, loud noises and being run over by our bigger dogs. Lucy, our Corgi, is sound sensitive, even phobic of some sounds such as thunder and applause. But both of my selectively fearful dogs are quite bold and confident in many other circumstances, so I wouldn't label them as generally fearful. While behaviors such as theirs can be debilitating, in some cases even life-threatening, and cry out for behavior modification, they aren't enough to land a dog in the "Fearful" category.

This fearful Chow mix at the Humane Society of Washington County, Maryland, was a good candidate for a Do-Over. Lita was adopted by animal care tech Christy Crone, who worked hard to successfully modify her fearfulness, then adopted her.

Unsocialized and under-socialized dogs are truly *neophobic*—a term behaviorists use to mean persistent or abnormal fear of new things or experiences. A list of symptoms associated with neophobia include:

- Irrational fear of new things
- Feeling of panic
- Feeling of terror
- Feeling of dread
- Rapid heartbeat
- Shortness of breath
- Nausea

- Dry mouth
- Trembling
- Anxiety
- Extreme avoidance measures taken

Just as all the rational, logical discussion in the world won't help a neophobic human get over his fears, similarly the neophobic dog can't be fixed by having his human tell him to sit, pay attention, and behave himself. It's a long road to help a fearful dog become braver, and even then he's likely never going to be as bold, confident, friendly, and outgoing as he might have been if he had received proper socialization.

The neglected dog

Many Do-Over Dogs have been subjected to varying degrees of neglect. Prior to the advent of the Internet, dog lovers had little awareness of the true extent of animal neglect and abuse in our world unless they had close ties to animal protection and animal law enforcement. Now it's frighteningly easy to find dozens of news reports online each week with the gruesome details of our inhumanity to our animal companions:

- Three Saint Bernard puppies seized from a home will likely be put up for adoption, Massachusetts SPCA officials said. The puppies were three of six dogs seized from a home after they were found kept in small cages with little or no food, water, or exercise.
- Five dogs were rescued from a Toronto home, in a disturbing case of animal abuse. The Toronto Humane Society found the dogs in a pitch-black shed with no ventilation, and two bigger dogs were wearing shock collars so tight they could barely breathe. The floor was covered in the dogs' own feces and urine.
- In Maryland, Duncan, an eight-week-old Shepherd mix pup with a severe case of sarcoptic mange was found by a passer-by one winter, frozen to the ground in a small makeshift enclosure where he'd been left by his owner's boyfriend one evening in hopes that someone would find him and care for him. The abandoned puppy's cries alerted the neighbor and saved him from death from hypothermia that night as the temperature dropped to near zero. Duncan recovered under the care of the Humane Society of Washington County, Maryland, was adopted, and the boyfriend pled guilty to animal cruelty charges filed by the humane agency.

Duncan as he appeared as a pup, shortly after being rescued from his frozen prison where he was abandoned and suffering from sarcoptic mange.

Duncan after one year with his new forever family, the Falteiseks.

- A Virginia couple pleaded no contest Tuesday to charges they neglected six pet dogs that were seized from their home in April. Four of the dogs have since been placed with new owners, including two that were emaciated when they arrived at the humane society. Two of the dogs had to be euthanized. The charges were based on the type of neglect found, namely deprivation of medical care and tethering in an inhumane or detrimental manner.
- Neighbors notified animal shelter in Ohio, that a young dog was being neglected and had been chained to a dog house for months. The Chief Dog Warden says she found the ten-month-old Retriever mix running loose with what appeared to be a huge tumor growing on her neck. Further examination by a vet revealed the tumor was actually infected skin that was forced through a dog collar which had twisted because it was too tight. The dog was taken into custody. A vet was able to repair her neck and she was spayed and put up for adoption.

Some cases are prosecutable, but many are not: a matted Cocker Spaniel with infected ears found roaming the streets; the litter of Pit Bull mix puppies found abandoned in a county park, bellies swollen with roundworms; an apparently healthy adolescent Shepherd/Lab mix left behind on a college campus at the end of the school year...the variations are endless. Examples of neglect abound in every community, resulting in thousands of dogs who are in search of their second chance for a first-class life.

These neglected Do-Over Dogs often have exceptional medical needs—huge loads of parasites and parasite-borne illnesses such as Lyme disease and heartworm, developmental problems from improper nutrition, injuries from ingrown collars, and dental disease. Not to mention the range of diseases even well-cared for dogs can suffer from. You name it, they could have it.

Behaviorally, neglected dogs run the same gamut of potential problems that dogs who *haven't* been neglected could experience, but sometimes to the very extreme. The good news is that you can find a badly neglected dog who can turn out to be a perfectly healthy ready-made companion as soon as she recovers physically from the neglect. The bad news is you could have long term significant behavioral problems *in addition to* the medical ones. Sometimes a neglected dog appears well-behaved at first because she's too weakened and shell-shocked to act as she normally would. You'll see the real dog, for better or for worse, when she's healthy.

Tied to a tree with a short leash and no access to water—this would be prosecutable neglect in many jurisdictions. Owners often lose custody of neglected canines upon conviction, and dogs such as this one become Do-Overs looking for new humans who will treat them well.

Bottom line is, if you take in a dog with a history of neglect you need to go into the relationship with your eyes open, knowing that you may be facing lots of damage repair to turn your Do-Over Dog into the canine companion of your dreams.

The abused dog

There's no doubt many Do-Over Dogs have suffered from unintentional cruelty. The difference between neglect and abuse is *intent.* In legal terms, abuse or cruelty requires *specific intent*—the perpetrator deliberately did the act in order to harm the animal, while neglect refers to *general intent*—the perpetrator intended to do the act, but didn't deliberately intend to harm the animal.

Abused dogs, too, are much more in the public eye these days, thanks again to modern technology. Another cruise across the Internet turns up a never-ending list of examples of deliberate dog abuse:

- Veterinarians say that an American Bulldog Pit Bull mix found on a highway in Rhode Island, badly beaten and severely burned, is holding up considerably well. The five-year-old dog, named Yugo by the vet staff, was picked up by a woman who was driving in the area. The woman took him to an animal shelter. Vet officials say they have received over 100 calls, and nearly $1,000 dollars in donations to help in Yugo's recovery. Officials say the animal had severe burns on his leg, one injury was infected, he had a bite wound, and injuries around his ears. Veterinarians say because his wounds were so severe they thought they might have to put him down. However, because the mix breed dog was wagging his tail and seemed to be in good spirits, the vets decided to save him and treat his injuries. Police are investigating this cruel case of animal cruelty and will press criminal charges against the person responsible. Yugo continues to recover at the local animal hospital.

- A juvenile could be facing felony animal cruelty charges after allegedly throwing a dog from a Kentucky bridge. Officials from the local humane society discovered the black Cocker Spaniel in the weeds below a bridge after a witness reported the alleged crime to the Kentucky State Police. Totzie, as she was later named, was reportedly seen by a passer-by being thrown from a bridge by a juvenile. Humane society workers searched for an hour before finding Totzie, who had crawled out of the river and was hiding in weeds. The six-month old dog was taken to an animal hospital where it was found she had a fractured pelvis after an estimated 30-foot drop from the bridge. According to a statement from authorities, the juvenile said he threw the animal from the bridge because it was sick. But the dog was in good health when she was found; nothing wrong with her other than a fractured pelvis caused by the fall.
- Animal control officers charged a Montana man with abandoning a puppy in a dumpster. A woman found the 3-week-old Border Collie in a dumpster while she was taking out her garbage. The puppy was inside a sealed garbage bag lying in vomit and near death, police said. After local media reported the incident, community tips led police to a suspect, who was cited with two misdemeanor counts of animal cruelty. One count charged him with injuring the puppy and the second count alleged he confined the puppy in a cruel manner. City staff named the puppy Piper. A veterinarian examined the puppy and said Piper suffered brain trauma and bruising. Piper recovered and was adopted.
- A college student was charged with felony animal cruelty after she allegedly taped her boyfriend's puppy to the side of a refrigerator in a bid to teach the rambunctious animal a "lesson." According to police, the suspect used clear packing tape to adhere the eight-month-old dog (a Shiba Inu named Rex) to the appliance in the kitchen of her boyfriend's apartment. The young woman allegedly was angry at her boyfriend for failing to get rid of the puppy, which she claimed, bitten her a few days earlier. According to police reports, when cops responded to a report of a male and female yelling at the apartment, they discovered that Rex's body was completely encased in packing tape. When asked how long the puppy had been taped upside down to the side of the refrigerator, the suspect replied, "Not long. Like 20-30 minutes. It was just until he calmed down." The animal, whose paws had been bound with elastic hair ties, was clearly in pain and yelped and screamed loudly as cops worked to free him. The puppy was handed over to the humane society.

Like neglected dogs, dogs who have been abused can be physically and psychologically traumatized, fearful and suspicious of humans, and perhaps defensively aggressive. Yet sometimes they are surprisingly resilient, ready to bounce back and trust people despite the horrific treatment they may have received. You may need to work through the period of physical recovery before you know how much of a behavioral project you're facing. And again, if you take in a dog with a history of abuse you need to go into the relationship with your eyes open, knowing that you may be facing lots of damage repair to turn your Do-Over Dog into the canine companion of your dreams.

So there you have it; lots of reasons why dogs need Do-Overs. Perhaps by now you're counting your lucky stars that your Do-Over Dog is on the milder end of the continuum, or at least relieved to realize the behaviors of your frustratingly difficult Do-Over Dog are not your fault. Of course, the best news is that there are almost always lots of things you can do to make it better; if not all better, at least somewhat better.

Chapter 2
THE SHELTER WORLD AND MORE

You might get your Do-Over Dog directly from a friend or neighbor who for some reason has to give the dog up. However, most Do-Over Dogs have spent at least some time being cared for by an institution such as a shelter or a breed rescue group. Knowing more about what these organizations do and how they function will help you become a more successful Do-Over Dog owner.

Animal shelters

Say the words "animal shelter" to ten different people and you're likely to get ten different responses—spanning the continuum of emotions from a warm, happy smile to sadness and tears, to anger. Why the disparity? Because the sheltering profession takes the "no two alike" approach to service providing, and those ten people likely had ten very different shelter experiences. When you've had one experience with a shelter, good or bad, you might think all shelters are the same. You couldn't be more wrong.

Many people think that shelters must all come under some national governing body that regulates what they do, a universal "mother club" like Red Cross, Boy Scouts, and Girl Scouts. In fact, the exact opposite is true—with a few rare exceptions, every shelter is its own entity, complete within itself, with its own policies and procedures, its own governing body, and its own list of services offered—or not offered.

National groups like the Humane Society of the United States (HSUS), The Humane American, United Animal Nations (UAN), the American Society for the Prevention of Cruelty to Animals (ASPCA), In Defense of Animals, Friends of Animals, Animal Welfare Institute, etc., do little to dispel the confusion. With the exception of the ASPCA, none of these organizations has anything to do with the management of shelters around the country—they are primarily *educational* organizations, offering training, materials and conferences at a price to local shelters and issue-based information to the public. (The ASPCA does have a shelter in New York City.) Some have offices around the United States and sometimes the world, many of them participate in disaster response efforts, and many are heavily involved in lawmaking, sometimes pursuing legislation whether local agencies support it or not.

These groups offer paid memberships. Shelter staff and volunteers are frequently members of one or more of them, but the organizations have no direct role in how shelters across the country are structured or run other than in an advisory capacity. Well-meaning animal lovers often join and support these national organizations, believing that donation dollars sent to those groups somehow find their way back to help animals in shelters in their own communities. They may be dumbfounded to discover that this is rarely the case. Oh, once in a great while, during a disaster or a high-profile cruelty case perhaps, but not to assist with the day-to-day costs of feeding and caring for sheltered animals. Rarely a penny.

The players: Types of shelters

Although every shelter operates independently, you can group them into similar types according to how they are structured.

Municipal shelter: This type of shelter is owned and run by your government—city, county, township, parish—and is completely supported by tax dollars. It usually has a name like "San Francisco Animal Care and Control," "Chattanooga Animal Services," or "Multnomah County Animal Control."

The shelter is part of the municipal "animal control" program, charged with protecting citizens from animals and vice-versa. They are usually responsible for enforcing city or county laws and regulations regarding animals, may also investigate cases of animal cruelty, and sometimes offer education programs. Their enforcement staff may be called "animal control officers," "animal services officers," "dog wardens," "dog law officers," or some other such regulatory-sounding name.

"Animal Control" may be its own department in local government, or can be housed under the police department, department of public works, health department, department of parks and recreation, or some other division. Priority of services often depends on what department oversees their work. If under the health department, high priority is placed on "rabies control" efforts; if under the police department, enforcement of animal control laws may take center stage. If you travel up the organizational tree, you eventually reach a Board of Supervisors, a Mayor, or whatever office is at the top of your particular governmental hierarchy.

Full-service private non-profit shelter: As the name implies, this is a 501(c)3 not-for-profit organization with a Board of Directors and by-laws that govern the mission and policies of the group. Its mission is to protect animals from people, which often includes a strong educational component. When applying for non-profit status in most states, these agencies are incorporated for the "prevention of cruelty to animals." They may have members, and members may or may not have voting privileges.

These groups have names like "Marin Humane Society," "Houston SPCA," "Chicago Anti-Cruelty Society," "Denver Dumb Friends League." Same type of organization: non-profit animal protection agencies—just different names. To emphasize the point, note that "SPCAs" across the country have *no* affiliation with the ASPCA, and your local humane society is *not* a branch of the Humane Society of the United States.

The full-service shelter, sometimes also called an "open admission" shelter, usually accepts most if not all animals that owners bring to them, and may (or may not) also accept stray animals of all kinds. These shelters usually keep animals as long as they can, have active adoption, education and spay/neuter programs, and strive for low euthanasia rates, but can't always succeed in that effort. While the most diligent of these may be able to achieve a sometimes tenuous "low-kill" status, most, by choosing to accept all animals that are brought to them, are compelled to regularly euthanize for a number of reasons including health, behavior and space, at least some of the time, if not on a daily basis. They may also be involved in humane investigations, rescues and cruelty case prosecutions. Cruelty enforcement workers are often given titles such as humane officer, humane agent, humane investigator, or cruelty investigator. At the top of the non-profit organizational chart is the President of the Board, Chair of the Board, CEO, or other such title.

Full-service non-profit shelter with animal control contract: Some full-service shelters contract with local community government to perform the function of animal control alongside their humane society mission. Under this arrangement, the shelter is still governed by its Board of Directors, but must respond to the contracting government over issues related to the contracted services.

The Marin Humane Society in Novato, California has long been a shining example of a full-service non-profit animal shelter with an animal control contract.

The contract may be only to *house* stray animals for one or more municipal animal control agencies, or it may be to perform field enforcement services as well as sheltering services. These services involve issues such as animals running at large, barking and other "nuisance" complaints, enforcement of licensing and "sanitation" (pooper scooper) laws, etc., and sometimes include enforcement of anti-cruelty laws. Non-profit shelters sometimes take on government contracts for financial reasons—some rely on government dollars to survive—sometimes for humanitarian reasons, in the belief that the non-profit shelter can do a better job of caring for the animals. Or both. Because the two missions are in conflict—protecting humans versus protecting animals, this arrangement can have a deleterious effect on community support for the shelter: actions such as issuing citations for leash-law violations; charging a fee for people to reclaim their impounded dogs; or declaring dogs "dangerous or potentially dangerous." These tend to not endear the organization to potential supporters. The issues are often no-win for the shelter—regardless of the action taken, someone is likely to be unhappy.

Non-profit shelters that have government contracts usually euthanize greater numbers of animals, since they are compelled to accept all stray animals as defined by the contract. This group of animals is likely to include some of the least potentially-adoptable animals in any given community.

Limited admission non-profit shelter: Also a 501(c)3 tax-deductible organization with a "protect animals from people" mission, this type of shelter is sometimes called "Selective Intake," "Guaranteed Adoption," "Low-Kill," or "No-Kill." Also governed by a Board of Directors, this shelter may limit the number of animals accepted, usually with some kind of screening test for potential adoptability. There may be a long waiting list to place a dog or cat in one of these shelters, as the responsible ones only accept a new animal when kennel space opens up, and their low-kill/no-kill policies may mean that some animal companions occupy kennel space for many months—or years.

Know that almost every so-called "no-kill" group sooner or later will euthanize or will have someone else euthanize some of their dogs. The sheltering industry has accepted a definition of "no-kill" that most of the general public doesn't understand—that *adoptable* dogs aren't euthanized. But which illnesses or injuries one shelter has the resources, willingness and ability to treat, or which behavior challenges one shelter has the resources, willingness and ability to treat, varies widely from one to the next. So a dog who is *unadoptable* and euthanized for upper respiratory infection at one so-called no-kill shelter might well have been declared *adoptable*, treated and rehomed at the next. A dog with a broken leg might be treated at one, and not at the other. A dog displaying resource guarding behaviors might be euthanized at one shelter, rehomed at the next, and rehabilitated and rehomed at a third. They can all call themselves "no-kill."

Another caveat of low-or-no-kill shelters is that *some* facilities keep dogs in their kennels far longer than is appropriate or humane—many months, even many years. It's well-accepted in the behavior field that a kennel environment can be highly stressful for some dogs, and that the resulting stress can cause a multitude of serious behavior problems, including aggression, and compulsive behaviors such as spinning and self-mutilation. If your Do-Over Dog has been a long-term resident at one of these facilities, you may be looking at some very significant long-term behavior modification programs.

Animal rescue groups: These may or may not be 501(c)3 not-for-profit organizations, and they may or may not be so-called "no-kill." Some rescue groups have an actual shelter; but many others house their dogs in foster homes and at boarding kennels.

Breed rescue groups that operate under the auspices of their breed clubs are usually not-for-profit with a governing Board of Directors, and for the most part are realistic about euthanizing dogs who aren't good adoption prospects—although not always. They tend to use scarce resources wisely, and make thoughtful and difficult decisions about how to help the most number of dogs with those limited resources.

Non-breed-affiliated rescues and mixed-breed rescues can run the gamut from 501(c)3 legitimate non-profit rescues to private adoption agencies to hoarders masking as rescues. We'll discuss hoarders at greater length shortly.

Meanwhile, the bottom line is that your Do-Over Dog can come from any of these sources, as well as from "free-to-good-home" ads in the paper, breeders dumping non-productive breeding stock, friends and family members who pressure you to take a dog they are trying to rehome, and impulse pet store purchases. Perhaps you took in a stray Do-Over Dog who appeared on your doorstep. Even puppies purchased from carefully researched responsible breeders can become Do-Overs! Whatever the pros and cons of the various shelters, private adoption agencies, rescue groups, or other sources of canine companions, they can all produce dogs who need a second chance at a first-class life.

Please don't misunderstand me. I don't want you to think all shelter dogs are "damaged goods." One of the most wonderful, never-put-a-paw-wrong dogs I've ever had the privilege of sharing my life with was our Terrier mix, the lovely Josie, adopted from the Marin Humane Society. You can find some wonderful ready-made dogs at shelters, and you can inherit some whopper Do-Overs from friends and neighbors. I want you to be prepared, in case...

I am a strong supporter of shelter adoptions—four of our own dogs were adopted from the shelter here in Maryland. (We found the fifth, our Scottie, as a stray, several years ago when we were living in Chattanooga.) Regardless of where you find your next canine family member, go into the adoption with your eyes wide open and your commitment strong, and I guarantee you can find a Do-Over Dog who needs you, and who has the potential to become a well-loved lifelong companion.

Puppy mills, pet stores and hoarders, oh my!

You can find some of the most challenging Do-Over Dogs from puppy mills and hoarders. A puppy mill is a large-scale commercial dog breeding facility that operates under substandard conditions, often with little regard for breed standards, quality of breeding stock, or genetic or physical health of their "product." As offensive as it is to animal-lovers to have dogs referred to as a product or "livestock," for a puppy-mill, in business for the sole purpose of making money, that's exactly what they are. According to Wikipedia, there are an estimated 4,000 puppy mills in the U.S. that produce more than half a million puppies a year. Many of those puppies end up at shelters or with rescue groups, by virtue of impoundment by increasingly frequent raids by humane law enforcement, rescue efforts without enforcement, and owner surrender or stray impound of dogs previously purchased as puppies from pet stores or directly from puppy mills.

The horrors of puppy mills

The majority of puppy mill puppies are sold through pet stores, puppy brokers, and other commercial outlets. *No* reputable breeder sells her puppies to the commercial mass market. Not one. Let me be perfectly clear. If you buy your puppy from a pet store, a puppy broker, or any other entity that collects and sells puppies from another source, you are almost guaranteed to be buying a puppy mill puppy. I recommend you *never* do this. Puppy mill breeder dogs have a miserable existence. They live in intensive confinement, often matted and dirty, under-socialized or poorly socialized, usually in cages with wire flooring so the feces and urine can fall through—sometimes on the dog below, if the cages are stacked. If you buy a puppy from a pet store, even if you believe you're doing a good thing by rescuing the puppy in the window, you are *supporting* the cruel puppy mill industry with your consumer dollars, and perpetuating puppy mill misery. It a simple equation—if there were no consumer market, there would be no puppy mills.

Pet store puppies like these almost assuredly came from a puppy mill.

The largest puppy broker in the U.S. is Hunte Corporation, located in southwest Missouri, heart of puppy mill country. They receive and process puppies from breeders in staggering numbers. According to one newspaper account, they sold more than 88,000 puppies in the year 2005. While Hunte Corporation has a slick on-line presence with a website that assures quality loving care for the puppies they broker, according to petstorecruelty.org, the Hunte Corporation's USDA (license number 43-B-1023) 2003 and 2004 inspection reports found numerous violations, primarily for inadequate cage size:

- Keeshond puppies E033096 and E033097 were each measured at 15". They require a cage with 6.12 square feet and were in [a] cage that measured 4 square feet.
- Ridgeback puppy D092426 measured at least 26" long (squirming). The dog requires 6.67 square feet and was in a cage that measures 5.42 square feet.

- In the main puppy room, there were three Walker puppies in a four foot square cage. The puppies when measured required 10.08 square feet for the three total. This cage does not meet the requirements of this section.
- In the main puppy room there were two Rottweiler puppies in a 5.3 square foot cage. Both were approximately the same size. The one puppy was measured at 24" in length. The two puppies together would require a cage with no less than 12.5 square feet.

While most of the puppies escape puppy mill hell early in life, the parents are simply puppy-making machines, to be used until they're used up. The females are often bred twice yearly until they no longer produce and then dumped—either killed or given to a shelter or breed rescue group. These discarded adults are the greatest travesty of the puppy mill industry. Some puppy mills even have the gall to *sell* these horribly under-socialized victims to unsuspecting adopters, who don't realize how damaged the dogs are until they remove them from their own familiar environment, to a new home, where they are neophobic and terrified.

The groups who rescue these dogs, if they are well-run, treat all the medical problems they inherit, and implement behavior modification for these poorly socialized dogs who have never seen the real world. Groups that are less well-funded or less well-run may go ahead and place the rescues immediately, without addressing the numerous physical and psychological problems that are inevitable in these dogs.

The puppies often arrive at the pet stores with mental and physical challenges as well—heavily parasitized and under-socialized. Their immune systems, weakened by the conditions in which they're raised and the stress of travelling to their far flung destinations, makes them vulnerable to deadly diseases such as parvovirus and distemper. Usually shipped at about 8 weeks, their most important socialization window from the age of two to fourteen weeks is already half gone, and while they will get handled and socialized at the store, some puppies never recover from the absence of adequate handling in their first several weeks. Some of them are Do-Over projects from the moment of purchase.

If you've already acquired a puppy mill puppy, don't despair. There are lots of dog owners who, before they knew better and realized the suffering that goes into pet store puppies, purchased the "puppy in the window" and are perfectly happy with their four-legged family members. A good percentage of puppy mill pups do manage to emerge from their poor start in life with minimal repercussions. I don't recommend you buy one, but if you already have and are dealing with the fallout from his early experiences, read on. Behavior problems aren't always fixable, but there is much you can do to repair the damage that was caused.

Hoarders—even worse

As bad as puppy mills are, the owner has an investment in his "inventory" and it behooves him to at least keep his dogs alive. Hoarders are even worse. While they claim to love the animals they neglect so horribly, they are often so out of touch with reality that they can't recognize the suffering they're bestowing on the animals they claim to love.

When I started my career in animal protection work in 1976, I had never heard the term "hoarder." Staff called them "collectors," and while we realized there was something horribly wrong with a person who could purport to love animals and at the same time watch them die of multiple preventable causes including starvation, we didn't realize how deep-seated the condition was. Today, animal hoarders are widely recognized in the animal protection world, and every day brings new cases to light.

My first collector case, more than 20 years ago, was a woman living in her Volkswagen van with 18 Siberian Huskies. As in every hoarder case I've been involved with since, part of the defense strategy was to present testimony about how much the defendant loved her animals. The words of prosecuting attorney Linda Witong's closing argument still ring loudly in my ears even to this day.

"Louise Ritchie claims to have loved her dogs. God help us if she had hated them." A jury found Ritchie guilty of neglecting her dogs.

It's incomprehensible how human hoarders can live like this, much less force animals to live in these conditions. Reports of horrendous animal hoarding cases are increasingly common in the animal protection world. These cases contribute significantly to the growing population of Do-Over Dogs.

"Hoarding" is a long-recognized psychological condition when it comes to the extreme collecting of inanimate possessions. Only beginning in the 1990s has the term been applied to animal collectors, and animal collecting is still not universally recognized as a hoarder syndrome. An animal hoarder has been defined as "someone who accumulates a large number of animals; fails to provide minimal standards of nutrition, sanitation, and veterinary care; and fails to act on the deteriorating condition of the animals (including disease, starvation and even death) or the environment (severely overcrowded and unsanitary conditions), or the negative impact of the collection on their own health and well-being."

In a 2009 study of the hoarding phenomenon, Dr. Gary Patronek of Tufts University estimates approximately 3,000 animal hoarders per year, and suggests that as many as one-third of *all* hoarder cases include animals. He estimated that there were between 700 and 2,000 new hoarder cases every year in the United States. Dr. Randall Lockwood at the ASPCA in New York suggested in 2009 that there were approximately *five thousand* new hoarder cases reported every year. That's approximately fourteen new cases *every day!* In 69 percent of the cases Dr. Patronek surveyed in 1999, animal waste accumulated in living areas. Over 25 percent of the hoarders' beds were soiled with feces or urine. Hoarders' justifications for their behavior included an intense love of animals, the feeling that animals were surrogate children, the belief that no one else would or could take care of them, and the fear that the animals would be euthanized. According to Patronek, a significant number of hoarders had nonfunctional utilities (i.e., bathroom plumbing, cooking facilities, heat, refrigeration and electricity).

These are clearly troubled humans. One theory is that hoarders suffer from obsessive compulsive disorder. The classic picture of the compulsive hoarder is the individual who saves everything and can throw nothing away. Possessions may be saved by both hoarders and non-hoarders for a variety of reasons, including sentimental value (emotional reasons or reminders of important life events), instrumental value (potential usefulness), or intrinsic value (beauty or attractiveness). The difference between people who hoard possessions and those who do not is that hoarders judge more possessions to have these values. This may also be true for people who hoard animals. Their attachment to animals is, in all likelihood, similar to other people's attachment, but it is applied to a much larger number or wider array of animals.

Like people who hoard possessions, animal hoarders have little or no awareness of the problematic nature of their behavior. They commonly share a persistent and powerful belief that they are providing proper care for their animals, despite clear evidence to the contrary, and are in complete denial about the suffering they are inflicting. Patronek reports that in some cases, the home environment is so seriously impaired that the house must be torn down after the animals are removed.

While one can be sympathetic to the plight of humans who are so disturbed, that doesn't change the fact that thousands of animals suffer as a result. A conservative estimate of 1500 cases per year, 20 animals per case, would total 30,000 animals. More realistically, a mid-range estimate of 2000 cases, 50 animals per case yields a total of 100,000 animals per year. That's an incredible amount of animal suffering. These aren't all dogs, of course. Cats are probably the most frequent hoarder animal of choice, but dogs, horses, and any number of other livestock, reptiles, exotics and small companion animals are included in the hoarder tally reported by animal control and humane agencies each month.

It's hard to know whether hoarder cases are on the rise, or if access to the Internet has just allowed us to share the information more easily. I have tracked such cases for the past two decades, and it seems to me that there are exponentially more of them than there once were. Dr. Lockwood's estimate seems to support my observations. Absent evidence to the contrary, it's my belief that the rise of the so-called "no-kill" movement has contributed significantly to the increase. More and more hoarders masquerading as rescuers are legitimized by shelters that are desperate to avoid euthanizing "adoptable" animals and welcome with open arms almost anyone who offers to rescue them. Even more tragically, many hoarders fail to spay or neuter their charges, so a multitude of new puppies and kittens are produced, and more often than not are given little to no socialization.

As more animal protection agencies investigate hoarders, more and more of these damaged animals enter the adoption pool and are rehomed with well-meaning, big-hearted adopters who may have little or no idea of how needy their new family members are. The four-legged victims of hoarder cases are often the most tragically desperate of Do-Over Dogs.

Chapter 3
ADOPTING A DO-OVER DOG

Some people adopt their Do-Over Dogs deliberately. Others do their best to avoid a Do-Over but end up with one anyway. And some are totally oblivious to the possibility that their new family member-to-be might bring baggage along that will require significant management and modification. If you're looking to adopt and you're reading this book, you probably don't fall into the third group, but if you already have a dog and are reading this, you very well might.

Assessment: identifying potential problem behaviors

If you're still looking to adopt, assessing the behavior of your adoption prospect can help you identify potential problem behaviors. Some, anyway. There's not an assessment protocol on earth that can present every possible stimulus to a dog in every possible environment to determine every possible behavioral response, so there's a huge certainty that some will get missed. Plus, problem behaviors can arise as a result of future events, again, completely unpredictable in a behavior assessment. The assessment simply gives you a snapshot of the dog's behavior in a moment in time. It can help you identify behaviors that appear in a particular dog on a given day. It's not perfect, but it's better than nothing.

Some dog behavior and care professionals use the term "temperament test." I much prefer "behavior assessment" for these reasons:

- We are really more concerned about the dog's responses to internal and external stimuli (behavior) than we are about his nature (temperament). While his natural predispositions are important, we really are observing, analyzing and drawing conclusions about his *behavior* in this process.
- The word "test" implies pass/fail. While there are certainly things a dog can do in the assessment process to "fail," we are primarily concerned with gathering information than we are with grading a test. Of course, a dog may "fail" on the hopefully rare occasion he does something completely unacceptable, like bite or attempt to bite the assessor (or the fake hand), but that's not our primary focus.

In fact, in some cases, like our own Scooter, a dog may bite and still be a good candidate for rehabilitation in a shelter behavior program, a rescue group, or a knowledgeable Do-Over home.

Many shelters and rescue groups conduct their own assessment procedures either before or after accepting a dog to rehome. Always ask if a behavioral assessment has been done on any dog you are thinking of adopting. Your adoption agency should be willing and eager to share the results of those assessments with you.

Commonly used protocols include Sue Sternberg's "Assess-A-Pet" and Dr. Emily Weiss' "Safer/Meet Your Match" program. Sue Sternberg, who operates her own non-profit shelter, Rondout Valley Animals for Adoption in New York, was a pioneer in the field of shelter dog assessment. Dr. Emily Weiss, the Senior Director of Shelter Research and Development at the ASPCA. Other notables in the field are Dr. Amy Marder, currently Director of Animal Behavior and Training Services at Animal Rescue League of Boston, Sarah Kalnajs, CDBC, CPDT, of Blue Dog Training and Behavior, and Kelley Bollen, on the Faculty at Cornell University, previously with the behavior department at the Massachusetts SPCA. Dr. Marder, Dr. Weiss and Kelly Bollen at the MSPCA have all conducted studies and/or surveys to confirm the validity of their assessment protocols.

It also makes sense to conduct your own standardized behavior assessment when you meet your prospective new canine family member. If you're not confident in your own abilities to analyze the behaviors you see, take along a very dog-knowledgeable friend, or hire a good, positive behavior professional to go with you. Many trainers bemoan the fact that people don't take advantage of the pre-adoption services they offer.

A shelter or rescue should not object to you implementing an assessment procedure, although they will most likely want to observe, and may stop you if they think you are doing something that puts you or the dog at risk. You might even be dealing with a private owner. Whoever is responsible for the dog, share the protocol with them before you do it, so they know what to expect.

Things you'll need for the assessment

1. A second person to help record observations and ensure your safety.
2. A sturdy leash and limited-slip (martingale collar) or a slip lead.
3. High value training treats. (Appendix 1)
4. A ball, a soft squeaky toy, and a tug toy.
5. A bowl of dry dog food with canned food mixed in.
6. A floppy hat and sunglasses, raincoat, or other unusual outerwear.
7. An Assess-A-Hand or three foot long device to safely work with the dog around high value resources.

Here are the steps of an assessment protocol you could use to evaluate some behaviors in your potential adoption dog. This protocol generally follows the one used by Kelly Bollen, but is not exactly the same. *Use caution! If at any time in the process you think the dog might bite you, or otherwise get too aroused or stressed, stop what you're doing and let him calm down, then make a prudent decision about whether to proceed. You can always skip parts of the protocol you think might be too much for the dog you're working with. For safety reasons, always have at least one other person in the room with you when doing an assessment on a dog you don't know.*

During the first part of the assessment you are simply making observations. With each piece of the protocol, write down how the dog responded. At the end you'll review your results to draw conclusions about the dog's behavior.

The protocol

Note: This protocol assumes you are conducting the assessment in a shelter environment or rescue facility. However, the same concepts/procedures could apply elsewhere as well, even at your own home. If you are conducting an assessment at your home, *always* have at least one other capable adult present to assist you if problems arise.

1. **Observe the dog in his kennel from a distance.** In this first step, you're looking to see how the dog handles himself in a stressful environment. Does he seem calm, friendly, and relaxed; excitable and aroused; stressed and nervous; or timid and fearful? What does he do when people or other dogs walk by?
2. **Walk up to the kennel and stand sideways at the kennel door in a neutral position.** In Steps 2, 3, and 4, you're exploring what he does when he's in a stressful environment and confronted by a stranger with various body postures. Don't talk to him or make eye contact as you stand sideways. Does he come to the front of the kennel with a happy face and friendly wagging tail? Charge the front of the kennel barking aggressively? Slink to the back and avoid eye contact? Stand or lie down quietly, looking at you?
3. **Turn and face him in the kennel.** Make direct eye contact, stare, and don't smile, but don't actively threaten him. Is he happy and friendly? A little worried? Very fearful? Does he stare back and growl or bark?
4. **Kneel down and make happy talk.** Is he still friendly? Less fearful? More aroused or aggressive?
5. **Have another person take him out of the kennel on-leash.** You're watching to see how he walks on leash, and what he does when he encounters new environments. Does he walk with confidence, or does he

Observe how the dog responds to you when you kneel down and interact with him.

have to be coaxed through doorways and across new surfaces. Is he pulling ahead of the person walking him, or lagging far behind? As he walks past other dogs does he try to greet them happily? Aggressively? Is he aroused (tail up, wagging stiffly, standing on tiptoes, leaning forward, staring at the other dog) or appropriate (soft body language, tail wagging at half-mast, body lowered, averting eyes), or does he try to avoid other dogs altogether? Be sure to take him outside to give him a chance to eliminate. Does he bolt through doors? Is he marking every object he passes, or does he try to "hold it" until he gets outside? Does he jump all over the handler, biting at the leash or the human?

6. **Take the dog to a separate room—preferably a relatively quiet room with few distractions.** Steps 6 and 7 help you gauge his social attraction to humans. Remove the leash, sit on a chair and let him explore for several minutes, without trying to engage with him. Is he curious and confident? Tentative and cautious? Excited and boisterous? Does he try to leave the room? Does he check in with you, or is he totally engrossed in his surroundings? If he doesn't check in with you at all, walk rapidly back and forth across the room. If he joins you, talk to him and give him a scratch under the chin. Then sit on the chair again, without inviting his attention, and see if he checks in with you.
7. **Sit on a chair in the center of the room and solicit his attention.** Does he come to you when you call him or does he ignore or avoid you and continue to explore the room? Is he polite when he greets you? Does he jump all over you? Does he seem fearful when you try to interact?
8. **Put his leash back on and sit on the chair again.** Now for some handling. You want to see how tolerant—or not—he is of the kinds of touching and attention he's likely to receive from people in the real world. Stroke his back, his far side, and touch, lift, tug on (gently!) and hold various parts of his body—his tail, his ears, his feet. Restrain him a little and look at his teeth a few times in a row. Does he enjoy or resist the handling? Get excited or fearful? Does he put his mouth on you in play, or in resistance? Try a gentle hug, making sure you protect your face should he decide to snap at you. Does he try to pull away from you, or does he calmly accept your attentions?

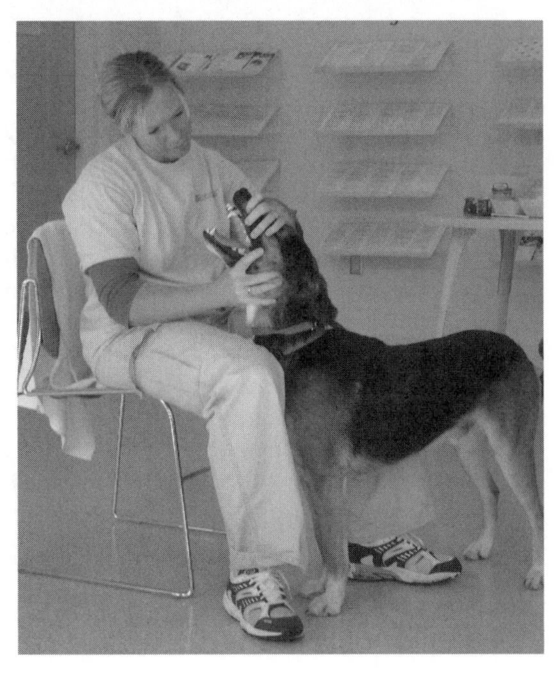

What does he do when you handle him all over, hug him, look at his teeth, play with his feet?

9. **Training.** You want to see if he knows anything. This gives you some clue of his prior relationships with humans. In some cases, the dog being assessed will get quite excited and happy when he hears a human using verbal cues for behaviors that are familiar to him, as if he's saying, "Finally! Someone who speaks my language!" *(Note: Many positive trainers use the term "cue" rather than "command" to mean a request for a behavior, verbal or otherwise. A "cue" means the dog has an opportunity to be reinforced for a behavior. "Command" is an old-fashioned training term that often means, "do it, or else!")* Without food at first, ask the dog to perform various behaviors that he may already know, such as sit, shake, and lie down. Use common owner body language cues (hand at your chest for sit, pointing to or patting the floor for down, offering your own hand for shake). Then try to get him to do some behaviors he doesn't know for a tasty food treat—sit, down (if he didn't do them for you without treats) and maybe a spin or twirl, where you lure him in a circle to see if he'll follow the treat. Does he know anything already? Does he seem willing to try new things? Is he fearful of your attempts to elicit new behaviors, or too stressed to even consider eating a treat?

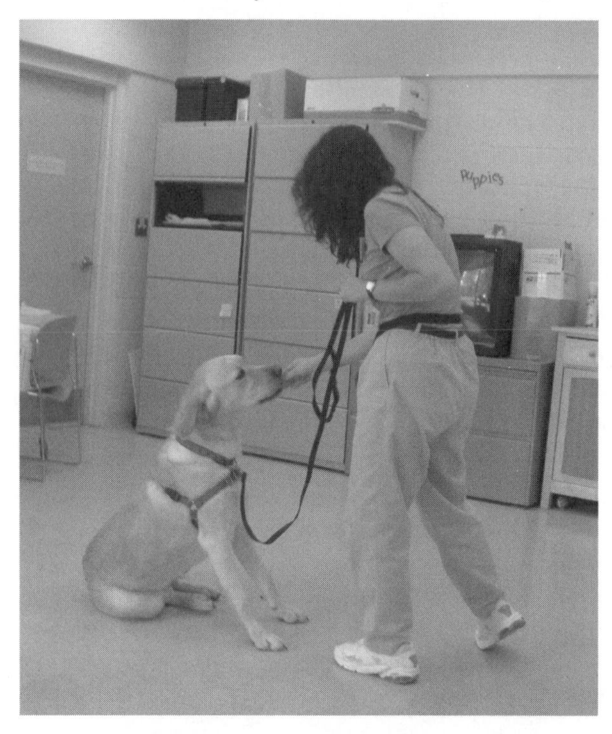

The dog's responses when you ask for behaviors he may know—and try to get him to do ones he doesn't—will help you decide if you can work with him.

10. **Playtime!** A tragically large number of dogs in shelters and rescue seem to not know how to play with humans. If the dog you're assessing has been outgoing and friendly, try normal play with him. If he's seemed cautious or fearful, play very gently. See if he'll chase a ball. Does he bring it back? If he shows no interest in a ball, try a soft squeaky toy, and offer to play tug with a tug toy. If he won't play with toys, try running away from him and see if he'll run after you, or get down on the floor and invite him to play. If he'll engage with you lightheartedly, he's playing, even if he doesn't know how to play with toys. On the other end of the scale, does he get *too* excited during play? Is he biting at you, grabbing your clothes, jumping on you, perhaps even mounting you? When you stop playing, hide the toy in your hand and fold your arms in front of you. Does he stop what he's doing or continue to interact inappropriately with you?

11. **Now for a startle.** Let the staff or rescue person know you're going to do this, in case they have any objections. Wait until the dog is otherwise engaged—sniffing the floor, looking out a window, countersurfing on a table—and *not* near a human. You don't want him to associate the startle with a person. If he has been

confident and outgoing, do a loud startle. If he's somewhat timid or fearful, a soft one. If he's excessively fearful; skip the startle. For the startle, *simultaneously* clap your hands, stomp one foot on the floor, and loudly yell "Hey!" As soon as you've done this, drop to your knees (do not bend over at the waist—that's intimidating to a dog!) and invite him to come to you. Was he startled or frightened by your noise? Did he even notice? Is he willing to come back to you? Immediately? With coaxing? Quickly? Slowly? Did he creep or run away? Does he not recover from the startle at all?

12. **Check for resource guarding.** While the tendency to guard one's valuable stuff is a natural, normal behavior—for humans as well as dogs!—it's one that's highly frowned upon when dogs guard their possessions fiercely from humans. This is often a controversial piece of the assessment procedure. Different organizations have varying tolerance levels for this behavior, but many otherwise highly adoptable dogs are euthanized at shelters because they don't do well on this piece of the protocol. If you choose to assess this behavior, *be careful!* It is easy to get bitten by a dog who is guarding food, for example. The pros use a fake plastic hand on the end of a stick to determine if there is tension in a dog's body language when approached while eating. You should always have a second person holding the dog's leash, and be *very observant* as you approach. Watch for any signs of tension in the dog—eating faster, looking at you sideways, a freeze (a very brief total stillness), trying to block you from the food or chew object. The professionals who do this will push a dog when they see signs of tension, using a fake plastic hand on a stick to determine how far the dog is willing to go to protect his stuff. I recommend you don't push him that far. Just seeing the early signs of tension is enough for you to know the dog has some propensity to guard—and for you to decide if this is a behavior you want to live and work with. If you *do* choose to explore further and you don't have access to a fake hand, any long stick—such as a yardstick—will do the job. Do *not* use your own hand unless and until you are *very confident* the dog is completely comfortable with you near his valuable resources. If you see resource guarding tension and are considering adopting anyway, I urge you to work with a positive behavior professional to determine the extent of the dog's guarding behavior, and to help you work on modifying it. Note: If you did see signs of tension around the food bowl, have your assistant lead the dog away from the bowl with the leash before you try to pick it up.

There are varying degrees of resource guarding—some guarders can be quite dangerous. Decide if this is a risk you want to take!

13. **Stranger danger.** Instruct your helper to go out of the room, don the floppy hat and sunglasses, and knock at the door. Respond by saying, "Who's there? Come in!" in a loud, somewhat alarmed tone of voice. Have the person enter the room, and move slowly, stiffly, arms raised to shoulder height, staring at the dog. Be sure to hold the leash tightly, in case the dog lunges forward. When the person reaches the halfway point they should stop, remove the hat and glasses, kneel down and invite the dog to them in a friendly manner. It's okay for the dog to act fearful or protective as the person approaches; your main concern is whether he recovers and is friendly when the person is no longer threatening.

Evaluating the results

Steps 1-7 of the assessment help you evaluate the dog's level of socialization and confidence. The easiest dogs to live and work with are those who are calm, relaxed, and unflappable even in the chaos of a shelter environment. Dogs who appear fearful or timid in this part of the assessment, who aren't interested in being social with you, or who are over-aroused and reactive are Do-Over candidates. They are the dogs who will need help, sometimes considerable help, learning how to be braver or act more appropriately when faced with new, scary, or exciting stimuli.

Steps 8-10 will give you information on how the dog accepts routine touch handling, training, and husbandry procedures. Again, the easy dogs are the ones who tolerate your fussing and invasion of their space with equanimity or perhaps even joy, dogs who have already had some training or catch on quickly when you try to lure new behaviors. They appear to understand and enjoy the concept of playing with humans. Dogs who are tense or fearful about handling, or resist with violent struggles, perhaps even a show of teeth, are the Do-Overs.

Step 11 gives you some idea of how easy—or difficult—it might be to interrupt the dog if he's doing something inappropriate, as well as how resilient he is. Does he ignore the startle and continue on his merry way? Does he stop what he's doing and cheerfully return to you? Does he appear fearful, or perhaps even aggressive when you try to interrupt him? The easiest dogs stop what they're doing and happily return to you—no hard feelings. The others are more challenging, either because it will be difficult to intervene and stop them when they're doing something inappropriate, or because they are easily traumatized by an unexpected startle.

The Step 12 Resource Guarding piece of the assessment gives you information about how a dog responds when a human is near his good stuff. Tension over resources does not have to rule out a dog as an adoption candidate. Remember that resource guarding is a natural, normal behavior; it's just not acceptable when directed toward humans. Depending on the intensity of the guarding behavior, you may be able to manage by restricting your dog's access to high value items, only giving him stuffed Kongs and other goodies when he's safely enclosed in his crate. If, however, he guards every little crumb that falls on the floor, the risk to human or other animal safety is greater. Guarding behavior can be modified, and you may want to discuss your potential adoption with a qualified positive behavior professional to determine how much of a project the dog might be. If there are children in the home, guarding presents a greater risk, as you would need to manage the children's behavior as well as the dogs.

I don't generally recommend families with small children adopt dogs with significant resource guarding behaviors. The risk is just too great.

The final piece—Stranger Danger—is less about evaluating the dog's response to the person approaching (although if someone approached me threateningly I think I'd *like* for my dog to protect me) and more about how easily he recovers. Whatever his emotional state when he feels threatened, you want to know how quickly he can get over it and be social with the now-friendly, non-threatening person. Of course, the dogs with the most solid personalities should recover quickly, while those in the Do-Over class are more likely to hesitate or even decline to interact with the now-friendly stranger.

Let me reiterate that your assessment protocol does *not* tell you everything the dog will do in the future. It only tells you what he did in this environment on this day in response to a specific, limited set of stimuli. If he does well on the assessment, you may want to evaluate how he is with children, other dogs, and cats, if you have those in your lives. If you're female and all your assessment assistants were female, you might also want to bring a male friend along to see how he responds to men. Some dogs, especially dogs with behavior challenges, will behave significantly differently with men than with women, because men tend to be bigger, have deeper voices, may wear beards, and carry themselves more assertively than most women, and can therefore sometimes be perceived as threatening to some dogs.

If you have small children, your adoptee should light up with joy when he sees them. Whatever Do-Over issues he might have, he *must* love children if he's going to live in a home with them. The risks are too great if he's cautious or overtly aggressive around them. A dog who loves kids will tolerate typical kid behavior, which is sometimes not as respectful to a dog as we would like. A dog who merely tolerates, actively avoids, or is openly aggressive toward children is likely to bite, sooner or later. When that happens, the child can be mildly or seriously injured, might be mildly or significantly psychologically traumatized, or in worst cases, *killed,* and the dog usually dies.

Evaluating potential problem behaviors

Now that you've collected this information, what does it all mean in relation to the possible adoption of a potential Do-Over Dog? Here are some of the common potential Do-Over behaviors you may have seen during your assessment process:

1. **Fearfulness.** Also described as shy or timid, fearful behavior is often, but not always, a function of under-socialization. It can also occur as a result of abuse, but often people assume a dog has been abused when in fact his fearfulness is due to lack of proper socialization. A dog may be neophobic—fearful of all new things—as a result of inadequate or improper social exposure during the first few months of his life, or he may be fearful of specific things as a result of bad experiences with those things. A dog who is generally fearful of all new things will usually be a bigger rehabilitation project than one who is wary of specific, identifiable stimuli. It's easy to lose your heart to the frightened pup huddling in the corner of his kennel. If you want to take on one of these, be sure you have the time, skill and patience to help him overcome his fears. A dog who runs

away from you and hides in the corner will be a massive Do-Over project. Your love alone will not be enough.

2. **Stress.** Manifests as one of more of these behaviors: panting, pacing, circling, whining, biting, barking, digging at the door, shutting down (not willing to do anything), and/or lack of interest in eating. You might also see yawning, lip-licking, whale-eye, unwillingness to make eye contact, and other more subtle signs. It's not unusual for dogs in shelters or kennels to be stressed—it's a difficult environment for them. The way your potential adoptive dog deals with his stress will give you clues as to how he'll react in the real world. The more shut down he is—the harder it is to get him to interact with you while stressed—the more challenging he's likely to be as a Do-Over project. You might take him outside on leash to see if his signs of stress diminish outside. If he seems more relaxed and acts more normal outside, his prospects are better for a less intensive rehabilitation.

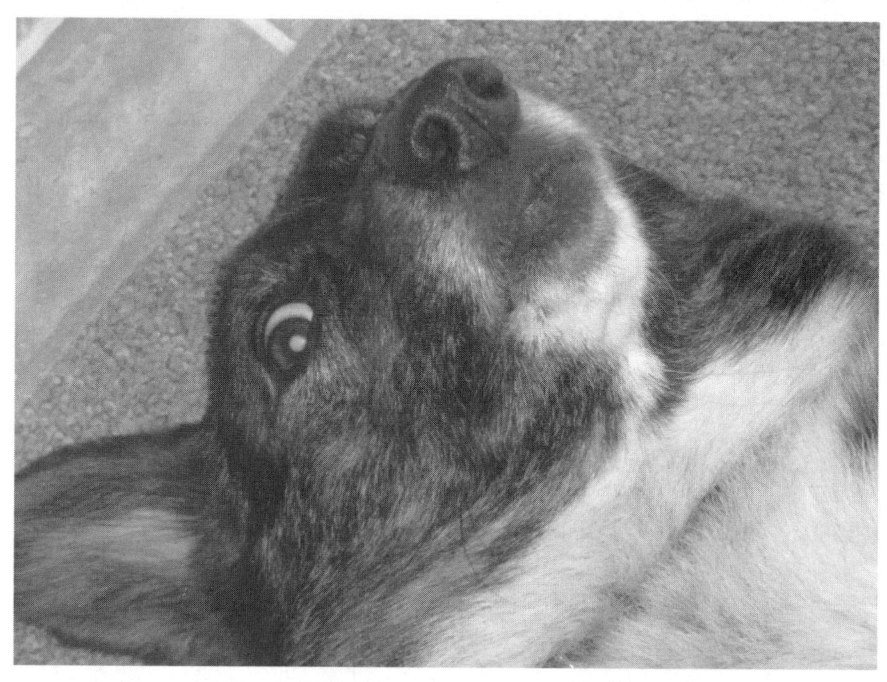

"Whale eye," when the whites of the dog's eyes are showing, is usually a sign of stress.

3. **Arousal.** When he easily gets excited and has trouble calming down. This is the dog who jumps all over you in greeting, perhaps mouthing your arms and nipping at your clothes, maybe even mounting you. The more you physically try to stop him the more aroused he gets. (Hint—don't try to physically stop him!) These dogs often do well when quickly removed from the over stimulating environment, especially if provided with adequate exercise and consistent management, positive training, and structure.

A dog who easily gets aroused and is slow to calm down can be a Do-Over challenge!

4. **Aggression.** Covers a long continuum of behaviors from slight tension, an intense stare, perhaps a low warning growl, all the way to full-out attack. I don't recommend adopting a potential Do-Over Dog who has seriously injured or worse, killed, a human. There are too many dogs available for adoption at risk of being euthanized who *haven't* mauled anyone to take on a dog who presents a very significant risk to yourself, your family, friends and neighbors, and your community. Dogs with lesser levels of aggression can be appropriate Do-Over candidates *in the right hands.* If you're considering adopting a dog with even *mild* aggression issues, please consult a qualified, positive behavior professional first to make sure you're not biting off more than you can chew.
5. **Isolation/separation distress or anxiety.** These include a continuum of related behaviors that can be exceedingly problematic in an adopted Do-Over Dog. Much of what is identified as "Separation Anxiety" is, in fact, a lesser manifestation of this very challenging behavior. Here are the distinctions:
   - Isolation distress—the dog is somewhat stressed about being left alone.
   - Separation distress—the dog is somewhat stressed about being separated from the one person he has bonded closely with.
   - Isolation anxiety—the dog becomes seriously panicked when left alone.
   - Separation anxiety—the dog becomes seriously panicked when separated from the one person he has bonded closely with. It's generally not unbearable to live with a dog at the "distress" end of the two behaviors, but the severe manifestation—anxiety—includes extreme destructive behavior, excessive vocalization, house soiling, and even self-injury. "Isolation" is also often easier than "separation." A dog with isolation distress can be calmed by the presence of another person—virtually any reasonable person will

> do—and sometimes even another animal is enough company to keep him happy. I would rather live with a dog who has aggressive behaviors than one with true separation anxiety. Aggression is easier to manage, and often much easier to modify.

When assessing your prospective Do-Over Dog, look for isolation/separation clues such as high-stress and clinginess—signs the dog is easily subject to stress and anxiety, bonds quickly and strongly, and is very needy. Try leaving the dog alone in a room and see if it seems to cause him distress.

There seems to be an inordinately large number of dogs at shelters who have separation or isolation issues. There is some speculation that the trauma of being abandoned by an owner and subjected to the stress of a shelter may trigger this constellation of difficult behaviors. Others suggest that the dogs end up at a shelter *because they've already manifested* these difficult-to-live-with behaviors and owners are happy to give them up or, alternatively, not come looking for them if they go missing. Chances are it's a combination of both. If a dog has a predisposition for separation anxiety, even if he hasn't had the opportunity or need to demonstrate the behavior, the stress of the shelter experience could well bring it on. In any case, know that it is quite possible for a shelter or rescue dog to come with separation or isolation baggage. If there's any question, this is another good time to consult your friendly positive behavior professional.

Evaluating potential medical problems

I'm certainly not a veterinarian, nor is it the purpose of this book to help you diagnose medical problems in your dog, pre-or post-adoption. You are wise to have your veterinarian examine your prospective Do-Over Dog *before* you make your final adoption decision, if that's possible, so you can weight the future cost and potential impact of any medical conditions into your decision. If that's not possible, at least schedule your vet visit for as soon as possible after the adoption. It's critically important to recognize that medical challenges can have a huge impact on behavior and on your dog's ability to adjust to his new life and fulfill your expectations for his role as your companion and partner in training.

For example, pain-causing/structural conditions such arthritis, hip dysplasia, spinal misalignments, and joint problems can contribute to aggression and anxiety, as well as interfere with a dog's ability to perform physical activities—run, jump, climb stairs, even sit and lie down. Parasites and parasite-related diseases can also cause significant behavioral problems and result in physical limitation: heartworms, untreated, damage the heart; ticks can transmit Lyme disease (which causes joint pain), Rocky Mountain spotted fever, and ehrlichiosis. Fleas and mites can cause raw, painful open sores. The list is almost endless. The population of dogs in shelter and rescue situations is a microcosm of the dog population in the larger world, so you can find every physical/medical problem known to humankind, from acne to zinc-deficiency.

Anything that causes your dog to feel "not right" can be a contributor to behavior problems. Think of how cranky you can get when you don't feel well, have a headache, back pain, arthritis, or the flu. Even hormonal imbalances (menopause, anyone?) such as a thyroid condition, can affect behavior. In fact, there's a large and growing body of evidence that low thyroid levels, thought clinically normal, can affect a dog's behavior. Anxiety and aggression may begin to occur even before the dog shows clinical signs of hypothyroidism.

Be aware, then, that if you're adopting a dog with known medical conditions, you'll need to address those as you work with your Do-Over Dog. If your own vet is skeptical of a possible health-related component to your dog's behavior when you suspect the possibility, ask him/her to do a phone consult with a veterinary behaviorist (most will do this for free). Many "regular" veterinarians are unaware of how some conditions, such as thyroid, can affect behavior.

Even when a medical condition is treatable and ultimately resolved, that doesn't magically make related, unwanted behaviors go away—you may still need to do behavior modification to help the dog unlearn behavioral strategies that were useful to him in the past. A dog who has learned to snap to keep children or other dogs from hurting his arthritic bones may continue to snap at children and other dogs even if he's given pain-relieving medication.

Also, be aware that many Do-Over Dogs come from home or shelters that may not have had the resources—or the inclination—to do diagnostics, treatment or prevention for common canine medical conditions. If you have hopes for competing in canine sports activities, it is really important to have the complete veterinary exam done *before* you adopt. You may have to pay for it yourself, even if you don't ultimately take the dog home, but it may help you avoid disappointment and costly treatments later. If you can't do it before, at least do it immediately *after* you adopt, so you can identify and begin treating any conditions as quickly as possible.

Identify and treat medical conditions as quickly as possible to remove one significant source of stress for your Do-Over Dog.

When we had radiographs done to determine why Missy, our newly adopted Australian Shepherd, limped, we discovered a previously-broken right-hind leg that had healed two inches shorter than the other leg. Fortunately, we adopted her simply as a companion. If we were thinking of agility, we would have been in trouble. Scooter (our resource-guarding Pom) was in dire need of a dental cleaning and was having difficulty urinating even before we took him home. While our vet had him sedated to clean his teeth she took radiographs and found and removed a bladder-stone the size of a large grape. Our pint-sized rescue dog cost us $800 in vet bills in his first 60 days with us, but his cranky personality (and his ability to pee) improved considerably!

Many years ago I adopted a seven-year-old Do-Over tri-color Rough Collie from the shelter where I worked at the time. Mandy was owner surrendered. She was extremely overweight as well as incontinent. Her coat was matted and her hind legs were raw with urine burns. A Collie fan from early childhood (thank you, Lassie!), I offered to foster her. I groomed her, put her on a diet, and put her on medications to control the incontinence. She walked into our house and laid down like she'd lived there all her life—and she stayed with me, a wonderful girl, for her remaining five years on this earth.

Once you have evaluated all the information, made sure your entire family is on board with the program, and decided to proceed with an adoption, you may still have one more step. If you already have canine family members at home, you'll need to do careful introductions on neutral ground to be sure that they are as excited and happy—or at least warmly accepting—of a new dog as you are. I strongly urge you to have a very competent dog person, preferably a professional, help you with this, both to avoid injury to dogs and humans, and to accurately analyze the interactions in order to determine if the dogs are a good match.

How to improve your odds

It's easy to lose your heart to a Do-Over Dog. Cautions and common sense aside, its human nature to want to rescue the doggie in distress—the pup who shrinks away from human contact and looks at the world with fear in her eyes. If you are the rescuer type, you have my respect and admiration. I know of many poorly socialized pups who, once rescued, go on to live happy and normal lives because their rescuers recognized the daunting task they faced, and made a solid commitment to do the work. I also know of many who don't make it. Here are some tips for you if you know that your heart will be captured by the challenge of a poorly-socialized Do-Over Dog:

1. Acquire him when he's as young as possible. If he's still a pup, and in a bad situation, the benefits of staying with his litter until eight weeks of age are outweighed by the benefits of getting started with socialization at five or six weeks. (Know that adopting a very young or singleton pup can present additional socialization and behavior modification challenges.)
2. Or, give him the best of both worlds: take the entire litter, or at least several of the pups, and start them *all* on the road to a happier life. Then be sure to find capable, knowledgeable adopters for his siblings when they turn eight weeks—adopters who understand the Do-Over challenges and will continue with remedial socialization.

3. Avoid the temptation to keep more than one pup. They are likely to bond to each other more closely than to you, which makes your socialization challenge many times more difficult. Even *well*-socialized littermates or same-age pals can have separation problems if raised together.
4. Whether a puppy or adult Do-Over, have a solid understanding of counter-conditioning and desensitization, and make a strong commitment to practice this with her *every single day.* (These subjects will be covered later in the book.)
5. Read *The Cautious Canine* by Patricia McConnell, *Help For Your Fearful Dog* by Nicole Wilde, and *Dogs Are From Neptune* by Jean Donaldson, as well as two of my books, *The Power of Positive Dog Training* and *Positive Perspectives 2.*
6. Be prepared to assertively protect your Do-Over Dog from unwanted advances by well-meaning strangers who want to pet him. You must not let people pet or harass him until he is well socialized enough to tolerate petting and harassment.
7. Know that love is not enough. Many well-meaning rescuers think that giving a psychologically neglected pup a home filled with love will be enough to "fix" the problem. Don't fool yourself. Love is an important part of the equation, but it will take a lot of work as well.
8. Be prepared for heartache. Some poorly socialized dogs—most likely those who are genetically sound—do respond well to remedial socialization and turn into reasonably well socialized companions. Others don't. If you don't succeed in enhancing your dog's social skills, are you prepared to live with a fearful dog who may be at high risk for biting—you, visitors, children…? Or to make the difficult decision to euthanize, so he doesn't have to live a life of fear and stress?

Think long and hard before opening your heart to a Do-Over Dog. If you fail him, he may not get another chance.

Always remember that there are Do-Over Dogs, and then there are DO-OVER DOGS. You can do as much of a good thing by adopting a dog with small Do-Over issues as you can one with large Do-Over challenges. Both dogs are in desperate need of a human to call their own, one who won't give up easily on them, and one who will, at some point in their lives, whether sooner or later, be there to give them a gentle good-bye.

Chapter 4

Welcome Home!

The decision is made. Congratulations! Whether you've gone through a search-and-assessment process or simply decided to keep the foundling who showed up on your doorstep, you are now the proud parent of a new furry family member. But wait a minute. Let's back the truck up. Before your Do-Over Dog even sets foot in the door, you want to have a lot of things ready for him.

Pre-arrival preparations

It's important to put some serious thought into your new dog's lifestyle long before he gets there. Family members need to agree on house rules for the arriving canine, including things like what and where he'll eat, who will feed him and when, where he'll sleep, who will walk him, if he will be allowed on the furniture, and much, much more. Your new guy is likely to be stressed by all the recent changes in his life, and the sooner he finds an environment with structure and consistency, the easier it will be for him to relax and settle in. If one family member invites him to sit on the sofa and another yells at him for it, it will add stress, not reduce it. Here are some suggestions for some of the more important decisions.

Where will he live?

I am an unwavering advocate for dogs living inside, in the house, with access to as much of the house as possible. It's hard to create a strong bond with a dog who is excluded from much of your world. Ample social time with you is vital for all dogs, and even more important for a dog who had a poor start in life. If your dog is only allowed in the kitchen and the basement, and you spend no more than an hour a day in those rooms, there's not a lot of hope for a strong relationship, or ever overcoming his Do-Over issues. It's not even worth mentioning the backyard dog arrangement—if he's outside 100% of the time, the prospects are even dimmer. Chaining him up dims the lights even further. A fenced back yard is a great convenience for a dog-owning family, but should not be the dog's primary residence.

Don't even try the "but the kids play with him in the yard" argument. If you work an eight hour job and commute an hour each way, 42 percent of your time is already gone. If you spend an hour with him in the kitchen/basement, and the remaining 13 hours sleeping, running errands, or doing things in the non-dog part of the house, he gets to be with you exactly four percent of your day. This, for a dog who, given the choice, would be in the company of his packmates close to 24 hours a day. Even if you take him for a couple of half-hour walks or your kids give him a couple of play sessions, you're only up to two hours, or eight percent of the day.

At minimum, if you crate train your dog and let him sleep in a crate in your bedroom you can add eight hours to those two, bringing him up to ten hours, or a full 42 percent of the day in the company of his humans. Way better than eight percent! In the best of all worlds he could even go to work with you, or stay home with a retired family member, bringing his human social time to near 100 percent. Now *there's* a happy dog! Of course, not everyone can do this, and since dogs spend a good part of their day sleeping anyway, you don't need to feel too guilty about leaving him home when you go to work—as long as you let him hang with you when you are home.

I am also fanatical about not leaving my dogs outside in their safely-fenced yard when I'm not home to monitor them. Twenty years working in an animal shelter convinced me that there are far too many hazards facing a home-alone dog in the yard: jumping over, digging under, chewing through the fence, gates accidentally or deliberately opened, malicious poisonings and shootings, close encounters with poisonous snakes, birds of prey, coyotes, skunks, rabid animals...need I go on? At worst, your dog can die, or vanish forever. At best, your neighbors may complain to you—or to Animal Control—that your dog is a nuisance barker. They could issue you a citation, or even force you to rehome your dog.

Fences are great, and can make dog-keeping easier—as long as you use them responsibly.

What kind of fence, if any?

Please build your dog a solid, physical fence—a privacy fence if at all possible. The fence should be high enough to make it difficult for him to jump over. Some dogs are quite athletic and determined to escape, but for "normal" dogs, a minimum six-foot fence is ideal for all but the teeny guys, most of whom can do fine with three to four feet. Even some small dogs, like the Jack Russells, need a substantial fence to discourage jumping and climbing. A high fence also deters outsiders from reaching over to pet your dog. This will give him a reasonably safe space to call his own, free from the teasing, tormenting, and arousal from visual stimuli that can happen with a chain link fence. If you must do chain link for financial reasons, you'll need to monitor your dog more closely to be sure he isn't getting into trouble with increasing reactivity as the world whizzes past his doorstep.

Don't even think about an underground shock fence. I'd rather you have no fence at all and resign yourself to taking your dog out on leash to potty at 2:00 am in the pouring rain than have you think that a non-visible underground shock system is in any way shape or form a safe or humane means of confining your dog.

There are a ton of reasons why an underground shock fence is a wretched idea:

- It doesn't keep your dog from running through the non-solid barrier when there is a stimulus enticing enough on the outside. Then he's stuck outside the fence and can't get back in.
- It doesn't protect your dog from intruders—human and otherwise—who can enter his space and injure or be attacked by him.
- It requires that he be shocked in order to be trained to the fence. Some dogs are so traumatized by just one shock experience that they are afraid to go back into their yard. You don't know until it's too late if your dog will be one of those.
- Even if he's only shocked one time and then "respects" the fence, every time he hears the warning tone he can have the same emotional and physiological responses as he did to being shocked—so it's as if he's being shocked again.
- He can generalize that same pain/fear response to other beeps that sound similar to the fence beep, and exhibit extreme fear behavior to the beeping of watches and electronics.
- Repeated associations between the emotional response to the shock or tone and passers-by can cause him to think *they* are causing the shock, or shock-associated tone, and can give rise to aggressive responses to those passers-by—children, other dogs, bicycles, skateboards, mothers with strollers, mail carriers. Then, when the fence fails (and they do fail) or when your dog otherwise encounters those stimuli outside the fence the potential for dog-biting-human is high.
- Shock fences fail. Batteries go dead, wires break, power goes out…shelters routinely house stray dogs who were picked up running at large with their shock fence collars on.
- Shock hurts. Why would you hurt your best friend?

I know there are plenty of testimonials out there about how great the underground shock fences are. There are also plenty of horror stories and tragedies. Don't risk it.

Where will he sleep?

Contrary to advice you may hear from some trainers, I'm fine with having BooBoo on the bed. I'm also a fan of crate-as-den, and I'm just as fine with dog-on-the-floor. We have a variety of sleeping arrangements in our pack of five. Scooter, the Do-Over Pomeranian, sleeps on our bed. Lucy the Corgi (who would love to harass the cats all night) is crated so the feline family members can relax. Bonnie, the Scorgidoodle (Scottie/Corgi/Poodle) is just too active and licky early in the morning—she's crated so the *humans* can relax. Missy and Dubhy, the mature and sedate Aussie and Scottie, usually sleep on dog beds on the floor, although Dubhy sometimes deigns to join us on the bed. Whatever your preference, I encourage you to have your dog sleep in *someone's* bedroom—it prevents him from being lonely at night, allows someone to hear him if he needs a nighttime bathroom break, and most importantly, gives him eight hours of social companionship.

What, when, and where will he eat?

I'm a firm believer in feeding meals rather than having food available all the time. It can be helpful to your relationship if your dog realizes that most good things come from you. For the same reason, I say "no" to the convenience of dog doors. If your furry guy has all the food, water, and access to outdoors he wants, he won't need you for much. *(Note: dogs generally should have access to water at all times, except possibly not at night.)*

I recommend regular meals for all dogs, and *especially* for a Do-Over Dog who needs to learn how to relate to humans. In fact, sometimes I suggest hand-feeding all meals to a dog initially, to *really* help him understand that all the good stuff comes from his human. As an added bonus, you'll be better able to notice if he's not feeling well—it's much quicker to know the *instant* he doesn't eat a meal, as opposed to realizing the level in the food bowl hasn't dropped for a couple of days.

Our adult dogs get two meals a day. Of course young puppies are fed more often than that; follow your vet's instructions for puppy meals. I feed our dogs *before* I eat. The common myth that the leader always eats first is simply absurd. (Even more absurd is the bizarre myth that you have to spit in your dog's food before you give it to him to show him it's yours.) I like to relax when I eat, and I'm much more relaxed knowing my dogs are already fed and I don't have to jump up to feed them just when I want to lean back and let my meal settle. In reality, the leader gets to eat when he or she *wants* to eat.

I also happily feed my dogs a combination of high quality dog foods combined with some healthy "human" foods like pieces of fruits and vegetables (no chocolate, grapes, raisins or onions please!), and bones and meat. Where did the silly concept arise that it's bad for your dogs to eat so-called "human" food? Our own physicians tell us it's healthier for us to eat fresh, unprocessed—or at least less-processed—foods. Why wouldn't the same be true for our dogs?

There is, of course, much discussion in the dog world about raw food versus cooked or commercially prepared food. I'm not going to tell you what to feed your dog, you can research that and make your own choice. But based on your research you should decide what your feeding strategy is *before* your Do-Over Dog arrives, and then be consistent. If you decide at some point there's a legitimate reason to change his diet, do so thoughtfully and carefully—don't just grab the prettiest bag on the grocery store shelf.

Who will feed him?

The "who" isn't generally as important as making sure feeding is done on a regular schedule. That doesn't mean 6:00 am on the dot every morning, it just means regularly twice a day. Our dogs are feed breakfast anywhere between 7:00 am and 9:00 am, and dinner is usually sometime between 5:00 pm and 8:00 pm. If children are part of the feeding crew, an adult must supervise to be sure the dog gets his meal. Whatever responsibility lessons you may be teaching your child, the dog cannot suffer for it; he is ultimately *your* responsibility, not your children's.

If your Do-Over Dog has relationship issues with a specific person in your family, there *can* be value in having that person be the primary feeder and caretaker for your dog. This can help create trust and develop a bond where there is none, or strengthen one that is weak. If the relationship issue includes moderate to significant aggression, however, this may not be a wise idea.

What other house rules are important to you?

Will your dog be allowed on the furniture? All furniture or just some? Will he have to stay in just one room, or have access to the whole house? Whatever the rules, the entire family has to be consistent from day one. Your Do-Over Dog won't understand, and it will make life much harder for him than it has to be if you let him on the sofa for special occasions but yell at him for getting on the sofa at other times.

Oh, go ahead, let him on the sofa! Brad and Lisa Waggoner owner/trainers of Cold Nose College in North Carolina, happily let Cody and Gibson share the furniture!

Who will your canine-care providers be?

Research, interview and select your veterinarian, groomer, pet-sitter, and trainer *before* you bring home your Do-Over Dog. Ask for and check references, watch them in action if you can, and ask them who their hero(ines) are in the world of canine training and behavior professionals. (Names like Karen Pryor, Patricia McConnell, Kathy Sdao, Karen Overall, Terry Ryan, Sarah Kalnajs, Sophia Yin, Leslie Nelson, Ian Dunbar—even Pat Miller—are good.) Make sure they each have a strong commitment to gentle, dog-friendly handling methods before you entrust your canine pal to their care. Don't let *anyone* talk you into letting them hurt or intimidate your dog, regardless of how many letters may be after their name. I routinely recommend against sending your dog away for training unless you have *absolute confidence* in the training methods and philosophies of the trainers. Many will talk a good positive game but still resort to the use of force behind closed doors. Your dog relies on you to protect him from those who still function in the old-fashioned world of dominance and punishment. Don't let him down.

What supplies do you need?

Don't get caught empty handed! You may need to wait until the last minute on some items until you know what size you'll need, but before you walk out the shelter door and return to your own home with your new four-footed family member you should have:

- Food and water bowls
- Food
- Collar (flat or martingale/limited slip collar), *not* a choke chain, prong or shock collar
- Treats, lots, ranging from low value to very high value (See Appendix 1 for list of treats)
- A 6-foot regular walking leash
- A 10-foot "exploring" leash
- A 20 to 40-foot long line
- License
- ID tags
- Microchip
- Dog bed
- Dog crate
- Dog toys (a wide variety—balls, soft toys, rope tugs, interactive and stuffable toys such as Kongs)
- A card taped near the phone with numbers for all your animal care professionals as well as your local Animal Services agency
- Same phone numbers programmed into your cell phone
- Books on dog training and care you have already read (selected from the Resource Section at the end of this book)
- Videos on dog training and care you have already watched (selected from the Resource Section at the end of this book)

Be sure to stock up on high quality durable dog toys—your Do-Over Dog will thank you for it!

Introductions

Your Do-Over Dog's day-one introduction to his new life can set the stage—and the tone—for the rest of his days with you. As exciting as it is to bring home a new family member, it behooves you—and him—to make his arrival as calm and peaceful an event as possible. Save the "New Puppy Party" for at least a couple of weeks down the road until you've gotten to know each other a little better and can predict how he'll react to the frenetic attentions of the three-year-old Wilson twins next door and the overly-strong hugs of 93-year-old Aunt Mildred.

Immediate family members—at least the humans, and ideally other dogs—should already have met the new dogs prior to adoption. If circumstances didn't allow for that, go slowly, especially if there are children who are understandably excited about the new arrival. If your new guy isn't very outgoing and social, have the rest of the family wait indoors, so he's not overwhelmed and frightened by the reception. If his Do-Over issues aren't about socialization, then you don't need to be quite so cautious, but still, take care not to overwhelm.

You'll want to manage your new dog's behavior from the moment you take possession of the leash, even before you deposit him in your car to take him home. You're laying the foundation for future behaviors—making new associations as positive as possible, avoiding fear-triggering associations, reinforcing behaviors you like, and making sure unwanted behaviors aren't reinforced.

Ask your dog's current caretakers in advance not to feed him the day you're picking him up to avoid a potential unpleasant carsick association with his ride home. When your paperwork is completed, spend some time with him so he can get comfortable with you before you start home. If he's abjectly fearful, this won't help, but anything short of that and a little "getting to know you" time will help ease the stress of the ride. In fact, if you can visit your dog several days in a row before taking home, that will make it even easier—it won't feel so much like stranger abduction to him.

Plan to crate (ideally) or seatbelt your dog in the car, or at least have someone hold his leash. It would be a very unpleasant association indeed to have a car wreck as you merge onto the freeway because your Do-Over guy decides to jump on your head!

Unless you have a long ride and need to stop for potty breaks (yours or his), take your new dog directly home. You should already have all your needed supplies ready and waiting, so no quick stops at the grocery store. When you arrive home, take him out of the car on-leash *if you can* and let him stretch his legs and explore the front yard, then enter your fenced yard (if you have one) and walk the fence line with him still on leash. Watch for any signs that he's looking for an immediate escape. If he's measuring the top of the fence for jump-ability, nudging loose boards, or testing the compactness of the dirt with a paw to see if he can dig under, you can add "escape artist" to your list of Do-Over behaviors to manage and modify.

If your new guy is high energy and eager to explore, grab a couple of his toys and play fetch or tug to wear him out before you take him indoors for the first time. By taking the edge off outside first, you're setting him (and you) up for a more successful first-time indoor experience. When you're done playing, hang out with him outside for another five or ten minutes to help him settle down from the excitement of play before you take him in.

Be sure to give your Do-Over guy time to relax and relieve himself before you bring him inside when you first arrive home.

If your newcomer is very fearful and won't walk on leash, you may need to carry him to your fenced yard, or to your nearest grassy area. Set him down, attach the ten-foot exploring leash to his collar and sit on the ground with him. Just sit there, for 20-30 minutes if necessary, to see if he'll get brave enough to get up and walk around a little. If he does, stay seated—just hold the end of his leash. If you stand up, you may scare him again, just when he thinks it's safe to move.

Whether walking with you or moving tentatively on his own, you will want him to empty his bladder and bowels before you take him indoors. No point in starting his housetraining program with an accident! A dog who is not accustomed to eliminating on leash, even one who isn't fearful, may be inhibited about emptying within six to ten feet of you. You may need to attach his long line at first, and let him wander farther from you, until he decides it's safe to do it in your presence. As long as you have a safely enclosed area, you may even need to take the leash off (if you're sure you can connect up with him again) or let him loose with a drag line—a long, light nylon cord—if you think he may run away from you.

Continue your careful management when you're ready to take him inside. First, put other non-human family members away in rooms with doors closed. You're going to orchestrate those introductions one at a time, under close supervision. Have the humans he hasn't met sitting quietly in one room. Bring the dog in, on-leash, and let him walk up and meet each person, and explore the parts of the house that don't have closed doors. Make note of potential trouble spots. Does he stick his nose in the trash receptacle? Stash them all in cupboards or closets, or invest in covered garbage cans. Does he put his paws up on the table, or kitchen counter? He may be a budding—or veteran—counter surfer. Keep all unattended surfaces clear of edibles until you can modify the behavior. Is he angling toward the bookcase with that leg-lift gleam in his eye, use indoor supervision and/or belly bands, until housetraining is complete.

Hey dogs!

When your new canine companion appears ready to relax and settle, you can consider non-human introductions. Take a deep breath, it has to happen sooner or later.

It's best to introduce him to other canine family members on neutral territory. If you can't find neutral, at least do it outside. Perhaps you already took your other dogs to meet him at the shelter or rescue, to see if they were compatible. If so, this step will likely be much easier, although it is still not without pitfalls.

While dogs are genetically programmed to get along with pack members and the odds are therefore good that canines will be compatible, that doesn't necessarily mean instant warm fuzzies every time two dogs meet. When you are adding a new member to your personal pack, it is especially important that the introductions go well. Here are some suggestions to tip the odds in your favor:

1. **Have a helper, don't introduce new dogs alone.** You need to have at least one other adult there to help you in case there is trouble. Be sure your helper is comfortable and confident with dogs, and let her know, step-by-step, exactly what you plan to do and what you want her to do. Do not have children with you when you are doing introductions.

2. **Introduce dogs on neutral ground if at all possible.** This is especially important if one or more of your dogs tend to be territorial. A neighbor's fenced yard, unused tennis court (if dogs are allowed) or other securely enclosed area works well.

It's best to introduce your new dog to your resident dog(s) on neutral territory, if possible.

3. **Introduce dogs outdoors.** There are less likely to be territorial issues outdoors than indoors, and the "great outdoors" provides more space and fewer traps—if the new dog feels threatened he can move away more easily in wide open spaces, not get stuck behind the sofa.
4. **Introduce dogs one at a time.** If you are adding a dog to a home-pack of several hounds, identify the home-dog most likely to offer an easy greeting for the newcomer. When those two have hit it off, remove the first home-dog and bring on the next most likely candidate. When the new dog has met each home-dog individually, introduce pairs, again starting with the two most congenial home-dogs. Keep adding one more dog at a time to the introduction groups until all the dogs are together. If you see tension at any point, don't add new dogs until the tension resolves. If necessary, manage by keeping the tension-inducing combinations separated until you can get professional help with the introductions.
5. **Present dogs at a distance.** Have your helper hold the new dog at the far side of the yard when you bring the home-dog in the gate. Let them see each other from opposite sides of the yard, then approach until they are six to eight feet apart. As long as there is no obvious aggression, release them so they can meet at their own speed, on their own terms, offering natural body language signals.

6. **Leave lightweight leashes attached to both dogs' collars.** If there is a problem, you and your helper can each grab a leash and separate the dogs without putting your own body parts in harm's way. When it's clear that the dogs are getting along—usually after just a minute or two, remove the leashes so they don't get tangled around legs—yours *and* the dogs—as the playmates begin to romp.
7. **Ignore minor scuffles.** A snap and snarl with minimal contact is one dog's way of telling the other to "Back off, Bub!" This is how they sort out their relationships and decide who can do what to whom. If you intervene when scuffles happen, you make it more difficult for the dogs to figure each other out, and it takes much longer for them to become comfortable with each other.
8. **Intervene when appropriate.** If one dog is fearful and appears traumatized by the encounter, or is clearly getting trounced by the other(s) beyond a mild scuffle, then you need to step in, grab a leash, separate them, and rethink your introduction program. Have tools readily available to break up a fight if necessary. (See Appendix 2—Tools and Techniques to Break up a Fight.)
9. **Be calm.** If you are stressed, your dogs will read your body language and become more stressed themselves. Stress causes aggression. Speak calmly and cheerfully; move slowly and deliberately. Avoid sudden movements and loud verbal corrections, which can contribute to stress and aggression. If you need to intervene, use a cheerful, positive interrupt such as "Fido! Over here! Good boy!" rather than a verbal punisher such as "Fido! No! Bad dog!"
10. **Be careful.** If you are not confident about your introduction skills, or you have extenuating factors such as a huge size disparity (introducing a Great Dane to a Chihuahua, for example) or a dog who has demonstrated aggression toward other dogs in the past, seek the assistance of a positive behavior professional to help with your introductions. Also, remember that there may be space issues indoors that didn't occur outdoors. Watch your pack closely when you bring them inside. If necessary, manage behavior in the house in small groups until they are all more comfortable with each other.

Here, kitty kitty

Cats tend to be the other greatest challenge, especially if your Do-Over pal has strong predatory behaviors. Of course, that also puts other small companion animals at risk, but at least hamsters, Guinea pigs, rabbits, birds, fish, and reptiles are usually in pens, cages, or tanks. You *will* need to manage scrupulously to ensure that doors are closed and baby gates are in place unless and until you decide your Do-Over Dog can be trusted with your other-species family members. But cats usually enjoy sharing the same living space that your new canine will occupy, and you need to be sure they're safe, as quickly as possible. That also demands good management.

Good management requires effective barriers (doors, Dutch doors, baby gates), sturdy containment units (crates, pens), restraints (leashes, tethers), and unwavering supervision (your eyeballs and awareness). However, all of your management tools are only as good as your ability to ensure their use. A moment's lapse can result in tragedy instead of warm breathing beings, and sooner or later there's likely to be a lapse.

You can use a baby gate to give your cats a dog-free zone.

If your housemates aren't good at heeding your warnings to keep doors closed, or if your talented canine can open doors, then you might need to add self-closing springs, child-proof latches, and/or padlocks to your list of management tools. You're likely to be more successful in the long run commingling species if you combine a foolproof management plan with an effective program of training and behavior modification.

Begin *before* you bring the dog home by creating safe places for the cat where the dog cannot go. Baby gates and cat doors are a big help, as are catwalks and other cat-friendly perches that are out of the dog's reach. Be sure your cat knows how to use them. Help Fluffy learn how to use kitty-doors by holding them open and luring her through with a treat. Gradually lower the flap as you lure Fluffy through so she starts pushing it open herself—a little bit at first, and eventually with the flap all the way down.

Make sure she can easily jump over the baby gate, by tossing her favorite treats over it and watching her sail. Baby gates are great for providing exercise for a sedentary cat, even without dogs in the home! Or, if your Do-Over Dog is larger than a cat, cut a cat-sized opening in the bottom of the gate for your felines to slip through. Putting feed bowls and litter boxes in a gated room keeps your dogs from chowing down on cat chow or cleaning litter boxes in search of "kitty rocca" treats (Yuck!).

Encourage Fluffy to explore perches and catwalks by baiting them with treats and catnip crumbs. When your cat is familiar with all her escape routes, you're ready to introduce the canine element. This could take days or even weeks, so plan ahead.

For your first introduction, hold your Do-Over guy on leash at the far side of the room, and have a friend or family member invite Fluffy to venture into the room under her own power. Both of you should have a handy container full of yummy treats. Watch your dog's reactions carefully. In a perfect world, he'll be slightly curious about the cat, but far more interested in the treats you offer him one at a time, as soon as he notices the cat. Ideally the cat does the same, "Ho-hum, there's a dog, and WOW—there's some tasty fish flakes!" If your Do-Over kid shows anything more than mild, controlled interest in Fluffy, then add "cat-related behavior modification" to your Do-Over list, and take extra precautions to keep Fluffy safe. Depending on how intense your dog's interest is in the cat, that could mean anything from simply shutting Fluffy in a safe-room (or crating the dog) when you're not home, to total lockdown while you work to determine if the two can ever be trusted together. If you do see intense interest, be sure to read the section in Chapter 7 on modifying your dog's behavior with cats and other small companion animals.

His own spot

"Everyone needs his own spot." That wise saying appears on a number of charming Mary Engelbreit products, and applies to dogs as much as it does to humans. You can help your Do-Over dude adjust to his new surroundings more quickly if you provide him with a spot of his very own—a crate, an exercise pen, or a bed in the corner. With our pack of five, we have a panoply of crates and dog beds—one each downstairs, one each upstairs. They know which ones are their own, and rarely is there a squabble about one dog occupying another's spot. Other squabbles, yes, but not about that.

They seem to take real comfort in their own beds, and the "go to bed" cue sends them flying to their respective places in my office to await a raw chicken wing or up the stairs to the crates for a bedtime cookie. A distant rumble of thunder sends sounds-sensitive Corgi, Lucy, to her safe-place crate, and it puts a smile on my face every morning to spy Dubhy, the Scottie, stretched out in the baby bassinet in the corner of our bedroom that he's claimed as his own.

Crates

I can recall when I first heard about crates, in the early 1980's. The Marin Humane Society where I worked as a humane officer, had agreed to purchase Australian Kelpie puppies for me and Donna Bosso, another officer, to be our Canine Field Agents. We would train the dogs to herd so they could help us with loose livestock calls, and they would also do education programs with us. My little red pup was a real treasure, and caring for her was a privilege. I wanted to do everything "state of the art" and so, while I had my reservations about this new-fangled crating idea, I was determined to try. For the first three nights, after brushing my teeth I carried my girl to her crate and put her in, generously plying her with treats. I was immediately impressed with the obvious—I could wake up in the morning without risk of stepping in a puddle of pee or piles of poo. On the fourth night, when I went to put Keli in her crate, Caper, my three-year-old Bull Terrier mix was lying inside, thumping her tail and grinning at me as if to say, "Gee Mom, these are really cool, can I have one? Please?"

Of course I got her one of her own, and within a few more nights, Keli, too, was already happily curled up in her crate by the time I finished brushing my teeth. Needless to say, I became a strong advocate of crate-as-dog's-spot.

Most dogs can learn to love their crates—which makes it an incredibly useful management tool as well as his own safe space.

A crate should be just large enough for your dog to stand up, turn around and lie down in comfortably. If it's too large, he'll be able to soil one end and stay in the clean end, defeating the housetraining value of the crate. Cover the floor of the crate with a rug or soft pad to make it comfortable and inviting.

Crates may not be the right choice for every dog. Dogs with isolation or separation issues often don't crate well. Dogs who have been overcrated or kept in an unclean environment are all too often perfectly happy to soil their crates and lie in the mess. And some dog owners do abuse the crate—keeping dogs in them far, far longer than is good for physical or mental health. Still, used appropriately, they are an impressively useful management tool. Used appropriately, dogs love them. If you can't crate, be sure to set up a spot for him with a comfortable bed. Every dog *should* have his own spot.

The social scene

A significant number of Do-Over Dogs are under-socialized. Lack of socialization creates shy, fearful dogs who can't enjoy the world around them, and who are at high risk for biting someone, sometime. Helping your dog learn to cope better with all sorts of stimuli soon after you bring him home is a must.

A dog's personality comes from nature (genetics) *and* nurture (environmental influences). If your dog is genetically confident, he'll still need *some* socialization as a puppy to become a well-adjusted adult. If he's genetically shy or timid, he'll need *tons* of socialization to become a normal dog. The best insurance against fearful, potentially biting adult dogs is to socialize the heck out of *all* puppies, to prevent them from becoming fearful Do-Over Dogs.

If your newly adopted Do-Over is under-socialized, you'll need to implement a very gradual behavior modification program. (See Chapter 7 for more details.) You can't ever really make up for the socialization he missed as a puppy, but you *can* help him become more comfortable by giving him positive experiences in a world that is overwhelming to him. Be sure you don't overwhelm him even more by exposing him to more experiences than he can handle.

Note the importance of *positive* experiences. You will want to protect your dog from painful or frightening experiences, especially when he is still getting accustomed to his new home. Don't expose him to excessively loud noises or extreme visual stimuli—like your town's 4th of July fireworks display or the loud band and scary costumes in the Halloween parade! Supervise interactions with children so they can't tease and torment him or encourage inappropriate puppy biting and chasing. Instead, have them feed him tasty treats for sitting politely—kids love to learn how to train dogs! Make experiences like trips to the vet for vaccinations as positive as possible—lots of treats in the waiting room, lots of treats while he gets the shot, lots of treats from the vet and clinic staff. In fact, make it a point to visit your vet's waiting room when you *don't* have an appointment, so going to the hospital doesn't always mean being poked and prodded.

See a pattern? Using tasty treats generously to give your dog a positive association with many potentially aversive stimuli and experiences is called *classical conditioning* —creating an association between two stimuli. Behavioral scientists have identified the period from two to fourteen weeks as the most important socialization window for a puppy. After the age of fourteen weeks that window starts to close, and it closes pretty quickly.

Present any aversive stimulus at a low intensity at first—far away, low volume, and associate it with yummy stuff. Every time the scary thing appears, feed your dog tasty treats—lots! As long as he can see the scary thing, feed tidbits. When the thing leaves, stop feeding. When your dog realizes that the thing *makes* good stuff happen, he'll *want* the scary thing to appear. Then you can increase the intensity—closer, louder—and keep feeding treats, until the pup is completely happy about the sight or sound.

Do this with things that are neutral, making sure your dog has a positive association with those things too. Children are the most common victims of dog bites. Start creating your dog's positive kid association the first time he sees them by feeding treats *whenever* young humans are around—don't wait to find out if he is afraid.

If you're not careful during your socialization efforts, you may inadvertently set your pup up to create *negative* associations. In that case, you can actually *sensitize* your pup to the things you're introducing him to—that is, you can make him afraid of them—the exact opposite of the outcome you want.

Think of the well-meaning soccer mom who takes the family's brand-new nine-week old Portuguese Water Dog pup to watch her son's team practice. The entire team suddenly spies the adorable black-and-white fluffball and charges toward mom to oogle over him. The terrified puppy screams, pees, and tries to run away when he sees a dozen giant human creatures coming toward him at a dead run. He can't escape; he's trapped by the leash, which panics him even more. Mom sees the pup flailing at the end of the leash and scoops him up in her arms to calm him so the boys can pet him. Now he's even *more* trapped! One boy reaches to pat him on the head, and the pup, thinking he may be about to die, as a last resort snaps at the lowering hand that appears poised to grab him. The boy yanks his hand away, and mom scolds the puppy for being "bad."

How much worse could it get? This puppy now has an extreme fear of children, especially boys, thanks to at least three negative classical associations in rapid succession:

1. Boys/children are scary—they run toward you in large packs.
2. Boys/children are scary—they try to grab your head.
3. Boys/children make bad things happen—when they are nearby, the pup's mom becomes aggressive too!

The pup may also have developed negative associations with the collar and leash, wide open fields, being picked up, and mom. In addition, he learned one important *operant* lesson—snapping is a successful behavioral strategy for making scary hands go away. Not the lessons we want a young pup to learn!

The bad news is the puppy is now "not good with children" and a "fear biter." While we often talk about how slow dogs can be to generalize operantly conditioned behaviors (if I do "X" I can make "Y" happen), classically conditioned associations, especially those that produce strong emotions, are great candidates for "one-time learning experiences."

The good news is that at nine weeks this pup's socialization window is still open, and if his owner is smart she has time to repair the damage. The other bad news, however, is that most owners don't realize the importance of taking immediate steps to change a pup's association if he has a bad experience at a young age. They think "tincture of time" will fix it—that he'll grow out of it. He won't. Or they think having the soccer team feed him cookies once a week, or forcing him to accept their attentions will be enough to make him love them. It won't.

Remember, socialization is the process of giving a puppy *positive* associations with the people, places and things in his world. You need to be sure he's having a great time, playing fun games, getting good stuff, and is protected from scary stuff while you're teaching him that the world is a safe and happy place. You need to be attentive to him any time he's in public or otherwise exposed to new things, and, if he's looking worried or overwhelmed, remove him from the action to a distance where he can relax, and make really good things happen for him there—treats, toys, massage. When he seems more comfortable, move slowly back toward the thing that worried him, stopping every few feet—or few inches, to help him relax again. If it all seems too overwhelming for him and you can't find his comfort zone, take him home.

If your fearful Do-Over Dog is beyond the puppy socialization stage, your challenge will be even greater. Not impossible, but large. You'll find detailed fear behavior modification programs for Do-Over Dogs in Chapters 7 and 8 of this book.

Chapter 5
Science Lessons for the Do-Over Dog

Although Do-Over Dogs often *seem* to behave differently from "normal" dogs, they really are subject to the same scientific behavioral principles that affect all beings with a central nervous system. We all want to get good stuff and avoid bad stuff, and we all make associations—positive or negative—based on our past experiences. When your fearful Do-Over Dog has a panic reaction to some environmental stimulus, it's either because he's had a past experience with that thing or because he has a generalized neophobic association with unknown things as hurtful or scary. When your Do-Over Dog checks out the kitchen counter and scores the roast beef sandwich that you carelessly left there unattended, it's because he's learned that checking out the kitchen counter is sometimes/often reinforced by the presence of "good stuff."

Training philosophies

All dog training techniques fit somewhere on a long continuum, from seriously harsh and abusive punishment-based methods at one extreme, to purely positive reinforcement at the other. As is often the case with extremes, neither of these is likely very practical, nor will you find many trainers who recommend either extreme. Most trainers use a combination of techniques that place them somewhere between the two ends of the continuum. Which side of center they are on defines them as primarily compulsion-based trainers or primarily positive ones.

Within the dog training community the debate about methods is spirited. Hackles get raised when trainers, who tend to be an opinionated lot, disagree on the very best method to resolve a particular canine behavior challenge. Why the huge diversity in training philosophies? Because there are, in fact, several different training approaches that can successfully teach a dog to do what you ask. You can teach your dog to sit by saying the word "sit," jerking up on the collar and pushing down on her rump to force her to sit, then patting her on the head, verbally praising or giving her a cookie. Alternatively, you can *lure* her into the sit position by moving a treat over her head, then saying "Yes!" and giving her the treat when she does. You can *shape* a sit using a *click and treat* technique to reinforce small steps toward what will eventually be a complete "sit" behavior. Or you can *capture* the behavior by waiting until she decides to sit on her own and then giving her a click or verbal marker followed by a treat reward. Each technique can work. There are pluses and minuses with each.

Behavioral terms

In behavioral terms, training is known as "conditioning behavior." You really aren't teaching your dog any new behaviors when you train him. He already knows how to sit, lie down, stay in one place, walk by your side, roll over, or come running to you from far away—when he wants to. He just may not know how to do it (or may not choose to do it) when you ask him to. Training is conditioning (or teaching the dog) to reliably give you the behaviors you ask for, when you ask for them.

Classical conditioning, as first described by the Russian scientist Ivan Pavlov (1849-1936), creates an association between a stimulus and a response or behavior. A stimulus is something that elicits a response. This is the famous "ring a bell, the dog salivates," experiment that most of us are familiar with. Classical conditioning is generally used to create or change emotional responses or associations. When you socialize a puppy to convince him the world is a wonderful place, you're doing classical conditioning.

Operant conditioning, most closely associated with the American scientist B.F. Skinner (1904-1990), is most commonly used for training specific behaviors. With operant conditioning, the dog does something in anticipation of an expected consequence. There are four principles of operant conditioning, often called "quadrants:"

Conditioning your pup to love children greatly reduces the likelihood that he'll ever bite one.

1. **Positive reinforcement.** The dog's behavior makes something good happen, so the desired behavior increases. For example, when the dog walks next to you without pulling on the leash, she gets a treat (treat = good thing, loose leash walking increases).
2. **Positive punishment.** The dog's behavior makes something bad happen, so the undesirable behavior decreases. For example, if the dog pulls on the leash, his neck gets jerked to bring him back to the heel position (jerk on neck = bad thing, pulling on leash decreases). *Note: I do not recommend this method.*

3. **Negative punishment.** The dog's behavior makes something good go away, so the undesirable behavior decreases. For example, you hold up a Frisbee to throw for your dog and when he jumps up to grab it out of your hand, you hide it behind your back. Frisbee = good thing; hidden = "goes away," therefore jumping up to grab Frisbee decreases, especially if followed by throwing of the Frisbee when the dog stays seated.
4. **Negative reinforcement.** The dog's behavior makes something bad go away, so the desired behavior increases. For example, a no-pull harness puts pressure on the dog's chest as long as the dog puts pressure on the leash. When the dog stops pulling, the pressure stops. Pressure = bad thing; no pulling = bad thing "goes away," pulling on leash decreases.

Use operant conditioning to teach your dog to offer behaviors in expectation of a desirable consequence.

Compulsion training

Old-fashioned, compulsion-based training works on the philosophy that you have to be the "alpha" and show the dog who is boss. He must do what you say, and quickly. If he doesn't, you immediately correct him or he will learn that he can ignore your commands. An important tool for compulsion trainers is positive punishment, often followed by a treat, a pat, and/or verbal praise to keep up the dog's enthusiasm for the training process. Twenty years ago, traditional trainers abhorred the use of food treats in place of praise. This thinking has changed in the last decade. As more and more "foodies" have demonstrated the effectiveness of food as a training motivator, more and more compulsion trainers have added the use of food to their training repertoire.

Compulsion training can work, as demonstrated by decades of well-behaved dogs who were trained using those methods. A skilled trainer uses the minimum amount of force necessary to get the job done. Proponents argue that the small amount of discomfort this may cause is worth the end result of a reliable, promptly responsive dog. It can be problematic, however, with very assertive or independent dogs who don't take kindly to being pushed and pulled around and may decide to argue back, and with very sensitive dogs—as are many Do-Over Dogs, who are intimidated by the use of force.

If you use compulsion methods with an assertive dog, you must be prepared to use enough force to get your message across quickly, and be willing to escalate the level of force if necessary. Techniques like scruff shakes and alpha rolls (forcing a dog down and trying to hold him there) only appear to work when the trainer is strong enough to persevere if the dog fights back. Many owners and trainers are either unwilling or unable to use this kind of force with their dogs—thank goodness.

Forceful corrections can also cause timid, submissive or sensitive dogs to shut down and become fearful, and a slight miscalculation can cause irreparable damage to the owner's or trainer's relationship with the dog. You may not know how much is too much until it's too late.

Yet another concern about compulsion training is the possible damage to a dog's throat from a standard choke chain collar, which can exert tremendous pressure on a dog's trachea. They are not recommended for puppies under the age of six months, yet it is more and more widely accepted that starting puppies in training classes at eight weeks is ideal, in order to take advantage of a pup's important socialization and learning period. I don't personally use or recommend choke chains *ever*, and if you are taking your *puppy* to a training class or a trainer who insists you use one, turn and run away fast. Prong collars reputedly distribute the pressure more evenly around the neck and are less likely to do damage, but they work because they hurt, and many owners understandably shy away from using the medieval looking spikes on their dogs.

Clicker training/positive training

"Clicker trainer" is a slang term for trainers who use positive reinforcement as their first method of choice, combined with an audible reward-predicting signal to mark desired behaviors. The click is always followed by a treat, so your dog knows that when he hears the click, a reward will always follow. These trainers operate on a different training philosophy from the compulsion trainers, preferring to get the dog to offer behavior voluntarily, then mark and reward when he does. The *marker signal, or bridge,* can be the click of the clicker, a whistle, some other mechanical sound, or a word. A verbal "Yes!" is frequently used to mark a reward-earning behavior. Since all living creatures tend to repeat behaviors that are rewarding, behaviors that are repeatedly marked and rewarded by a dog's owner get offered more and more frequently. Behaviors that are not rewarded tend to go away, or "extinguish." *Note: Ignoring an unwanted behavior isn't enough to extinguish it. You need to manage your Do-Over Dog's environment to be sure he's not getting reinforced for the behavior by the environment—i.e., the roast beef sandwich left out on the kitchen counter.*

Take, for example, the puppy who wants to jump up on everyone. Dogs often greet each other's faces (sniffing noses, licking lips), so it is natural for your dogs to want to greet your face. Plus, when he's a cute little puppy you pick him up and cuddle him in your arms, thereby rewarding him for being "up." Small wonder that so many dogs jump on people!

Some of the suggested compulsion approaches to correcting jumping behavior actually reward the very behavior you are trying to extinguish. When the dog jumps up, he touches you. That's a reward. You look at him. Eye contact is reinforcing. You speak to him to tell him to get off. You're paying attention to him—that's a reward! You reach down to push him away. You touched him—another reward! For some rowdy dogs, even the time-honored "knee him in the chest" is an invitation to start a rousing game of body-slam.

The positive reinforcement approach relies on the principle that behaviors that are not reinforced will extinguish. But how do you ignore an enthusiastic, obnoxious canine who is leaping up to greet you nose-to-nose, inflicting multiple bruises and lacerations in the process? Just standing still doesn't work—he gets all kinds of self-rewards by jumping all over you.

Instead, turn your back on the dog and step away. As he tries to come around to face you, do it again. Turn away and step away. Turn away and step away. Over and over. If necessary, step through a door (or some other barrier) and close it with him on the other side, or practice with your dog tethered so he can't follow you and keeping jumping on your back (and be reinforced for touching you) as you walk away. Sooner or later—and with most dogs this happens much sooner than you would imagine—your dog gets frustrated and confused, and sits down to puzzle out your bizarre behavior. Bingo! Now turn toward him, tell him "Yes!" and feed him the treat from the stash you keep in your pockets at all times in anticipation of opportunities just like this. You can also pet and praise him—assuming petting and praise is reinforcing to him. This may not be the case, especially with many Do-Over Dogs. If he jumps up again, repeat the process. Before you know it, he'll figure out that in order to get the attention he craves, he needs to sit when he approaches you, not jump.

Clicker trainers use primarily positive reinforcement, but will also use varying degrees of negative punishment, negative reinforcement and (hopefully very little) positive punishment. This usually will vary depending on the dog, the individual trainer's own comfort level and skill with the various methods, and commitment to positive training. The jumping up example above actually uses negative punishment—the dog's behavior (jumping up) causes something good (you) to go away. Then, when he sits and you give him a treat and attention, it is positive reinforcement—the dog's behavior (sitting) causes something good (treat and attention) to happen. Negative punishment works best if you can follow it with positive reinforcement for a desirable behavior in place of the unwanted one.

Proponents of positive reinforcement training know that a training approach based on rewards rather than punishment builds trust in the human-canine relationship and encourages the dog to think for himself and freely make deliberate choices of rewardable behaviors, rather than living in anticipation of being punished for making a wrong choice. Positive-trained dogs tend to be more willing to think for themselves, choose "right" behaviors, take risks, and offer new behaviors than do dogs who are routinely corrected for making mistakes.

Of course, it's not always possible to ignore a dog's inappropriate behavior. Some unwanted behaviors are self-rewarding, destructive or unsafe, like barking at the mail carrier, chewing electrical cords, or chasing cars. All trainers use a variety of approaches to correct unwanted behavior, but by definition clicker trainers apply methods that stop short of physical or harsh verbal corrections.

One such method is *management.* It's easier to prevent unwanted behaviors than it is to correct them. It's far easier to keep your dog properly confined in a fenced yard or on a leash than it is to stop a dog with strong predatory behaviors from chasing cars, cats, joggers, or skateboarders. While you're managing the behavior, you also work to train a better level of control so your dog becomes more reliable around highly arousing stimuli.

Positive trainers may also use a *"No Reward Marker,"* or *NRM,* also called a *"Loss of Opportunity Marker,"* or *LOM.* This is a signal to let the dog know he made a mistake. It's not applied angrily, just used in a neutral tone to let the dog know that the behavior didn't earn a reward. Commonly used NRM's include "Oops," "Try Again," or the sound "Uh!" or "At!" I prefer "Oops!" because it's hard to say it in an angry tone of voice. "Uh" and "At" can easily become aversive if the trainer is angry or stressed. A properly-used NRM is not aversive, but simply tells the dog that the behavior offered didn't earn a reward because it was not the one requested, and encourages him to try again.

Yet another positive behavior correction method, is to reinforce an incompatible behavior. A dog can't lie on his rug in the living room and jump up on the visitor on the front porch at the same time. If you teach him that the doorbell is his cue to go lie down on his rug and stay there, he will no longer greet your guests with his sometimes unwelcome exuberance.

The ongoing debate

There's no lack of debate between trainers about the effectiveness of their various training approaches. Compulsion trainers believe that an aggressive dog must be physically corrected for the least sign of aggression: hackles raised, intense stare, growling. This purportedly teaches the dog that the behavior is not acceptable, or at least serves to suppress the behavior so it's less. Many modern, educated behavior professionals argue that a growl and other signs of aggression are important canine communication tools; that punishment suppresses the dog's warning signals, but the aggression is still there, and can erupt without warning in the future on some hapless victim.

Positive reinforcement trainers suggest that a better approach is to change the way the dog thinks about the aggression causing stimulus by associating it with positive things. Consider a dog who wants to bite children. If every time he sees a child he gets a treat before he has a chance to act aggressive, he'll begin to associate the presence of children with "Good things happen." Eventually he'll be eager to see children, and the aggression will fade. Aggressive behavior is not lurking beneath the surface, because the dog no longer thinks of children as a threat; they are now a reliable predictor of good things. You still won't want to leave him with children without direct supervision, but he will be much more relaxed around them.

Clicker trainers believe that force-based training dampens a dog's enthusiasm for learning, and "stifles their creativity." Compulsion trainers may assert that reward-trained dogs won't perform reliably under stress. Clicker trainers say that violence elicits violence, and that many dogs who are euthanized for biting were often made worse by physical corrections. Compulsion trainers argue that their methods are faster, and that sometimes the use of force can cause quicker behavior changes that save a dog's life whose owner is at the breaking point and on the verge of sending the dog to a shelter.

Most trainers, regardless of training philosophy, agree that owners apply whatever training methods they are using with varying degrees of skill and success. Trainers from both sides of the continuum talk about some of their client-owners who "just don't get it." Other arguments aside, it would seem logical to conclude that much more harm can be done by an underskilled owner improperly jerking on a collar or applying other coercive techniques such as the "alpha roll" than by one who tosses a few extra treats at the wrong time.

Deciding on what training methods to use is a personal choice. Pet owners left to their own devices are more likely to follow their hearts and choose a gentle, non-violent training method, while those owners who have been conditioned by past trainers and the pressure of competition to believe that a little "pop on the collar" won't hurt the dog, will more quickly accept force-based training.

In the end, the dogs tell us the truth. You can find pet dogs and obedience show ring competitors from both training styles that are happy, reliable, willing workers. You can find dogs from both training styles that are poorly trained and out of control. But you're likely to see more dogs in a compulsion-based class who grudgingly comply with commands or look bored or disgruntled than in a positive reinforcement class, where enthusiasm usually abounds among two-and-four-legged students alike. More importantly, methods that utilize coercion, force and intimidation have a significantly higher likelihood of creating behaviors such as learned helplessness, in which the dog simply shuts down, and aggression, in which the dog fights back. Given all that your Do-Over Dog went through before joining your family, it only makes sense to use gentle, dog-friendly methods as you work to convince him he really has a second chance for a first-class life.

Emotion and behavior

Fear, anger, joy, love, jealousy—these emotions can play an important role in your Do-Over Dog's behavior. Just think how your own emotions sometimes contribute to or even control what you do—and you're human, with a much greater cognitive ability to analyze your feelings.

There was a time when scientists said animals didn't feel pain. We know now how ignorant and cruel that was. Then they said animals didn't use tools. But Jane Goodall and other ethologists have presented irrefutable proof that apes, birds, dogs, and other animals do, in fact, use tools. Emotion and cognition were the last holdouts, but increasingly, scientists are agreeing that animals have a range of emotions quite similar to ours. After all, a dog's amygdala (the part of the brain that controls emotion) appears very similar in size and function to the amygdala of a human, supporting the theory that the two species experience very similar emotions. Anthropomorphism is no longer a dirty word! It's even becoming widely accepted that dogs have much greater cognitive abilities than we once gave them credit for, although the fact that the canine cortex is considerably smaller than ours probably means they'll never do calculus. But I could be wrong.

Other important behavior concepts

In addition to the basic principles of operant and classical conditioning, there are many additional behavior concepts that can help you help your Do-Over Dog adjust to his new life with you. Here are some that you can use while training.

Reinforcers—the dog decides

It doesn't matter how wonderful *you* think something is, if the dog doesn't like it, it's not a reinforcer. Some things can be reinforcing to your dog sometimes, and not at other times. Again, your dog gets to decide, not you. A high value food treat is not reinforcing if your dog is too stressed to eat, has an upset stomach, or is so full he can't eat another bite. The opportunity to chase a ball is not reinforcing if your canine pal is tired, in pain, or never learned to love chasing balls. Petting and hugging—something we touchy-feely humans *love* to do to dogs—are only reinforcing if your dog has learned to love petting and hugging. Many dogs do not. If you try to reward your dog with something you think is reinforcing but he doesn't, you may actually be *punishing* his behavior—which means it will decrease rather than increase—the opposite of the effect you're striving for when you're attempting to reinforce a behavior.

Reinforcers are divided into two types: primary and secondary. *Primary reinforcers* are things that have innate value, and are linked to biology and survival—food, water, air, sex, social contact and interaction, exercise, and comfort—protection from heat and cold, emptying bowels and bladder, relief from pain and fear. *Secondary reinforcers* are things that take on value because of their association with primaries. A ball is reinforcing because your dog associates it with social interaction (with you) and chasing. Your praise is reinforcing to your dog because he associates it with social interaction and treats. A leash is reinforcing because he associates it with walks—social interaction and exercise. Trained behaviors can be secondary reinforcers because of their association with you, and high value food rewards.

"Tug" is a high-value secondary reinforcer for many dogs.

The more you develop your dog's repertoire of secondary reinforcers, the more ways you have to reward him without using food. Although there's nothing wrong with using food as a reinforcer, there are times when it's more convenient, and/or more beneficial, to have other reinforcers at your disposal as well. A dog who is too stressed to eat might be reinforced by a game of tug, a "Find it!" cue, or an invitation to ride in the car.

Take the time to make a complete list of your dog's reinforcers, as well as those you might be able to add to his list of secondaries (See Appendix 3). Then remember to make full use of the list as you help your dog through his Do-Over challenges.

Generalization

Whether you're doing basic training with your Do-Over Dog or behavior modification protocols, you need to know about *generalization*—a dog trainer term that means you have to practice in lots of different places, with lots of different variables, if you want your dog to understand that whatever you're doing happens anywhere and everywhere. This holds true for classical conditioning as well as operant conditioning, and goes triple for Do-Over Dogs who have difficult past experiences to overcome. If your dog is fearful of children and you give your dog a new, positive association with them, but you only do it in your own home, he may still be fearful of them out in the "real" world. You need to generalize his positive association with children everywhere you take him. If your dog is a star at performing his basic good manners behaviors in your living room, but you never practice anywhere else, it's likely to fall apart when you take him out in public. You need to practice all of his training and modification exercises in a wide variety of environments in order to help him generalize those lessons. The good news is that many dogs seem to generalize the concept of generalization. The further you progress in your dog's training, the easier it gets to generalize his new behaviors.

This training class is generalizing their dogs' good manners behaviors to the real world.

Counter-conditioning thresholds

For a detailed discussion of counter-conditioning, please refer to Chapter 8, page 128. At this point, let's focus on the concept of *thresholds* as they often come into play when working on generalizing behaviors.

When you're doing any behavior modification protocol that involves changing your dog's behavioral response to something in his environment (a stimulus), the process is most successful—and least stressful to dog and human—if you stay below *threshold*—the level of intensity of stimulus that causes the dog to react strongly. Whether you are doing counter-conditioning to change the dog's emotional response with a resulting change to his behavior, or operant conditioning to change his behavior with a resulting change to his emotional response, you'll be most effective if you can present the stimulus *sub-threshold*—at an intensity that he notices and is a little concerned, but is not so stressed that he barks, lunges, bites, tries to run away, shuts down (won't eat high value treats), or shows other signs of extreme stress.

For auditory stimuli (things he can *hear),* start with the volume of the sound, very low, and gradually increase the volume. With tactile stimuli (things that *touch* him) start with low intensity by briefly touching where he's tolerant of your touch, and increase intensity *when he's ready* by gradually moving your hand to more sensitive places. You can also increase intensity by increasing *duration* (touching him longer in the same spot) and/or amount of pressure.

If you do accidentally go over your dog's threshold (it happens to the best of us!), back up, take a break until the dog has calmed, and start again at a reduced intensity.

The Premack Principle

While we're on the subject of reinforcers, let me introduce you to an interesting and useful principle. *The Premack Principle* says that you can use a more desirable/rewarding behavior—from the dog's perspective—to reinforce a less desirable one. It's also called Grandma's Law: "You have to eat your broccoli before you can have your ice cream." For your dog, you could use it like this:

- "Come to me first, and then together we'll go chase the squirrel."
- "Give me your paw for clipping *one* toenail and then you can chase the ball."
- "Sit politely in front of me and then I'll throw the Frisbee."
- "First put on your sweater and then we'll go for a walk."

You can practice Premack exercises to help your dog understand the concept, and then use Premack in real life when that squirrel—or deer, or bicyclist—speeds across your path. Here's one way to practice, with a dog who has already learned a reasonably good recall. You'll need one or two friends to help you.

1. Give your partner a handful of very yummy treats. Have her feed one to your dog.
2. Have your partner hold your dog, on-leash, on the far side of your fenced yard. Tell her that when you call your dog you want her to drop the leash. Or—if your dog does a solid sit-stay, tell her to stay and walk to the other side of the yard.
3. You stand on the opposite side of the yard, facing your dog.
4. Ask your partner to stand halfway between you and your dog, holding several treats in his hand. (You will need a third person for this part if your dog doesn't have a strong "stay" behavior.) Tell him that if your dog stops to try to get treats from him when you call her, he should hide the treats and keep turning his back on the dog.

5. Call your dog. If she comes directly to you, praise her, pick up her leash and run back to the treat-guy, who then feeds several treats to your dog. If she stops at the treat guy, keep calling, and when she finally comes to you, pick up her leash and run back to the treat-guy for her "dessert."
6. Repeat until she runs quickly to you every time you call, in order to get your permission to go see the treat-guy.
7. When you have reliable and consistent recalls to you past the treat-guy enticement try it in real life, first with your dog on a long line until you get the same response even with squirrels (call your dog to you, then you *both* chase after the squirrel), then eventually without the long line. Make sure you are in a safe area when you try it off-leash for the first several times!

One cautionary note when you use Premack with your dog: be sure you don't get a reverse effect. If the less desirable behavior is *very* aversive to your dog, she can learn through association to dislike what was previously a desirable behavior. If she hates nail trimming she could come to dislike chasing the ball through its association with the hated nail trim. If you gag when you eat vegetables you could learn to hate ice cream if you have to eat broccoli every time in order to get your ice cream: "Ice cream? Ugh, never mind…"

Poisoning the cue

Let's stick with the ice cream here for a moment. What if you loved ice cream (an easy assumption for me) and you had a good friend with whom you regularly share your ice cream experiences. In fact, she frequently makes homemade ice cream, and often calls you up and invites you over to share her latest creation. You love her ice cream so much that whenever she calls you drop whatever you're doing, wherever you are, and race to her house. But one day when you race to her house and walk in the front door, for no reason whatsoever that you can discern, she slaps you in the face.

"Wow," you think to yourself, "She must be having a really bad day!" You give her the benefit of the doubt, and eat the ice cream, but your enthusiasm for the treat is dampened a little by her unexpected violence.

Five more ice cream sessions occur without incident, and you're just beginning to forget the strange anomaly when you walk in the door the sixth time and she yells at you and calls you bad names. When you ask her about her odd behavior she shrugs and says, "Oh, you just didn't get here fast enough."

The next three times you break speed limits to get there, but you realize your pure enjoyment of the ice cream sessions has been significantly damaged by the stress you're now feeling over the uncertainty about the reception you'll get.

On your fourth arrival, despite the fact that you got to your friend's house in record time, she gives you a knuckle punch in the arm when you enter the house.

"What was *that* for?" you complain.

"Oh, I don't like the shirt you're wearing," she says.

You're now convinced that your friend has lost her mind. You can barely eat the ice cream, despite the fact that it's Chocolate Chip Cookie Dough—your favorite flavor. During your conversation with her you recommend she get counseling. She apologizes for her behavior and promises it won't happen again. Still, the next time she calls, you almost don't even go, but you do, hoping your talk with her has been effective. You drive very slowly because you're so ambivalent about going. You're thinking about telling her you can't do ice cream with her anymore. But when you finally get there she apologizes again for her past bad behavior, and greets you with a warm hug and an extra large bowl of ice cream, with hot fudge sauce, cherries, and whip cream.

"Wow," you think. "She really is sorry. Maybe we *can* still do ice cream!"

The next time she calls you, you drive your normal speed, thinking the problem has been resolved. But when you go in she screams at you again for being too slow. You turn around and walk out the door. The next time she calls you hang up on her. You have no intention of ever coming again when she calls you, because you don't know if the ice cream invitation predicts good stuff or bad stuff.

She has *poisoned* her "ice cream" cue.

Now substitute you and your dog in this scenario, and your recall cue. If "come!" sometimes means the equivalent of "ice cream" to your dog, and sometimes means verbal and physical punishment, your dog will likely become ambivalent about coming when you call him. Your recall cue is poisoned.

It doesn't just have to be the recall cue. Any cue you use with your dog should ideally have a completely consistent "Yay, good stuff!" association if you want your dog to respond eagerly and happily every time he hears it. You want your cues to be reliable predictors of good stuff. Everything from his regular training cues to his everyday "real life" words: Sit, down, stay, heel, his name, his "go to bed" cue, his "put the leash on," and "get in the car" cues…all should mean "good stuff." Always.

A study done under the direction of Dr. Jesus Rosales Ruiz at the University of North Texas demonstrated that it's easier to teach a new cue than to rehabilitate a poisoned one. The ambivalence and anxiety your dog feels at not knowing whether this time the cue will mean "good stuff" or "bad stuff" is powerful and long-lasting.

There's a good chance that your Do-Over Dog's association with commonly used words have been poisoned, especially if he came from a background of abuse or neglect, his prior human was a compulsion-style trainer or, if you are a "cross-over" owner, meaning you started your training with compulsion methods but are switching over to positive ones. In any case, if you have any reason to believe your dog's cues *may* be poisoned, it's time to create a whole new vocabulary that you are very careful to keep positive—starting with your dog's name.

Do-Over Dogs often come without names, in which case you're probably doing well with the one you've already given him. However, if you've already done a lot of "No, Fido! Bad dog!!" you might want to start over with a new one. If he did come with a name that *may* be associated with bad things from the past, then by all means change it. Dogs probably have less, if any, "I am my name" feelings than we humans do, so changing his name is not likely to create an identity crisis. It's far more likely to help him leave behind the bad associations from his past life.

Make a complete new vocabulary list for any cues that you think might have been poisoned: "Come" might become "Close," "Down" (meaning "lie down") might become "Park," "Drop it" could be "Trade!" Write them down so you and the rest of your family don't forget them. Then cherish all your new cues—don't let anyone give them a negative association for your dog. Now you're talking!

The poisoned "No"

Most dogs are familiar with the word "No!" It's one I try to avoid, doing my best to tell our dogs what *to* do rather than what *not* to do, except for emergencies when I *really* have to stop a behavior. If I find myself using "No" repeatedly, I try to take a step back and either manage or train for that situation to eliminate the need for no.

Do-Over Dogs are likely to have heard the word "No" even more than regular dogs. I've known dogs from abusive situations who had such a negative association with "No" that they became aggressive if they even hear the word. They were likely beaten or otherwise harmed in their past life as someone yelled "No!" at them, forming a very negative classical association with the word, and becoming defensively aggressive as a result.

It's always good to minimize the need for "No!" For your Do-Over Dog, you might be well-advised to come up with a new emergency "Stop that behavior!" word to avoid the possibility that he might react very badly in those *rare* emergency times when you do have to stop a behavior. It just needs to be a word or phrase you yell loudly enough to get his attention and stop him in his tracks when he's about to do something horribly wrong. Alternatives to "No!" could be "Stop!" "Whoa!" or "Phooey!"

Superstitious behavior/superstitious thinking

Superstitious behavior happens when your dog makes an association between two stimuli and believes that the consequence directly relates to the relationship between those two things, even though there is, in fact, no such relationship. Humans also engage in superstitious behavior. A football star might have a "lucky shirt" that he always wears before a big game because it's the one he wore the night before his team won the Super Bowl. Bingo players may have lucky dolls and statues that they bring with them to games, convinced they help them win.

In dog training, it might be the funny little flip of the head your dog does before he sits, because he's convinced it's part of a behavior chain that makes you click the clicker and feed him a treat. Superstitious behaviors can be harmless, funny, annoying, or significantly detrimental to your training and behavior modification, depending on their context.

Superstitious thinking is the belief that there is a correlation between two events where in reality there is none. The phrase we use in behavior and training is, "Correlation does not necessarily mean causation." Just because your dog peed on the floor after you let him lick your dinner plate doesn't mean that licking dinner plates causes dogs (or more specifically causes your dog) to pee on the floor. A superstitious belief commonly held by many dogs is that barking furiously makes the mail carrier go away.

This dog may think that staring at the restaurant door will make his owner reappear. If so, he's engaging in superstitious behavior.

The law of parsimony

Humans seem to like complex, convoluted explanations for everything, including dog behavior. *The Law of Parsimony,* also called "Occam's (or Ockham's) Razor" after a 14th century English logician and Franciscan friar, William of Ockham, says that when you have two competing theories that make exactly the same predictions, the simpler one is the better.

For example, you could theorize that your dog lies in the warm sunny spot in the middle of your hallway because he likes warm sunny spots. Or you could theorize that he lies in the warm sunny spot in the middle of your hallway because he's being dominant and he knows that blocking your pathway is an expression of his dominance, and puts him one step closer to ruling your household and your life. Clearly the first explanation is simpler, and more likely.

The Law of Parsimony is also sometimes expressed in simple terms with this phrase: "When you hear hoofbeats, think horses, not zebras" (unless you live in Africa). Understanding the behavior of a Do-Over Dog is complex enough. Avoid the temptation to make it even more so.

The parsimonious explanation for Lucy being on the sofa is that it's comfortable. The complex, convoluted, and incorrect one is that she's being dominant.

Behavior myths

Hang out with dog folks long enough and you're sure to hear some pretty interesting theories about dog behavior. Some are, of course, useful and accurate, but the dog training world is littered with myths, many of which are at least several generations old. Some of them are just silly, some have the potential for causing serious damage to the dog-human relationship, and still others are downright dangerous. It's time to get past the myths.

I am always exhorting my interns, apprentices, and clients to be critical thinkers. When someone offers you a nugget of alleged canine wisdom, regardless of *who* the someone is, you're wise to run it through your own rigorous filters before accepting it as real wisdom or adopting it as the basis for a training technique. These should include:

- **The scientific filter.** Does it make sense scientifically? If someone assures you that shock collar training is actually positive reinforcement training because the shock is no different than someone tapping you on the shoulder to get you to stop a behavior, does that concur with your understanding of positive reinforcement? (That a dog's behavior makes a good thing happen, so the behavior increases.) Don't be fooled by the euphemisms "e-collar," and "tingle," "tap," or "stim" for the word "shock."
- **The philosophical filter.** Is it congruent with your own philosophies about dog training and relationships? Positive punishment (dog's behavior makes a *bad* thing happen; behavior decreases) makes sense from a scientific standpoint. That still doesn't mean you want to—or have to—use it with your dog and risk the damage it can do to your relationship. Trainers with a positive training

philosophy generally try to avoid the use of positive punishment, or any methods that work through the use of fear, pain, aversives, and avoidance.

- **The "acid test" filter.** It may seem sound scientifically, and it may feel okay philosophically—but does it work? If you're comfortable trying it out and you don't like the results, feel free to continue on and explore why it's not working or simply toss it out. Just because it works for someone else doesn't mean it has to work for you.

A word about dominance, hierarchy, and relationship

Seems like everyone these days has heard about "dominance" and "alpha" as it relates to dogs. You'll hear, "If your dog jumps up, he's being dominant. If your dog bites, he's being dominant." In fact, in some circles, dominance is used to explain every single undesirable behavior. The sad fact is that those terms are overused and misused daily in respect to our relationships with our dogs, and their relationships with each other. A dominance perspective toward your dog can do serious damage to your relationship.

For starters, there's no such thing as a "dominant dog." While dominance and submission are indeed part of social interactions, status, in fact, can be fluid depending on context and circumstances. You may well find that in your kitchen, one of your dogs appears to have more social freedom and ability to claim what she wants, while in the yard it could be a different dog altogether. Dominance is not a personality trait, what you are seeing is relationships in action where both parties want the same thing.

Some people claim you need to be the "alpha dog," keeping yourself at the top of a hierarchy over your dog(s). Dogs know we aren't dogs. In fact, we may only be peripherally in their social group. We are so awkward at understanding their subtle social signals, and so gross in trying to repeat them, that I have to think they gave up a long time ago believing we were their social peers. There's little to be gained trying to be the "alpha dog," other than perhaps intimidating and frightening your dog.

Rather than worrying about social status, simply focus on behavior. If you control most of the good stuff in your dog's life and teach him to offer polite, appropriate behaviors (sit, down) in order to get good stuff from you, you'll naturally and gently create a relationship in which he defers to you—acts polite—in order to get good stuff. In fact, stable, successful social relationships work because of deference, not dominance. That's so important I have to repeat it again. Social relationships work because of deference, not dominance. When you are skilled at getting your dog to voluntarily defer to you, without the use of force, you will gently reign supreme in your multi-species social group.

Here are ten of my favorite behavior myths, with an explanation as to why these "busted" myths should not be used as the justification for a training or behavior modification technique.

Myth #1: "Puppies should not go to puppy classes/the mall/a friend's house until they have had all their vaccinations at 16 weeks/6 months of age." Fails all three tests. This one lands squarely at the top of the "dangerous myth" category; many neophobic dogs are in the Do-Over boat because their humans believed this myth. It's generally perceived as credible by new puppy owners because it's often offered by the pup's veterinarian or some other canine professional.

While it appears scientifically sound on its face (an unvaccinated puppy *is* at risk for contracting deadly diseases!), puppies who aren't properly socialized are at a much *greater* risk for developing behavior problems, including aggression, that are likely

Taking your puppy to a well-run positive puppy class will provide her with good opportunities for socialization, help you teach her good manners behaviors, and is one of the best things you can do to ensure that she has a long and happy life in your family—never to become a Do-Over dog.

to shorten their lives. The vet is right on one hand—the *best* way to ensure that your pup isn't exposed to dog germs is to avoid other dogs. It's certainly true that you want to prevent your pup's exposure to *unknown* and/or possibly *unhealthy* dogs (and their waste). But it's also critically important that your pup get *lots* of exposure to the rest of the world, including healthy puppies in a controlled environment, before the critical socialization period ends at 12 to 16 weeks. If he doesn't, he'll be at risk of developing serious, sometimes deadly, behavior problems.

In addition, during the period leading up to the age of four months, your pup has protection from his mother's immunities, and should receive "puppy shots" to cover that period of time when his mother's protection starts to decrease. Not only is it "okay" to take your pup places while exercising reasonable caution, you have an *obligation* to provide him with extensive socialization in order to maximize his chances of leading a long and happy life.

Myth #2: "Dogs pull on leash, jump up on people, (add your own favorite inappropriate behavior) because they are dominant." Fails scientific and philosophical tests. Like the first myth discussed, this one can be dangerous, because those who believe this myth are likely to believe that they need to use forceful methods to assert their own status over their so-called "dominant" dogs. Many Do-Over Dogs have aggressive behaviors as a result of coercion, force, and intimidation used by dog owners who unfortunately believed this myth.

No one disputes that dogs living in a group understand and respond to the concepts and dictates of a social hierarchy. The fact that canine social structures share elements with human social structures is probably one of the reasons that dogs make such wonderful companions for us. However, most experts in animal behavior today believe that canine social hierarchies are much more based on *deference* than dominance, and that most canine behavior that many misguided humans attribute to dominance simply isn't!

A dog's goal in life is to make good stuff happen. Behaviors often labeled "dominant" because they are perceived as pushy and assertive—like pulling on leash and jumping up—simply persist because the dog has learned that the behaviors are reinforced; they make good stuff happen. Pulling on leash gets him where he wants to go. Jumping up gets attention. Behaviors that are reinforced continue, and even increase—but *they are rarely about social status.*

If you remove all reinforcement for the unwelcome behaviors (pulling makes us stop; jumping up makes attention go away) and reinforce more appropriate behaviors in their place, your dog will change his behavior.

Myth #3: "If you let your dog sleep on the bed/get on the furniture/eat first/go through doors first/win at tug-o-war, he will become the alpha." Fails all three tests. This one is mostly just silly. Some sources even suggest that the entire family must gather in the kitchen and take turns buttering and eating a cracker before the dog can be fed. Seriously! While it's not likely to be the *cause* of many Do-Over Dogs, if you believe this myth, you may miss some golden opportunities to help improve your relationship with your Do-Over Dog.

See Myth #2 for the mythbusting response to this one. If you don't want your dog on the furniture, that's your lifestyle choice, but you don't need to defend it with the alpha-garbage argument. I feed my dogs before I eat so I don't have to feel guilty about them being hungry while I fill my own belly. I teach my dogs to sit and wait for permission to go through the door ("say please!") because it's a polite, safe behavior and reinforces deference, but not because I'm terrified that they'll take over the house. And I like to win tug-o-war a lot because it reinforces polite behavior. You can quit worrying about your dog becoming alpha just because you don't rule with an iron fist.

If you are concerned that your Do-Over Dog is too pushy or ill-mannered, you can implement a "Say Please" program (sometimes called "Nothing in Life is Free") where your dog asks politely for all good things by sitting—a nice, polite, deference behavior. If you think your Do-Over guy is potentially aggressive, it's even more important to avoid conflict—your attempts to physically dominate him are likely to escalate his aggression rather than resolve it. If aggression is a real concern, I recommend you consult with a qualified, positive behavior professional who can help you modify your dog's behavior *without the use of force.*

You really can let your dogs get on the furniture without worrying that they're going to stage a coup and take over your household!

Myth #4: "Dogs can't be trained with positive reinforcement. You have to punish them so they know when they are wrong." Fails scientific and philosophical tests; fails acid test unless punisher is *very* skilled. But how does one *become* skilled at punishing (why would they even want to) without damaging a lot of dogs along the way? And how do we define *skilled?* This myth has very high potential for causing serious harm to the canine-human relationship, especially to a Do-Over Dog who already has problematic behaviors. Research confirms what positive trainers hold dear: that positive reinforcement training is more effective and has far fewer risks than positive reinforcement training combined with positive punishment.

One study was conducted by scientists at the University of Southampton in the UK and the University of Life Sciences in Norway. The study evaluated whether punishment was a contributor to behavior problems, and examined the effects of reward, punishment, and rule structure (permissiveness/strictness and consistency) on training and behavior problems. Information was collected via questionnaires from 217 dog guardians. Those who used strong and/or frequent punishment had a significantly higher level of training problems and lower obedience in their dogs. A similar study, conducted at Britain's University of Bristol, also found that dogs trained only with positive reinforcement exhibited fewer problem behaviors.

For most humans, this makes sense. Do you learn better if someone acknowledges (and rewards) you when you do it right, or slaps you upside the head when you do it wrong? Even if you get rewarded for doing it right, if you *also* get slapped for doing it wrong, your fear of getting slapped will likely impede your learning and make you more reluctant to try things.

Of course, a good positive training program makes use of management to avoid giving the dog opportunities to be reinforced for unwanted behaviors, and will also make judicious use of negative punishment (dog's behavior makes a *good* thing go away) to let him know he made an unrewarding behavior choice.

Myth #5: "If you use treats to train, you will always need them." Fails all three tests. This just isn't so. A good positive training program will quickly *fade* (reduce the frequency) the use of food as a constant reinforcer while moving to a schedule of *intermittent reinforcement* (food rewards are used randomly instead of continuously) and expanding the repertoire of reinforcers to include things like toys, play, petting, praise, and the opportunity to perform some other highly reinforcing behavior. When you're working with a Do-Over Dog, you may need to keep food in the picture longer, as you work to change his negative associations to positive ones.

Food can be a very high-value reinforcer and quite useful in training a wide variety of behaviors, so it's plain silly to turn your back on treats. Just be sure to fade food lures quickly in a training program, move to a variable (intermittent) schedule of reinforcement when your dog will perform a behavior on cue eight out of ten times, and incorporate a variety of reinforcers so you're never dependent on any one particular reward choice.

Myth #6: "A dog who urinates inside/destroys the house/barks when he is left alone does so because he is spiteful." Fails the scientific and philosophical tests. Housesoiling, excessive barking, and destructive behaviors are often found in Do-Over Dogs. This myth definitely causes harm to the dog-human relationship, and does nothing to help modify the problem behaviors. Dogs don't do things out of spite, and to think so gives owners a negative perspective on their relationship with their canine family member. Dogs do things because they feel good, they work to make good stuff happen (or to make bad stuff go away), or because they are reacting to events and associations in their environment. While our dogs share much the same range of emotions as we humans, they don't seem to indulge in all the same motives. Spite requires a considerable amount of premeditation and cognitive thinking that science doesn't support as being evident in the canine behavior repertoire.

Assuming this only happens when you're not home, there are two rational explanations for the behaviors described in this myth. The first is that the dog isn't fully housetrained and hasn't yet learned house manners. In the absence of direct supervision, the dog urinates when he has a full bladder (an empty bladder feels good) and becomes destructive because playing with/chewing sofa cushions, shoes, ripping down curtains, tipping over the garbage, and barking are fun and rewarding activities.

The other explanation is that the dog suffers from some degree of isolation distress. These behaviors are often a manifestation of stress and the dog's attempt to relieve his anxiety over being left alone. If your dog regularly urinates (or worse) in the house or destroys things when he is left alone, he may be suffering from a moderate degree of isolation distress, or more severe separation anxiety. This condition can worsen without appropriate management, or with punishment. Behavior modification is certainly called for, but to perceive a dog's misbehavior as spite often gives the owner justification to feel angry and punish his dog—which is definitely not what your Do-Over Dog needs.

If it also happens when you *are* home, add "medical issues," and "lack of management" as possible additional explanations.

Myth #7: "If you feed a dog human food, he will learn to beg at the table." Fails all three tests. This is just plain silly! One dog owner's "begging" is another's "attention" behavior, eagerly sought-after and highly valued. In fact, many Do-Overs would benefit from the kind of dog-human relationship that elicits "begging." Behaviors that are reinforced continue and/or increase. If you fed your dog *his own dog food* from the table, he would learn to beg at the table—it has nothing to do with what *type* of food he's being fed. If you don't want your dog to beg at the table, don't feed your dog from the table.

Whether it's fed in a form that we recognize as something we might consume, or it's been transformed into something that more resembles our mental concept of "dog food," it all still comes from the same basic food ingredients. In fact, human-grade food is *better* for dogs than much of the junk found in many commercial brands of dog food: artificial coloring, preservatives, and sweeteners, and meat "by-products."

Myth #8: "He knows he was bad/did wrong because he looks guilty." Fails all three tests. This myth is damaging to the relationship, as it leads owners to hold dogs to a moral standard that they aren't capable of possessing. Most Do-Over Dogs can't withstand any more damage to the relationship than already exists!

When a dog looks "guilty," he is most likely offering *appeasement behaviors* in response to a human's tense or angry body language. He's probably thinking something like, "I don't know why, but my human looks pretty upset right now. I'd better offer some appeasement behaviors so her anger isn't directed at me!" Even when the "guilty" expression is a direct and immediate result of your dog's behavior because your punishment was timely—"Hey! Get out of the garbage!"—your dog's turned head, lowered body posture, averted eyes—are simply an acknowledgement of your anger and his attempt to reconcile with you.

A trainer friend of mine once did an experiment to convince a client that her dearly held "guilty look" belief was a myth. He had the client hold her dog in the living room while he went into the kitchen and dumped the garbage can on the floor, strewing its contents nicely around the room. Then he had the client bring the dog into the kitchen. Sure enough, the dog "acted guilty" even though he had nothing to do with the garbage on the floor. He just knew from past experience that "garbage on floor" turned his owner into an angry human, and he was already offering appeasement behavior in anticipation of her anger, and to divert her ire from his dog-self.

Finally, most owners who have punished a dog for something that was done in their absence can attest to the fact that the punishment generally doesn't prevent the dog from repeating the behavior another time. What *does* work is simple management. Put the garbage somewhere that the dog can't get to it; under a sink with a safety latch on it, for example. Keep counters clear of anything edible. Leave the dog in a part of the house that is comfortable but not easily destroyed. Hire a dog walker to come by in the middle of your dog's longest days home alone to let him out, give him some stress-relieving exercise, and leave him with a food-filled chew toy. These actions will result in an intact home, and a dog who is not afraid to greet you when you return. Help your Do-Over Dog succeed.

Myth #9: "The prong collar works by mimicking a mother dog's teeth and her corrections." Fails the scientific and philosophical tests. It's a little discouraging to think that people actually believe this myth. It would be silly if it weren't so potentially damaging to the relationship and dangerous as well.

The prong collar works because the prongs pressing into the dog's neck are uncomfortable at best, painful at worst. Because dogs will work to avoid pain and discomfort, the prong collar *does* work to stop a dog from pulling on the leash, and can shut down other undesirable behaviors as well, at least temporarily. However, like all training tools and techniques that are based on pain and intimidation, there is a significant risk of unintended consequences.

In the case of the prong collar, the primary risk is that the dog will associate the pain with something in his environment at the time he feels it, and this can lead to aggression toward the mistakenly identified cause. A dog's unmannerly, "I want to greet you" lunge toward another dog or person can turn into, "I want to eat you," if he decides that the object of his attention is hurting him. This is typical with a reactive Do-Over Dog, and a prong collar (or worse, shock collar) only makes the associations worse.

If you have used or are considering the use of a prong collar to control your dog, please consult with a qualified positive behavior consultant to learn about effective and less potentially harmful methods.

Myth #10: "Aggressive/hand-shy/fearful dogs must have been abused at some point in their lives." Fails the scientific test. This is a very widespread myth; I hear it so often it makes my brain hurt. Fortunately, while the behaviors described in this myth are problematic, the myth itself may be the most benign of our top ten.

There are many reasons a dog may be aggressive, hand-shy, or fearful. Lack of proper socialization tops the list, especially for fearfulness. If a pup doesn't get a wide variety of positive social exposures and experiences during the first 12 to 14 weeks of his life, he will likely be fearful and/or aggressive.

Widely accepted categories of aggression include:

- Defensive (fear-related) aggression
- Idiopathic aggression
- Maternal aggression
- Pain-related aggression
- Play aggression
- Predatory aggression
- Possession aggression (resource-guarding)
- Protection aggression
- Status-related aggression
- Territorial aggression

Note that there's no category for "abuse-related" aggression. Abuse *can* be one of several causes of fear-related/defensive aggression, but is much less common than the fear-related aggression that results from undersocialization.

Regardless of the cause of a Do-Over Dog's fearful or aggressive behavior, a myth-corollary to our Myth #10 is that love alone will be enough to "fix" the problem. While love is a vital ingredient for the most successful dog-human relationships, it takes far more than that to help your fearful Do-Over Dog become confident, or an aggressive one to become friendly.

Chapter 6
The Honeymoon Period

You have now made all of your "Welcome home" preparations from Chapter 4 and reviewed the 'Science lessons" from Chapter 5. You and your Do-Over Dog have survived your first day together. Congratulations—but now what?

What comes next is the "honeymoon period." Many rescuers suggest that this "honeymoon" lasts about a month and is important in that the dog's behaviors may be somewhat inhibited or suppressed during this time. Veterinary behaviorist Dr. Karen Overall has said that for some dogs this period can be as long as three to five months. This may also be a "trial period," where your dog is trying out a variety of behavior strategies, and selecting for the ones that seem to be working for him—those that are either positively reinforced or negatively reinforced. Over time, the successful strategies will increase in frequency and perhaps intensity. If you don't carefully manage your dog to be sure the behaviors you like are the ones that are getting reinforced, you may see the increasingly noticeable presence of undesirable behaviors. For some dogs, what rescuers refer to as seeing the "real dog" after the honeymoon period may be those behaviors becoming established over time through reinforcement, as well as an indication of the dog's growing comfort level in his new environment.

This is a good time to *carefully* explore how your dog reacts to different situations, to determine where you need to focus your rehabilitation efforts. After he's had a week or two to adjust to his new living situation, gradually expose him to new people and places, always careful to protect him and avoid overwhelming him. If you see signs of stress or tension, remove him from the situation before he reacts badly, and make a mental note (or better yet, a written note in your training journal) that he needs behavior modification work with that stimulus. *Never force him to endure situations that are frightening to him or that cause him to react badly. Depending on the intensity of his response, your behavior modification program could take weeks, months, or even years.*

Maximize the honeymoon period

I suggest you make good use of your honeymoon period with your Do-Over Dog by laying a solid foundation for the rest of your lives together. This means making sure the behaviors you want are the ones that are being reinforced, and managing the environment so unwanted behaviors *aren't* reinforced, and being consistent about which behaviors are reinforced and which are not.

Any time you find yourself repeatedly interrupting your dog in the middle of an inappropriate behavior, look to management. Is your dog constantly jumping up on the forbidden loveseat? Use a baby gate or a closed door to keep him out of that room—or put boxes on the seat—when you're not there to remind him to stay on the floor (and reinforce him for doing so!). Does he get in the kitchen garbage? Get a covered trash receptacle, or put the garbage can in a cupboard or closet.

If your Do-Over Dog gets reinforced for this behavior because you carelessly leave tasty food on surfaces for her to find, you can bet her countersurfing behavior will increase!

In 1996, I left my 20-year career in animal protection at the Marin Humane Society to launch my dog training and behavior business, Peaceable Paws, in Monterey, California. Early in my Peaceable Paws career I was doing in-home training with a couple who had adopted an Australian Shepherd mix from the Santa Cruz SPCA. Dog and owners were doing well together, and at the end of our second session the husband asked if we could train Winnie to stop drinking out of the toilet.

"We could," I replied, "But it would be a lot easier to train you to close the toilet lid, or the bathroom door."

Management. When I returned the following week for our third session, I noticed that the bathroom door was closed.

Remember that structure and consistency are key to helping your dog learn how his new world works—and the sooner he figures that out, the sooner he can relax and settle in. Therefore it is particularly important for the Do-Over Dog during the honeymoon period. You can refer back to Chapter 3 for a discussion on management.

Good manners training

Some trainers still call it "obedience" training, but for me that conjures up old images of marching my dog around in circles and yanking on his choke chain. The very word obedience implies strict compliance… or else! Many of today's modern, enlightened trainers call it, instead, names like "good manners training," "family dog training," and "companion dog training." Whatever you call it, it's critical that good manners training begins in the honeymoon period.

Remember that learning doesn't just happen in formal training sessions! Operant and classical conditioning are *always* happening (see Chapter 5). You're wise to take advantage of this knowledge, reinforcing behaviors you like, preventing or removing reinforcement for those you don't, and managing potential association-making, in order to influence your dog's behavior.

Meanwhile, be aware that your Do-Over Dog is training you by doing behaviors that get *you* to give *him* what he wants during this period. It's a symbiotic behavioral relationship; one that works best when the human is the trainer more often than she's the trainee. When you are always conscious of how your behavior is reinforcing to your dog, and you take care to manipulate his reinforcers so you're consistently delivering them for the behaviors you like and want, you are more likely to avoid having your dog train you!

Our first Pomeranian, Dusty, trained me to hang up my jackets. I was just entering the treat-giving phase of my dog-training experience, and tended to leave treats in the pockets of my jacket and hang them over the backs of chairs. After finding several jacket pockets chewed through by a treat-seeking Dusty, I learned to hang my clothes up. Dusty's long gone now, my jackets are once again hanging over the back of dining room chairs—but now I mostly keep my treats in my jeans pockets.

Some trainers recommend waiting a month before you begin training your new dog. When I hear that, my reaction is "Hunh?" Depending on your Do-Over Dog's "issues," you may need to wait a month—or even longer—before you can begin to even consider taking him to a *formal* training class, but his training should start the *instant* he sets his paws on your heart and in your home. The sooner he learns how to communicate with you—and you with him—the more his world will make sense to him.

Before you begin your good manners training, let's review how to get the most out of clicker training.

Charge the marker

The reward marker is an incredibly powerful training tool. It is simply a sound—like the click of a plastic box clicker—or a "mouth click," or a word, like "yes!" or "tick!" that will come to mean to your dog that whatever he was doing when he heard the marker sound earned him a reward. A reward marker allows for better timing! If you click your clicker the *instant* he does a desirable behavior and follow it up with a reward, your dog will quickly understand what he did to earn the reward—even if it takes a few seconds to deliver it.

I use the click of the clicker to mean my dog has earned a *food* treat and a verbal "Yes!" marker to mean she has earned some kind of reinforcement—sometimes a food treat, but sometimes the opportunity to chase a ball, get in the car, run out the back door, or some other "life reward." In the following section on training, I will use the term "click" to mean whatever reward marker you choose to use with your dog.

My preference is to use a clicker for formal training sessions, always reinforced with food treats, and a verbal marker for more casual real-life reinforcement opportunities—while we're hiking or working around the farm or hanging out in the house. I prefer food reinforcements most of the time during training because they are high-value for my dogs, and because I can reinforce and get back to work quickly. If I reinforce with a toy or a ball (which I do occasionally), we have to take time out to play before I can cue the next behavior.

There is some evidence that the clicker is more effective for training new behaviors than a verbal marker, partly because the sound is consistent no matter who is using it—your voice changes depending on your emotion, laryngitis, and other factors—and partly because it has only *one* meaning (it *always* means *treat!)* while our words send a wide variety of messages to our dogs, are sometimes poisoned, and often have no relevance to our dogs at all.

To charge your reward marker, set out a bowl of pea-sized treats, and have your dog on leash in front of you. This is probably the easiest thing you'll ever train your dog to do, because he doesn't have to do *anything*. You're simply conditioning your dog's brain to recognize that "click" means "treat." All you do is click and treat, pause for a few seconds, then click-and-treat again, over and over, until your dog's eyes brighten and his ears perk up when he hears the marker sound because he knows that means a treat is coming. Usually a dozen or so repetitions is all you need—your marker is charged and you're ready to train!

If you're using a box clicker, be sure not to click too close to your dog's ears (the sound is loud!) and watch for any signs that the sharp "Click!" is making him uncomfortable. When I introduce the clicker to a new dog I usually start with the clicker in my pocket to muffle the sound, and watch for any signs of discomfort, such as ears flattening, head turning away, or the dog just looking worried, frightened, or trying to leave. Don't worry if your dog looks at the ground—he may think the click is the sound of something falling on the floor until he realizes it means treats coming from your hand. If your dog is worried or frightened by the muffled click, stop using the clicker *immediately*—use a verbal marker instead, a "mouth click," or a very soft clicker sound, such as a ball-point pen.

If the dog I'm working with responds well to a few repetitions of the muffled click, I'll hold it behind my back for a few more clicks, just to be sure he's okay with it, then hold it in front of me at my hip, which is where I usually carry it. *Note: I like to put my clicker on a retractable badge holder, available at office supply stores, and attach it to my pocket, so I can let go of it when I'm not using it and still have it handy at my hip whenever I need it.*

Getting behaviors

There are several ways to get your dog to do the behaviors you want to reinforce. Here are the ones I recommend:

1. **Capturing.** Click and treat when your dog offers the complete behavior you want. Example: He sits—you click and treat. Capturing can be quick and easy. The disadvantage is that your dog might not offer you the behavior you want to reinforce.
2. **Luring.** Show your dog the behavior you want by leading him with a lure—usually a food treat. You click and treat when he follows the lure and does the behavior. Example: You hold a treat over his head. He sits—you click and treat. Luring can help you get behaviors faster. The disadvantage is that dog and human can become dependent on the lure. If you lure behaviors, you need to be sure to *fade* the lure as quickly as possible—by teaching the dog to offer the behavior on cue *without* the presence of the lure.
3. **Shaping.** Click and treat small steps toward the complete behavior you want until you have the complete behavior. You may lure to get the steps, or you may wait for your dog to offer tiny steps toward the final behavior. Example: Your dog lifts his head an inch. You click and treat. You keeping clicking and treating for small head lifts until he starts offering small head lifts on purpose because he realizes that behavior will make you click and treat. Then you gradually click for higher and higher head lifts. Eventually as he lifts his head higher and higher his read end will start to lower, until you've shaped him all the way into a sit. The disadvantage of shaping is that it can seem painstakingly slow when you first try it, but it's my favorite way to get behaviors—it really encourages the dog to think about what he needs to do to get you to click, and makes it much easier to get more complex behaviors in later training. Dogs who are skilled at shaping offer you lots of behaviors to choose from when you're trying to teach a new behavior. Alternatively, you can lure-shape, by using a treat to encourage your dog to give small steps of the behavior to reinforce. If you lure-shape you have to remember to fade the lure quickly so you don't become dependent on it to get the behavior, and your dog may be less creative about offering behaviors when you're teaching something new.

I *don't* recommend methods that employ the use of force, coercion, or intimidation to get your dog to perform behaviors.

With these skills in mind, the specific "good manners" behaviors to teach (or strengthen) during the honeymoon period are:

- Teach your dog his name
- Attention
- Sit
- Down
- Crate training
- Targeting

- Walk politely on leash
- Come when called
- Tug

Teach your dog his name

Your dog's name should mean "stop what you're doing and look at me for further instructions," and his association with it (and with all the cues you teach him) should be *"really good stuff!"*

It's normally very easy to teach your dog his name. While your dog is looking at you, say his name in a happy tone of voice and offer him a treat. Click as he looks at you. Do this several times to "condition" him to the reward marker and treat when you say his name. When you think he's made the connection that "name" equals "treat!" wait until he looks away, and say his name. If he looks back at you right away, click and give him a treat. If he doesn't look at you, spend more time conditioning him to his name, and then test his response again. You want him to love his name so much that eventually he'll snap his attention to you when you say it no matter *what* he's doing. Remember to always be cheerful when you say his name so you don't poison it!

When your dog responds easily to his name, you can play a game with other family members. Have everyone sit in a circle with your dog in the middle. In a designated order, have each person say the dog's name, click, and treat when he looks at them. The person who says the name should click and treat. After a few rounds, change the order so the dog isn't guessing ahead of time where the next click will come from.

Depending on your Do-Over Dog's behavior challenges, you can expect that teaching him his name, as well as his other good manners behaviors, may take longer than other dogs you, your friends and family, and your training class classmates may be working with.

Attention

If your dog sees you as the source of all good stuff in his life—or at least most of the good stuff—it will be easier to keep his attention focused on you. Be generous with your reinforcers!

Time and again, I see Do-Over Dogs who have no clue that there's any reason to have a relationship with humans. They often come to our trainer academies from the local shelter and on day one there's no connection between the dog and the trainer working with him. By day six, however, the dog is glued to his trainer, gazing at her with adoration. The trainer has clearly become the "Source of Good Things."

Like charging the clicker, "Attention" is often pretty darned easy. Sit on a chair with your dog on a leash. Wait. When he looks at you *or looks in your general direction,* click and give a high value treat. If he keeps looking at you, keep clicking and treating, frequently at first, and then more randomly and farther apart, to increase duration of attention. If he looks away, stop clicking and wait for him to look at you again. When you've reinforced his attention enough that you can predict when he's going to look at you, add a verbal cue such as "Look" or "Watch me" so you can elicit the behavior on cue.

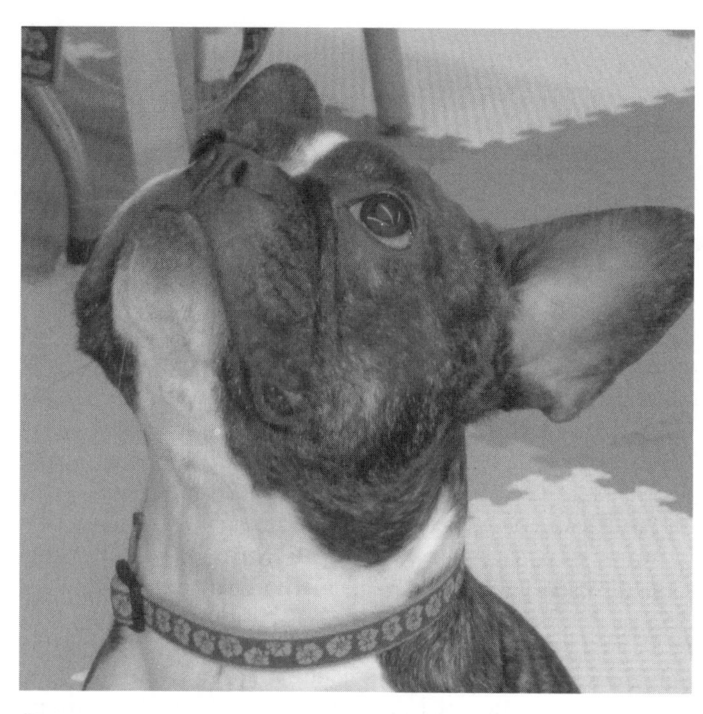

This French Bulldog, Oscar, has mastered the art of paying attention to his owner, Lori Kobayashi.

Sit

I like "sit" to be my dogs' default behavior. That means they get reinforced so much for sitting that they do it automatically, without being asked, when they don't know what else to do. It's a useful good manners behavior: they can't sit and jump up at the same time and it's a polite "Say Please" deference behavior—a lovely way of reminding them that non-assertive behavior makes good stuff happen. You can capture it by clicking (and treating) your dog anytime he happens to sit, and you can elicit it by luring:

Stand in front of your dog with a treat in your hand. Show him the treat and, holding the treat at the tip of his nose, slowly move it back over his head. As he tips his head back to watch the treat, he will sit. When he sits, click and treat, and tell him he's brilliant.

When you know he'll sit as you move the treat over his head, say "Sit!" in a happy voice (not a commanding one) just before he does it. After a dozen or so times of this, you're ready to ask for the sit without the lure. Rest your arms at your sides, or slightly behind your back, if your dog is too focused on the food. Say "Sit!" in a happy voice and wait three to five seconds. If he sits, click and treat. If he doesn't, move the food over his head to lure him into the sit, then click and treat. Practice three to four (or more) times a day, five to ten minutes per session. In short order he will sit when you give the verbal cue, without the food lure. You will still click and treat—on a continuous schedule at first (every time he sits on cue) and eventually on a variable schedule (sometimes, but not always). Remember that when you start using a variable schedule you will still treat every time you click, but you won't click every time he sits.

Teaching Lucy to "Sit"—a useful default and deference behavior.

> **Sits for the fearful dog**
>
> A fearful dog may be very uncomfortable with you moving your hand over his head. If that's the case, or if you have a dog who just doesn't sit easily when you lure, you will need to either capture sits until he is offering them freely, or *shape* the sit by luring a tiny bit at a time. You may need to click and treat several times at first simply for the dog sniffing the treat, then for lifting his nose a half-inch, or an inch—and gradually inch/shape your way to a sit. You can also try luring him to a down and then raise the treat slowly to lure him *up* into a sit.

Down

The down behavior is useful because it helps your dog park, settle, and relax. With your dog sitting, hold a treat in front of his nose, and slowly move it down toward his paws. Wait for him to follow it with his nose. When you get the treat all the way to the ground, hold it there until he starts to move his body down, then very slowly move it away from him so he can follow it and lie down all the way.

Careful—if you move it too fast he'll stand up! If he does, have him sit, and start again, moving the treat more slowly this time. You may need to lure-shape, by clicking and treating numerous times as he follows the lure to the ground. When he lies down (elbows touching the ground) click and treat and tell him how wonderful he is. When he will lie down easily and consistently for the lure, say "Down!" in a happy voice just before you lure him down.

After 12-24 repetitions, you are ready to start fading the lure. Stand straight, arms at your sides or behind your back. Say "Down!" in a happy voice and wait three to five seconds. If he lies down (he probably won't), click and treat. If he doesn't, lure him into the down, click and give a treat. Repeat in three to four brief sessions per day, varying the amount of time you wait between your "down" cue and your lure, to give him time to process the cue in his brain. You can fade the lure gradually by moving it only part way toward the floor to get him started, then whisking it behind your back and letting him finish the down on his own. In time, he will lie down for just the word, without the lure.

Note: The down exercise puts your dog in a very vulnerable position. If your Do-Over Dog has trust issues with humans, this can be a difficult exercise for him. You may want to wait until he gains trust and confidence with you and is comfortable in his environment before attempting to teach him to lie down on cue.

Crate training

One of the most valuable things to train your Do-Over Dog to do during the honeymoon period is to go willingly into his crate and remain there for as long as you require (within reason!). I've already mentioned how a crate can be used as an aid in housetraining, but a fearful or anxious Do-Over Dog may benefit from having a place to go and relax and calm down. For the owner, a crate can be a great place to send a dog for some period of time to avoid problems like a bunch of noisy kids coming over for a party. Make sure the crate's in a quiet room where the partygoers won't harass him!

With the crate door open, toss some irresistibly yummy treats inside. If your dog hesitates to go in, toss them close enough to the doorway that he can stand outside and poke his nose in to eat them. If that's still too scary, scatter treats outside the crate until he's more comfortable. If you're training with a clicker or other reward marker, each time your dog eats a treat, click the clicker, or speak your verbal marker. Gradually toss treats farther and farther into the crate until he'll step inside to get them. Drop them through the top of a wire crate, or the side grates of a plastic one, to position them deeper in the crate.

When he enters the crate easily to get the treats, click and offer him one while he's still inside. If he stays in, keep clicking and treating. If he comes out, just toss another treat inside and wait for him to re-enter of his own. Don't force him to go in or stay in. When your dog enters easily, add a verbal cue such as "Go to bed" so he'll learn to go in on cue. When he'll stay in the crate calmly, gently swing the door closed. Don't latch it! Click and treat, then open the door. Repeat, gradually increasing the length of time the door stays closed before you click. Sometimes you can click and reward without opening the door right away.

When he'll happily stay in with the door closed for at least ten seconds, close the door, latch it, and take one step away. Click, return, reward, and open the door. Repeat, varying time and distance. Intersperse long ones with shorter ones, so it doesn't always get harder and harder for him. Start increasing the number of times you click and treat without opening the door, but remember that a click *always* gets a treat.

Leave the crate open when you aren't actively training. Toss treats and favorite toys in the crate when he's not looking, so he never knows what surprises he might find. You can feed him his meals in the crate—with the door open—to help him realize his crate is a truly wonderful place.

To motivate him to *want* to go into the crate, take a particularly smelly, enticing stuffed Kong or marrow bone and tie it inside the back of the crate. Close the door so he *can't* get in. His frustration at not being able to get it will motivate him to go in later when you *do* open the door. Because the yummy object is attached to the back of the crate he has to stay inside to eat it even with the door open. *Note: Only do this when you are present, on the rare chance that he could somehow get caught in the tie you use to secure the object to the back of the crate.*

Some dogs and many puppies can crate train in one day. Some take several days; a few will take weeks or more. If your dog whines or fusses about being in the crate, don't let him out until he stops crying—*unless* you think he may have to go to the bathroom. If your dog's been asleep for a while, wakes up and starts to cry, he probably *does* have to go out. If he has a medical condition that requires him to go frequently or urgently, pay attention when he speaks to you from his doggie den. Otherwise, wait for a few seconds of quiet, then click and reward. Work with shorter periods of time between reinforcements, then increase the difficulty in smaller increments, and vary the times. Instead of going from 5 seconds to 10 to 15, start with 5 seconds, then 7, then 3, then 8, then 6, and so on. If your dog panics in the crate, you must let him out. You may have a dog with separation distress or anxiety. A crate is not recommended for this condition. Stop the crate training and consult an experienced, positive behavior professional.

When your dog is crate trained, you'll have a valuable behavior management tool, and he'll have his own spot. Respect it. If you abuse it by keeping your dog confined too much, for too long, or by using it as punishment, he may learn to dislike it. Keep your verbal "Go to Bed" cue light and happy. Reward him often enough to keep his response willing and quick. *Don't ever let anyone tease or punish him in his crate.* He's counting on you to protect him.

Targeting

Targeting means teaching a dog to touch his nose, paw, or other designated body part to a particular target. This is not a behavior we used to teach in old-fashioned training classes! I find that a majority of dog owners who attend our classes still aren't aware of the wonderful benefits of teaching a dog to target. One major benefit is targeting can help a fearful dog gain confidence. It's also handy for positioning a dog without having to physically manipulate him—very useful when you're working with a Do-Over Dog who is sensitive to touch.

The target can be your hand, a finger, or a "wand" or baton of some sort, a yogurt lid stuck to the wall, or almost any other object. I usually start with the palm of my hand—you can transition to other objects later. If your dog is too fearful to touch your hand, you can use a stationary object set on the floor. Encourage your dog to touch his nose to the target, held 4-6 inches from his face. Curiosity usually elicits a sniff, so you can capture the touch behavior. Be sure not to push the target toward his nose! If he's not interested in sniffing, you can lure the behavior by rubbing a yummy-smelling treat on it. You should be able to fade this lure very quickly.

When your dog touches the target, click and treat. When he's consistently and eagerly touching the target, precede offering of the target with the verbal cue "Touch." When he's clearly responding reliably to the cue, put the target in different places so he learns to move toward the target when it's farther away, when it's in motion, and when it is above and below his nose level.

Most dogs learn to *love* targeting. The positive association they have with this behavior can help them overcome negative associations when stressors appear in their environment.

"See that child? Touch my hand, click, treat. Yay!"

He can't be delighted about targeting and unhappy about the child at the same time. You can use targeting to your hand, or a target stick, to help modify behavior, as well as managing behavior by keeping your dog's attention focused on you while the scary thing goes away.

Walk politely on leash

An inability (at first) to walk politely on a leash is a common Do-Over Dog problem. Why? Usually because the previous owner failed to teach it successfully or never even bothered to try.

If your dog can learn to walk politely on leash, the easier it is to build your relationship with him. For example, you will be more likely to take him lots of places. It's no fun getting dragged everywhere by a fractious canine. It's important to remember that while a walk on leash is a good social outing and an excellent training opportunity for your dog, it's *not* adequate exercise for a healthy, active canine. I often counsel my clients to exercise their dogs well *before* they take them out on-leash to improve the potential for a pleasant and successful walk—at least until the dog has well-installed leash manners.

Dogs pull on leashes because it gets them where they want to go—which reinforces the pulling behavior. We are slow and boring on walks—if you let your dog off-leash (don't—unless you're positive he'll stay close and return when you call) he would run circles around you, and hike several miles for every mile you walk. Key to successful leash walking is using a high rate of high value reinforcement—lots of clicks and treats—so you are as fun and interesting as the things around him, and *not moving forward when he pulls, so he doesn't get reinforced for pulling.*

To teach polite leash-walking, keep your leash-arm by your side and your hand pressed against your hip so the leash stays loose. Use a happy voice, treats, toys and coaxing—*not force.* If your dog lunges forward and pulls on the leash, stop, and keep gentle pressure on the leash. When he stops pulling and looks at you, Click! or tell him "Yes!" and offer a treat *at your side.* When he returns to you, give him the food reward. If he's a hard puller you might want to invest in a front-clip control harness, where the leash attaches in front of the dog's chest. When he pulls, the pressure at his front end re-orients him back to you, making it difficult for him to pull.

If he stops *behind* you, keep walking, put gentle pressure on the leash to keep him coming with you, and click and treat when he takes even one step on his own. *Don't drag him though!* If he's truly put on the brakes, look for some small movement forward to click and treat, and shape him to start moving again.

Continue reinforcing randomly and very frequently with treats when he is not pulling. Decide on the word you want to use to tell your dog to walk, and use that word every time you move forward. Do several short practice sessions each day, first in a location with few distractions, working up to more distractions as your dog succeeds. Keep the walking varied with lots of changes of pace and direction to keep your dog interested. Remember—*you* have to be more interesting than the environment!

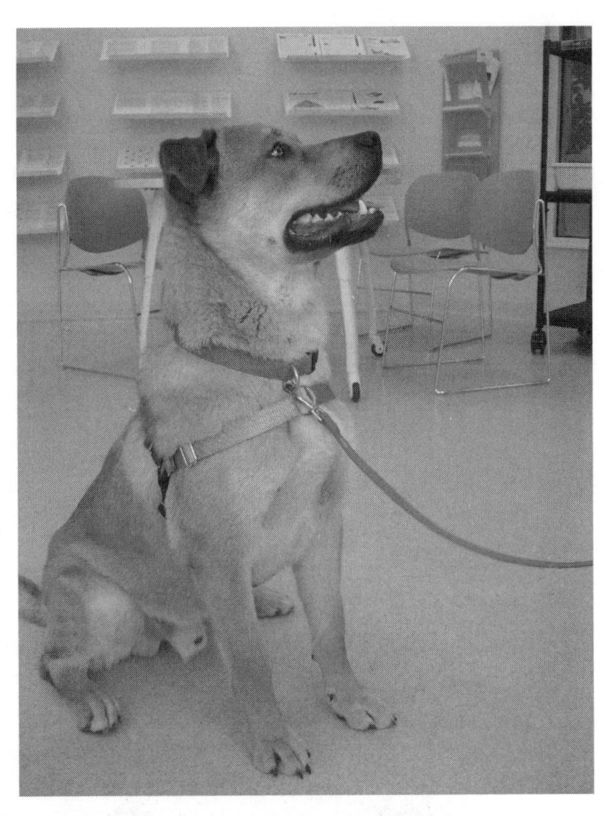

With a front-clip control harness like the one shown here, the leash attaches in the front, making it much harder for your dog to pull you.

The wonderful positive trainer Patty Ruzzo, now deceased, encouraged her clients and fellow trainers to be "variable and unpredictable" with their dogs as they strive to be more interesting than the environment. If you keep your dog guessing about when the next "good stuff" will suddenly appear, he'll keep a good eye on you so he doesn't miss it.

For example, if your dog loves to tug, leash-walk practice is a great time to use occasional games of tug as a reinforcer. Keep a small tug toy hidden in your pocket, and when he's walking particularly nicely, whip it out and invite him to play. Tug-loving dogs become *very* attentive to humans who unexpectedly initiate their favorite game.

If your dog is afraid, pulls back or panics on the leash, it's too soon to take him out in public. If he seems fearful even of having the leash attached to the collar, you'll need to do modification—counter conditioning him to the leash before you can even *think* about going for walks with him. If he's okay with having it attached but leery of walking with it, you can try cutting an old leash to a length of two to three feet, attaching to his collar, and letting him drag it around—but only when you are home to make sure he doesn't get it caught on something.

If your dog is out of control, leaps about, bites the leash, and wants to play, he just has too much energy. In a safe, enclosed area (house, fenced yard) play with your dog until he's tired. Give him five to ten minutes to settle after play, then go back to your on-leash work. You *want* your dog to be happy about being on the leash, so *do not* use harsh reprimands if he is playful on the leash.

Come when called

Coming when called, or the *recall,* as it's more formally known, can be a lifesaving behavior, and one that allows you to give your dog more off-leash freedom—in appropriate locations, of course. Responding to your call may initially be beyond the capabilities of your Do-Over Dog, especially if he comes with a history of undersocialization or abuse. You would be wise to hold off on practicing the recall until the two of you have a relationship of mutual trust. If you try too soon, the cue will quickly become poisoned.

When he's ready, with your dog near you, run away a few steps, with your back to him. You can do this on leash, but don't pull on the leash. When he follows you say "Come!" click and feed him a treat. When he gets the idea—that is, when consistently he bounds happily after you—run away several steps, *fast.* As he follows, say "Come," click and treat. The better he gets at this, the further he can be from you when you *start* to move away. When you think he's starting to understand, try saying "come" as you *start* to move. Then say it *before* you move. You will gradually be able to fade your motion completely, until you can stand still and call him to you. Remember that you want his "come" to be *very* enthusiastic—so keep running away as you practice until he always comes running to you as fast as he can when you call. Even when he's good at it, occasionally play the "run away" game with him to keep him excited about coming to you.

By running away when you call your dog, you teach him that "Come!" predicts having fun with his human.

The recall exercise is a great one to incorporate other reinforcers in addition to food treats. You can play tug when he speeds to you or toss a ball or favorite toy as his prize for coming. Be variable and unpredictable—he may never know what he'll get when he comes, but he knows it will be good!

When your dog understands "Come" and consistently returns to you quickly and happily, you can play the Round Robin Recall Game with two or more people. Each person has a clicker and treats. Stand a short distance apart and take turns calling your dog. Click and treat him for each recall in turn as he comes to you. Gradually increase the distance until he comes flying to each person in turn from far away.

When you think your dog's recall is solid in a safely enclosed area, take him out to open spaces and practice on a long-line—a thirty to fifty foot line for practicing distance work. When he'll recall to you reliably even with exciting distractions like bounding bunnies and darting deer, you're ready for off-leash recalls.

He only gets to play tug if he'll sit politely and wait for you to invite him to play. If he lunges for it, the tug toy disappears.

Tug

Tug is a great game to play with your dog to work off energy and allow the two of you to roughhouse safely. It won't make him "dominant" and it won't make him aggressive or unruly, as long as you play by the rules. And it's the process of being able to follow rules and exhibit a degree of self-control that makes this game such a great one for Do-Over Dogs. The rules are designed to remind him that you are in charge (the leader controls the good stuff), and to let him know which behaviors are acceptable, and which ones are not when he's playing exuberantly with humans.

Rules of tug

1. Use a toy that is long enough to keep your dog's teeth far away from your hands and that is comfortable for you to hold when he pulls. Keep the tug toy put away. Bring it out when *you* want to play tug.
2. Hold up the toy. If he lunges for it, say "Oops" and quickly hide it behind your back. It's *your* toy—he can only grab it when you give him permission.

3. When he'll remain sitting as you offer the toy, tell him to "Take it!" and encourage him to grab and pull. If he's reluctant, be gentle until he learns the game. If he's enthusiastic, go for it!
4. Randomly throughout tug-play, ask him to "Give" and have him relinquish the toy to you. If necessary, trade him for a yummy treat. After he gives it to you, you can play again (see steps 2 and 3). You should "win" most of the time—that is, you end up with possession of the toy, not your dog.
5. While you are playing, if his teeth creep up the toy beyond a marked or imaginary line, say, "Oops! Too bad," in a cheerful voice, have him give you the toy, and put it away briefly. (You can get it out and play again after a minute.)
6. If your dog's teeth touch your clothing or skin, say, "Oops! Too bad," and put the toy away for a minute.
7. When you are done playing, put the toy away until next time.
8. Children should not play tug with your dog unless and until you are confident they can play by the rules.

We have just scratched the surface here with your Do-Over Dog's training potential. For a more in-depth exploration of a positive training program, see my first book, *The Power of Positive Dog Training*. There are many more behaviors you can teach him, including a fantastic array of behaviors we call tricks. Of course, to your dog there's no difference between a trick and a "serious" behavior—it's all just behaviors he can do to get good stuff. But we humans think tricks are fun, so if you include tricks in your dog's behavior repertoire it helps you to remember that *all* training is supposed to be fun. Go ahead, teach him lots of tricks along with all his good manners behaviors. The more he knows, the more confident he will become, and the better the communication and relationship will be between the two of you. See Appendix 4 for a starter-list of tricks you can teach your Do-Over Dog. Be sure to choose ones that *he* will enjoy!

Tricks can remind dogs and humans to have fun with each other. Here's Dubhy playing the keyboard—one of his favorites!

Chapter 7

A Do-Over Repair Manual

Part I: The Basics

You have adopted your Do-Over Dog, brought him home, helped him adjust to the new changes in his world, instituted necessary management procedures, and started on an appropriate training program. In the best of all worlds, that would be all you'd need. But most Do-Over Dogs were in shelters for a reason. There are often behavior challenges that go beyond the simple need for basic good manners training.

Pre-owned dogs are more often than not surrendered to or left unclaimed at shelters and rescue facilities because of one or more difficult behaviors that the prior owner wouldn't, or couldn't, manage or modify. Even when the reason for surrender is "moving" or "landlord issues," there is often some underlying behavior challenge that prompted the owner to give his dog up rather than make the effort to find new living arrangements that could include the dog.

Some of the problem behaviors are "minor," relatively insignificant, easy to manage or modify, and/or not even a problem at all for you. People have different tolerance levels for different dog behaviors and what may seem perfectly normal and acceptable to you may have been a deal-breaker for the prior owner. Some behaviors are major, requiring a long-term strong commitment to management and/or modification. Perhaps you were informed about difficult behaviors before you made the decision to adopt—and perhaps you've discovered one or more behavior challenges after the fact. Perhaps you're still discovering.

In this chapter and the next, you'll find tools to start you down the behavior management and modification path for a variety of behavior problems. However, nothing replaces the eyeballs-on observations of a skilled behavior professional. If your dog's problem behaviors are putting himself or others at risk, or if they don't resolve with reasonable ease, I urge you to consult with a qualified positive behavior professional in your area.

I cannot give you a timetable or predict how long it will take for you to resolve your dog's problem behaviors. There are many variables that enter into the equation, including your dog's past history (which you may have little or no knowledge of), what his behavior issues are, how strong the genetic influence, how long he's been practicing inappropriate behaviors, and how successful they've been for him, as well as your own skill and commitment to applying management and modification protocols and the resources you have at your disposal. Many canine behavior problems are related at least in part to stress—the more stress, the greater the likelihood of significant problems. Most Do-Over Dogs have had more than their share of stress in their lives and behaviors that may have been mildly inappropriate at one time may have intensified with several rehomings or in a stressful shelter/kennel environment.

Behavior modification isn't linear—you'll see progress and think you're in the home stretch, then the behavior will occur again. It's useful to keep a behavior journal that you refer to on the difficult days to remind yourself how far you and your dog have come. Also, bear in mind that *good* behavior modification isn't fast. Avoid like the plague anyone who promises you a "quick fix" for significant behavioral issues. Quick fixes can intimidate a dog into submission and have the potential to create many more problem behaviors in the long run. You're very likely to regret cutting corners later. My friend and trainer/behavior specialist Jolanta Benal once quoted to me, "With behavior modification, when you think you're going too slow, slow down." Take your time, help your dog succeed, and appreciate the baby steps that move you toward your goal. It will be worth it.

Before looking at the details of training and behavior modification for problem behaviors, it is important to review some of the possible underlying causes of why they may be occurring.

Of canine morals and ethics

Whatever the underlying cause of your Do-Over Dog's problem behavior(s), it's important to realize that dogs don't do things out of spite and the concept of "guilt" does not really apply to dogs. This was mentioned earlier, but so many people seem to believe dogs act this way it is worth repeating. Their brains simply don't work that way. Rule both of these out right away. As with any behavior, your dog is doing it because he is somehow *finding it reinforcing.* Before you begin to try to solve the problem, you need to figure out why it is reinforcing to him.

Here is an example that shows why it so common for owners to feel that dogs do things out of spite and then express guilt: you've been gone for several hours and then arrive home to a dog-trashed house (you interpret as spite) and your dog is groveling at your feet (you interpret as guilt).

In terms of the trashed-house, I can pretty much bet he wasn't thinking about moral behavior when he was spreading garbage around the kitchen—he was probably fully engaged in garbage play. Nor was he likely thinking, "Mom's going to be really mad later, but it's worth it!" Dogs live in the moment and in the moment that he got in the garbage, he was just making good stuff happen. He found it reinforcing because perhaps he found something to eat or it just relieved boredom. The simple solution? Put the garbage can where he can't get to it or get a covered garbage can that he can't open.

In terms of what you interpret as guilt, the most likely behavioral explanation is that he can see by your body language that you're upset—and dogs are very good at reading body language. He offers deference signals—ears back, submissive grin, crawling on the floor, rolling on his back—in an attempt to divert your wrath away from him. He doesn't know why you're upset, but he can tell that you're about to be aggressive. His behaviors are about self-preservation, not guilt. Even if you haven't seen the damage yet, your tension over the anticipated destruction you *might* find could well be enough to induce him to go belly-up (literally), especially if he's a soft, non-assertive dog.

Reducing stress

Many of your Do-Over Dog's difficult behaviors may be related to stress. We all have stress in our lives, but too much stress results in problem behaviors. In humans, "road rage" and "going postal" are perfect examples of the behavioral result of too much stress.

I help my behavior clients create a complete list of all the stressors in their dogs' lives. Stressors can be internal or external and include things that might not even occur to the owner. A partial list might look like this:

1. Other dogs
2. Men with beards
3. Children
4. Sudden hand movements
5. Sensitivity to touch
6. Prong collar
7. Harsh verbal corrections
8. Physical punishment
9. Visits to the vet
10. Arthritic pain from old injury to leg
11. Itchy skin
12. Cold
13. Owner stress (doesn't have to be dog-related stress)
14. Stairs
15. Shiny floors
16. Doorways

Some of the items on this list, such as stairs, doorways, shiny floors, sensitivity to touch, men with beards, and children, may be stressful to the dog due to a lack of socialization. They can also result from prior bad experiences—children who teased the dog, men with beards who treated the dog badly, other dogs who attacked the dog—but owners often assume prior bad experiences when, in fact, the dog simply may not have been well socialized.

Other items on the list are a result of inappropriate training and handling practices. Well-meaning owners are often given poor advice about how to respond to their dogs' undesirable behaviors. Harsh verbal corrections, harsh or mild physical punishment, tools that cause pain, such as shock collars and prong collars, can all successfully *suppress* behaviors in some dogs, while in others, they can elicit aggression or other defensive responses to touch and movement. In either case, they carry with them the high price of adding to the dog's stress load. Stress causes aggression and anxiety and the more stressed your dog, the more likely he is to offer unwanted behaviors related to stress and anxiety.

Finally, some of the stressors on the list, such as heat, cold, pain, and itching, are physical—either internal or external.

Stress reduction is an important part of almost every behavior modification plan. The more stressors you can identify and eliminate from your dog's life, the farther away he is from going over his emotional threshold—"canine road rage" or some other equivalent of a stress-related breakdown. With your dog's complete list of stressors in hand, you can determine how to get rid of as many as possible. Some are easier than others to get rid of. Some can be minimized. Some are impossible to get rid of. Strategies for getting rid of stressors include:

- **Just get rid of it.** Don't use the tool anymore, don't physically punish anymore, don't have it around anymore. On our sample list above, you could easily get rid of harsh verbal corrections, physical punishment, and prong collars.
- **Treat medical conditions.** Provide pain relief for injuries and arthritis. Identify possible allergies to treat and reduce itching. A trip to the vet is always in order when working with a significant behavior problem, so your dog's doctor can look for medical issues that can contribute to problem behaviors and that may not be evident to you—such as low thyroid or Lyme disease.
- **Manage his environment to prevent exposure to the stressor.** Unless and until you can modify your dog's behavior around other dogs, children, and men with beards, put him away in a safe room when these stressor are present. Likewise, don't take him places where dogs, children, and bearded men are likely to congregate. If he gets cold easily, let him wear a sweater. Management may be short-term or long term, depending on the results of your modification program.
- **Change his "opinion" of the stressor.** This is done through a process called counter-conditioning and desensitization (covered in detail in Chapter 8, page 129). This process involves changing the association the dog has with something from negative to positive. If your dog was afraid of thunder, you could help him lose his fear if he were fed tasty treats every time a thunderstorm was to occur.
- **Teach a new behavior.** Undesirable responses to stressors usually persist because the consequence is reinforcing to your dog. He snaps at the bearded man, the man goes away. This is *negative reinforcement*—the dog's behavior (snapping) makes the bad thing (scary man) go away. The dog is more likely to snap at bearded men in the future, because the behavior strategy was successful. You can reinforce your dog for small indications of calmer, more relaxed behavior—like sitting, for example—in the presence of bearded men. This can ultimately

change his behavior *and* his emotional response to bearded men if sitting in their presence means a tasty treat.

- **Live with it.** We all have some stress in our lives. It may be mildly stressful to your dog when you leave to go to work every day, but he can live with it, as long as it's mild. We know owner-stress affects dogs and it's another one of those things they just have to live with. It *is* important that you recognize that when "live with it" stressors are present—perhaps things are going badly at your job—your dog is closer to going over his emotional threshold and having a blowup or a meltdown himself.

After we work our way through the list of stressors and strategies, and develop a plan for the modification pieces, I review a list of suggestions for general canine stress reduction as well as behavior modification. Remember, your dog's stress is not just about the *immediate* trigger for aggression or anxiety-related behavior; it's about *all* the things that pile up to push him over his threshold. The more you can do to reduce his overall stress, the less likely he is to go over threshold.

Stress reduction check-off list

These are topics I discuss with my clients as we discuss management, modification, and stress reduction, in addition to the specific needs of their individual dogs.

Management. Prevent the dog from practicing the unwanted behavior so it isn't reinforced, so the dog doesn't succeed and get better at it, to prevent exposure to stressors and decrease stress load and so no one gets hurt.

Removing stressors. Reduce stress load to help him stay below his emotional threshold.

Counter-conditioning and desensitization. Change the dog's opinion of various stressors so they are no longer stressful to him.

Positive training. The more a dog can make sense of his world, the less stressful life is for him. Positive training opens communication between you and your dog, helps his world make sense to him, and creates a less stressful and more rewarding relationship for *both* of you.

"Say please" program. Ask for your dog to sit or lie down in order to get all good stuff. Not only does this teach your dog to defer to you (sit and down are deference behaviors), thus strengthening the relationship, it also teaches him self-control and to offer good manners behaviors as *default* behaviors—the behaviors to offer when he's not sure what to do.

Veterinary exam. Rule out, or identify and treat, medical stressors, to reduce stress load.

Exercise. Aerobic exercise produces mood-regulating endorphins and plays and important role in the body's ability to make use of naturally occurring calming chemicals such as serotonin.

Comfort Zone (DAP-Dog Appeasing Pheromone). A synthetic substance that mimics the pheromones emitted by a mother dog when she's nursing her puppies,

DAP appears to have a calming affect on a significant number of adult dogs, although not all. Available as a plug-in, a spray, or a DAP-infused collar.

Diet. Poor quality protein can interfere with the body's ability to utilize serotonin—a naturally-occurring chemical that helps dogs (and humans) to relax. For best utilization of serotonin, feed foods that only contain *human-grade* protein.

Anxiety Wrap. A "jacket" made of stretchable fabric, using the technique of "Maintained Pressure" as used to calm autistic children. Studies show that babies who are swaddled cry less, indicating less anxiety and stress. You can accomplish much the same effect, at a considerably lower cost, with a snug T-shirt.

Calming Cap. Similar to the hoods used on falcons to reduce stress and prevent the easily-excitable birds from panicking and "bating"—trying to fly off perches or the falconer's wrist. The Calming Cap is made of a thin nylon material that allows your dog to see shapes but not detail, thereby reducing the intensity of stimulus, helping to keep him below threshold and allowing for successful counter-conditioning. Another option for reducing intensity of visual stimuli is Doggles—commercially-produced sunglasses for dogs.

"Through a Dog's Ear." A bio-acoustically engineered CD of soothing classical piano music, with tones removed that have been demonstrated to be arousing to a dog. This wonderfully soothing music eases *my* stress too!

Calming massage. Soothing touch feels as good to many dogs as it does to many humans. If administered in conjunction with aromatherapy, the scent association can be used to induce calmness in other environments.

Neutering. Spaying and neutering can help with behavior modification in some cases, especially when stress is related to reproductive hormones. Even when not directly related, in most cases dogs with significant behavior issues should not be used for breeding.

Medication. Only rarely do I suggest the use of behavior modification drugs on an initial consult. I do inform my client that drugs are a possibility if modification efforts aren't productive in reasonably short order. If that time comes, we will consult with a veterinarian, preferably a veterinary behaviorist.

Behavior modification drugs

The last point on the above stress reduction list merits more discussion. I used to be strongly opposed to using drugs in behavior modification except as a very last resort. That was years ago, at a time when the most widely used behavior drugs for dogs were Valium and Acepromazine. Those drugs have a strong sedative effect—creating a "groggy doggie" who is still very aware of the fear-causing stimulus; he's just too drugged to do anything about it. Still inappropriately prescribed by some vets today for behavior modification, they are quite likely to *sensitize* the dog even further and make fear-related behaviors *worse,* not better.

These days, I'm much more likely to suggest consulting with a behavior-educated vet sooner, rather than later, about the use of behavior modification drugs. I'm not a vet, so not only can I *not* prescribe drugs myself, it's inappropriate for me to even suggest to a client which specific drug might be just what her dog needs. What I can do is tell her that based on the behavioral history form she filled out for me, my observations of the dog, and our subsequent discussions regarding the success of our behavioral modification program, it's appropriate to talk to a veterinarian about the possibility of adding pharmaceuticals to our modification program. I am most likely to suggest this in cases where dog's and owner's quality of life are significantly impacted by a dog's fearful and/or aggressive behaviors.

Today's classes of psychotropic drugs are a far cry from the sedatives of the past. They are explicitly designed to help rebalance brain chemistry that's out of kilter—to enable ongoing behavior modification to be more successful. Admittedly, it's somewhat experimental—most of the drugs were designed for use in humans, and use in canines is an off-label application—more argument in favor of working closely with a veterinarian who is very knowledgeable about canine behavior and the likely effects of the various drugs on dogs.

Humans tend to have a knee-jerk "cringe" reaction when someone suggests "drugging" their dog. I understand and applaud a dog owner's caution—behavior modification drugs are not benign and they need to be used with care. There is potential for adverse reactions, and the dog needs to be monitored closely to determine if the drug's impact is beneficial, neutral, or harmful to the individual in question. All the more reason to work with a team that includes a caring owner, a knowledgeable behavior professional, and a behavior-educated veterinarian. So don't automatically say "No!" to drugs—just use them wisely, and with care and assistance from your animal behavior professionals.

Training and behavior modification: Minor behavior problems

Now let's take a look at some of the behavior challenges you might face with your Do-Over Dog, starting with the "minor" or simpler ones. *Note: just because they are simple doesn't mean they are easy to live with, modify, or are unimportant.* These include:

- Housetraining
- Chewing
- Digging
- Destructive behavior
- Barking
- Escaping
- Do-Overs and cats

Housetraining

Do-Over Dogs are frequently not housetrained or poorly housetrained at best. This is especially true of dogs who have been rescued from puppy mill or hoarder situations. Housesoiling is a common reasons why people give up on their dogs. In addition, a Do-Over Dog who was housetrained previously may, due to the stress of a new environment, regress and make mistakes in his new home. So even if your new dog comes with an assurance he is housetrained, be wary and ready to treat him like a new puppy in this regard.

The basics

Poop and pee outside, not inside. It seems like such a simple concept, and indeed, many dogs are easily housetrained. But not all. We adopted our Scorgidooodle, Bonnie, from the Humane Society here in Hagerstown when she was about six months old. She was surrendered to the shelter because her owners couldn't housetrain her. Now age four, she's *reasonably* reliable with her housetraining, but she'll never be one of those dogs you'll find waiting at the door with legs crossed if an emergency keeps you away from home for ten hours.

The basic premise of successful housetraining is: Take your dog out more often than he has to go, and supervise and manage to prevent accidents. For young puppies, that means outside every hour on the hour during the day, and crated or otherwise confined at night, where you can hear him if he wakes up and says he has to go out. As your pup matures, a general rule of thumb is that he can "hold it" for one hour more than his age in months. That is, a three-month-old pup might be able to go for four hours—up to a maximum of about eight hours on a regular basis for an adult dog. Remember, though, that it's a general rule—there are certainly normal three-month-old puppies who can only hold it for two to three hours and adult dogs who can't go longer than three or four. There are also canine saints who will maintain their housetraining when left alone for 10 or even 12 hours—but even with those I don't recommend expecting them to do so routinely.

You can use a tether—as long as you're there to supervise—to prevent housetraining accidents and keep your Do-Over dog out of all kinds of trouble.

You can rely on a dog's instinct to keep his den clean as the basis for housetraining. Your "den" (home) is huge compared to a dog's natural den, so your canine family member, until he learns otherwise, sees nothing wrong with using part of your vast empire as his bathroom. A crate appropriate to your pup's size—big enough for him to stand up, turn around, and lie down in—is a perfect den. He won't want to soil it, he will let you know when he has to go out, and he'll learn how to "hold it."

Along with the use of crates (discussed earlier), I recommend the "umbilical approach" to housetraining puppies and adult dogs. This means that your dog is always either in a crate or pen, on a leash attached to you (or restrained nearby on a tether), under the direct supervision of an adult or responsible teen, or outdoors, until he can be trusted with house freedom.

If your Do-Over Dog shows any evidence of not being fully housetrained, establish a daytime routine—go out *with* your dog every one to two hours. If you want him to use a particular bathroom area of the yard, always take him on leash to this same spot for bathroom breaks. Don't just send him out to "do his business" on his own. You won't know if he did anything or not, and you won't be able to reward him for doing the right thing. Go with him. When he urinates or defecates, click your clicker or tell him "Yes!" and feed him a treat. Be sure to wait until he's just about empty—if you interrupt his flow with a "click" you may think he's empty when he's not. Then play with him for a few minutes before bringing him indoors, as a reward for eliminating. If he doesn't go, bring him back in, put him in his crate, and try again in a half-hour or so. When you know he's empty you can give him some relative-but-still-supervised freedom for twenty minutes to a half-hour. Then he goes back under wraps.

If he makes a mistake indoors, do *not* punish him after-the-fact. It's your mistake, not his. He won't even know what he is being punished for! Quietly clean it up, using an enzyme-based product designed for clean up of pet waste, and vow not to give him so much freedom. If you must spank someone with a rolled up newspaper, hit yourself in the head three times while repeating, "I will watch the dog more closely; I will watch the dog more closely; I will watch the dog more closely."

If you catch him in the act, calmly interrupt him with a cheerful, "Oops! Outside!" and take him outside to his bathroom spot. Again, do not punish him. If you do, you'll only teach him that it isn't safe to toilet in front of you; he'll learn to run to the back bedroom to do it.

If your dog is quicker than you, or has housesoiling challenges that include marking and excitement or submissive urination, a belly band (for males) or panties (for females) are useful management tools. You still need to make the effort to housetrain, but at least your carpets will be safe!

Start keeping a daily log, writing down when (and what) he goes. Once you have this documentation of his routine, you can start reducing the number of times you take him out, based on his elimination schedule. As he becomes more trustworthy, you can start to give him more freedom. Continue keeping your log until he's reliably housetrained, so you know where you are in your program if he starts having accidents. If he backslides, you've given him too much freedom too soon. Back up to a more restricted routine and proceed more slowly.

At night, your dog should be crated in or near your bedroom. If he wakes up in the middle of the night and cries, he probably has to go out. You must wake up and take him out, click and reward when he goes, then bring him back and immediately return him to his crate. You don't want to teach him that crying at night earns a play session or a snuggle in bed with you.

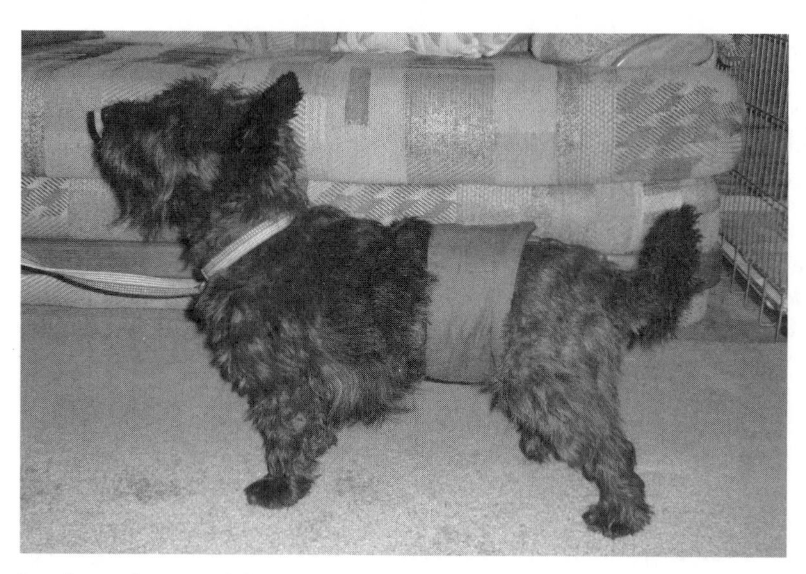

A belly band can be a useful management tool for marking and excitement urination behaviors.

Troubleshooting

If you're doing all the right stuff and still have trouble with housetraining your Do-Over Dog, a visit to your veterinarian is in order to rule out—or treat—any possible medical condition that may make it difficult for your dog to control his bowels and/or bladder. These might include, but are not limited to, things such as a urinary tract infections, parasites, bladder stones, and any condition that causes loose stools or diarrhea.

Other things that can make housetraining difficult include:

- **Overfeeding.** Too much food can cause too much "by-product."
- Free feeding. If your dog eats throughout the day, he has to eliminate throughout the day. Feed regular meals and pick up bowls after 15-20 minutes if your dog hasn't finished. If he eats on schedule, he'll eliminate on schedule.
- **Feeding too late.** It's best to feed your dog his dinner at least three hours before you go to bed. If you feed him too late, he won't have time to process it before bedtime and he'll have to go in the middle of the night.
- **Restricting water.** Unless there's a valid *medical* reason to restrict water, your dog should have access to clean, fresh water at all times, except not necessarily overnight. Restricting water can cause him to over-drink when he does get access, which will cause a very full bladder, making it harder for him to "hold it" until you take him out. Withholding water can also cause dehydration, which can create serious medical problems.
- **Switching foods suddenly.** Your dog's system may need time to adapt to new foods, especially if he's been on a single-food diet. If you decide to change foods, change gradually, adding small amounts of the new food to the old food, increasing the new food slowly until he's switched over. If you routinely feed

your dog a variety of foods and training treats (a practice I highly recommend), this is not so much of a problem.

- **Food allergies.** If your dog is sensitive to certain foods, they can cause digestive upset, which can cause accidents. Many dogs are sensitive to corn, soy, and other grains and some dogs are sensitive to a variety of other dog food ingredients. Good quality dog foods do not contain corn, soy, or meat "by-products."
- **Medications.** Some medications, such as prednisone, can cause increased thirst, drinking, and urination.
- **Too much freedom too soon.** Err on the side of caution. Your goal is to minimize the number of indoor accidents and maximize the number of successful outdoor potty trips.

Doggie doors

Many people view doggie doors as a solution to their Do-Over Dog's housesoiling issues. I'm not a big fan of doggie doors, for several reasons. While free access to the outdoors may seem like an easy solution to leaving your dog home alone longer than he can hold his bowels and bladder, it's fraught with risks. During my 20 years at the Marin Humane Society, I saw firsthand the tragedies that can occur when dogs are left outdoors, unattended. It should go without saying that chaining a dog up all day is unacceptable. But what would be wrong with a doggie door that gives a dog access to a safely fenced yard? Plenty.

For starters, if your dog can get out, others can get in. Raccoons, skunks, squirrels and snakes are just a few of the visitors you may find in your home when you give your dog free access to the backyard. In addition, dogs who are left in yards all day tend to bark. They bark out of boredom, they run and bark along the fence when they're aroused by people and cars passing by, they bark because they're lonely, and they bark when they're excited. Your barking dog is looked upon with disfavor by neighbors, especially neighbors who are home all day. They may report you to animal control, or worse, open your gate and let him run free, steal, or poison him. In addition, unattended back yard dogs can be teased and tormented, jump, climb over or dig under fences, and have perilous encounters with wildlife, including rabies carriers such as skunks, raccoons, and foxes, in your absence.

Chewing

While puppies are notorious for their ability to chew on anything and everything, your Do-Over Dog may come with built in chewing problems, whatever his age. What many dog owners *don't* seem to realize is that while puppies sooner or later get beyond the stage where they feel compelled to put their teeth on *everything* they see, mature dogs also need to chew to exercise their jaws, massage their gums, clean their teeth, and to relieve stress and boredom. As discussed before, Do-Over Dogs may have suffered from stress, boredom, and inadequate management in their former homes or in shelters. There's a good chance your new canine family member never learned appropriate chew habits. You could be way behind the starting line on this behavior—especially if he has found it reinforcing to chew on very inappropriate objects.

Thousands of years of domestication and a steady diet of packaged foods haven't extinguished the adult dog's need and desire to chew. Many dogs continue a significant amount of vigorous adolescent chewing until the age of 18 to 24 months as teeth continue to mature, and then still chew, but with somewhat less intensity, as they age. Chewing is as basic a behavior to a puppy as a human baby sucking on a pacifier. Humans, as they grow, transition to sucking on thumbs, then lollipops, straws, sports bottles, and perhaps cigarettes. Dogs, like us, can learn to transition to appropriate objects for mature oral attention, but they never completely outgrow the need to gnaw. Given the opportunity, mature dogs will chew for as long as they live and have teeth to chew with.

Case in point: Katie, our second Australian Kelpie who, at the advanced age of 15 could barely hear, had difficulty walking, and whose vision was failing, still happily chewed raw bones and chicken wings right alongside her younger packmates.

Building good chew habits

Puppies develop substrate preferences for elimination in the early months of their lives and they similarly develop chew-object preferences. Hence the inadvisability of giving your dog old shoes or socks as chew toys. If you give your Do-Over Dog the run of the house and he learns to chew on Oriental carpets, sofa cushions, and coffee table legs, you can end up with a dog who chooses to exercise his jaws and teeth on inappropriate objects for years to come. You'll find yourself crating him frequently, or worse, exiling him to a life of loneliness in the back yard, where he can only chew on lawn furniture, loose fence boards, and the edges of your deck and hot tub.

If, instead, you focus Fido's fangs on approved chew toys and manage him well to prevent access to your stuff, he'll earn house privileges much sooner in life. By the end of his first year with you, you'll probably be able to leave him alone safely while you go out to dinner, shopping, even while you're away at work.

If your adolescent or adult rescue or shelter dog comes to you with a history of inappropriate chewing, you'll need an intensified management program to overcome his already-programmed chew-object preferences. You may not know anything about his past chew behaviors, but his first few days in your home will tell you if he chews on the right stuff—or not.

Be sure to provide him with plenty of dog-desirable appropriate chewables. If you can prevent inappropriate chewing in his new environment through management and redirection to appropriate chewables, even if he chewed inappropriately in the past, you will reprogram that behavior more quickly.

As long as Do-Over Dan still snags the occasional shoe, knick-knack, or other off-limits possessions for a mid-day gnaw, it's too soon to give him unfettered freedom. When you're home, he needs to always be under your direct supervision. You may need to keep him on a leash or a tether, or simply close the door of the room you're in so he's shut in with you and can't wander into the parlor to shred your grandmother's antique lace doily while your back is turned. If you're momentarily too occupied to supervise, put him in his crate or exercise pen to keep him out of trouble.

At the same time, supply him with a variety of "legal" chew objects to keep his teeth appropriately occupied. Stuffed Kongs, Goodie Ships and Buster Cubes are just a few of the many interactive toys available that can keep your dog's teeth and mind acceptably busy. If you consistently supply him with desirable and acceptable objects upon which to chew, he'll eventually develop a strong preference for chewing on those same objects. He will seek these items out when he feels the need to gnaw and ultimately your personal possessions will be safe, even when your back is turned.

Beyond normal chewing

Some destructive chewing and other related inappropriate behaviors are a result of isolation distress or separation anxiety rather than "normal" chewing. Such chewing is often—but not exclusively—directed toward door and window frames, and occurs only outside of the owner's presence, by a dog who shows signs of stress at the signs of his owner's pending departure. Separation anxiety dogs often don't crate well, which makes managing the destructive behavior even more challenging. If you think your dog's chewing is related to separation anxiety or isolation distress, you'll need to work with a qualified, positive behavior professional to modify the behaviors.

Because different dogs chew with different levels of intensity, it's impossible to make definitive statements about which types of chew products are appropriate for your particular dog. The safety of chew objects such as rawhide, various bones, pig ears and cow hooves is a hotly debated topic. Rope tugs are wonderful chew toys for some dogs, but others chew off and ingest the strings and risk serious gastrointestinal complications, even death. Check with your own veterinarian and follow his/her recommendations regarding the use of these and other chew items for your dog. Regularly check the condition of any chew toys you do give your dog and discard them when they begin to show signs of wear and tear.

The trading post

You can reduce the risk of damage to occasional ill-gotten items from chewing by teaching your dog to exchange toys for treats, using something he loves that he's allowed to have, such as a favorite chew toy, or a stuffed Kong. The key to this game is he learns that, if he gives something up, he gets something *better* in return *and* he gets the original thing back as well. Two rewards for the price of one! Then, when he has a forbidden object, he's more likely to bring it to you to trade than to drag his prize to his cave under the dining room table for a leisurely chew. The rare occasion that he doesn't get "the thing" back, won't be enough to overcome the programming you've done by playing the "Trade" game with him frequently.

In order for this to work, you have to stop playing his game of "Chase the Dog" when he grabs the sofa cushion or some other forbidden object. This is often an attention-getting behavior; he's learned that grabbing "your" toys and dashing off with them initiates a rousing play session.

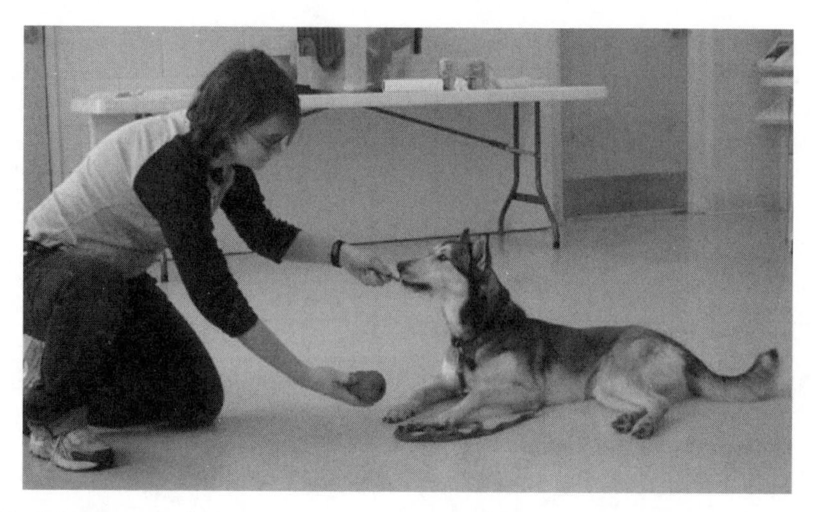

The "Trade" game can help prevent resource guarding and save wear and tear on your valuable possessions.

Here's what you do:

1. Offer him his well-stuffed Kong and say, "Take it!" Have him on a leash if you think he'll run off with it.
2. Give him a little while to get fully engaged in chewing, and then say "Give!" or "Trade!" in a *cheerful* tone of voice and offer him a handful of irresistible treats, such as small bits of chicken or low fat cheese.
3. Hold the treats under his nose and let him sniff. It may take him several seconds to think about it, but eventually he should drop his Kong and start eating the treats. Don't let him eat them in one gulp! Protect the tidbits in your hand a little so he can only nibble them one-by-one.
4. When he drops the Kong, say, "Yes!"
5. *While he is still nibbling the treat in your hand,* reach down with your *other* hand and pick up the chew toy.
6. Let him nibble a bit longer, then offer him the Kong again.
7. Repeat the exercise several times, then end the game by giving him back his Kong and letting him chew to his heart's content.
8. Play this game at every opportunity, whenever he's engaged in chewing on his toys on his own, or whenever you feel like initiating the game, until he'll give up his chew object easily, on your "Trade" cue.

The game may not always go as smoothly as you might like. Here are some of the challenges you may face:

- Your dog may not be willing to drop his toy in exchange for the treats in your hand. Try dropping the treats on the floor in a little Hansel-and-Gretel-trail. Lots of dogs are more willing to give up their valued possession if the treats are within easy reach on the floor. Then, while he is following the trail to your hand that's still holding a reservoir of treats, pick up the Kong with your *other* hand.

- Your dog may lose interest in his toy after he realizes you have yummy treats in your hand. Try using less valuable treats or a more valuable chew toy. Or simply play the game when he happens to be chewing on one of his toys.
- Your dog may guard resources. If he growls, snaps, or even stiffens and looks angry when you try to trade with him, you should *stop* practicing this exercise and seek the help of a qualified and positive training professional to help you resolve the resource guarding challenge. Meanwhile, supervise him very closely to prevent his access to forbidden objects so you don't put yourself at risk for being bitten because you *have* to take something away from him.

Choose your chews

For a chew toy to be effective it must meet three criteria:

1. It must be attractive to the dog. The dog must want to chew it, or it is useless.
2. It must be durable. If it only last 30 seconds it won't help with a long-term chewing problem.
3. It must be safe. It must not contain toxins, or break up (or break down) into pieces that can cause the dog to choke or do internal damage.

It is important to look at individual dogs when deciding which chew objects are safe. Aggressive chewers can splinter objects and swallow large pieces that can choke a dog, cause life-threatening bowel obstructions or tear the lining of the intestines. Delicate chewers can safely be given items that would be deadly for some dogs. A veterinarian friend gives her Greyhounds rawhide chips, which would not be safe for more aggressive chewers. Aggressive dogs and dogs that are left alone with a chew object are safest with a hard rubber, hollow Kong-type toy that can be filled with something tasty to hold the dog's interest. Very large carrots make ideal chew objects for many dogs.

Over time, any chew toy softer than your dog's teeth will become worn down. Any chew object harder than your dog's teeth will cause wear to the teeth. It's generally preferable to have wear to the toys than wear to the teeth.

Safety requires good judgment. Many chew objects may eventually become too small to be safe and should be disposed of before they reach a dangerous size.

"Leave it"

You can also teach your Do-Over Dog to respond to your cue to leave something alone *before* he sinks his sabers gum-deep into a treasured possession. This behavior has lots of other applications as well beyond just chewing problems. To teach "Leave it," have your dog on leash in front of you. Show him a tasty treat, tell him "Leave it!" and let him see you place it under your shoe. Freeze-dried liver cubes work well for this; they are high-value for most dogs, but firm enough that they aren't easily squished under your foot.

Your dog may dig, claw, and even chew at your foot to try to get the treat. Let him. This is an exercise in patience for you as well as an exercise in "Leave it!" for him. *Be sure to wear durable shoes for this exercise.* Sandals may leave you with bloody toes, and patent leather will be permanently scratched.

He may give up easily when he realizes he can't get the treat, or he may be very persistent. Either way, you're just going to wait for him to give up. The instant he looks away from your foot, click your clicker (or say "yes!"), and feed him a very tasty treat. If he continues to look away from your foot, keep clicking and treating at a high rate of reinforcement—lots of clicks and treats. If he returns his attentions to the treat under your foot, just wait for him to look away again. Do *not* repeat the cue. When he looks away again, click and treat—again, at a high rate of reinforcement.

When he can control his urge to maul your foot for at least five seconds, carefully move your foot off the treat. If he tries to grab it, simply cover it back up with your foot. You don't need to repeat the "Leave it" cue. In a surprisingly short time, he'll ignore the treat on the floor. Now pick it up, show it to him again, repeat the "Leave it!" cue and try it under your foot again, still with a high rate of reinforcement. Remember to keep your cue cheerful—you're not trying to intimidate him away from the forbidden object; you're just giving him information.

When he's reliably ignoring the treat, you can move your foot a few inches away from it. Don't get too confident! The farther you move from the treat, the more likely he is to think it's okay for him to have it. Take it slow, set him up to succeed, and in time you'll be able to tell him "Leave it" and leave the object unattended.

You can translate this exercise to real life as soon as your dog understands to look away from the object when he hears the "Leave it!" cue. Set some tempting items on the floor, put him on leash, and walk him past the objects, just out of reach. The instant he looks at an object, say, "Leave it!" in a cheerful tone, and stand still. He may stare at and strain toward the object. Just wait. When he gives up and looks away from the forbidden object, click and treat, and continue toward the next object. When he'll do this reliably without the leash tightening at all, you're ready to try it off leash. Then, as you supervise your pup's antics, if you see him coveting an inappropriate object, just say, "Leave it!" in that cheerful tone, and be ready to click and treat when he turns back toward you.

When you've taught your dog the "Trade" and "Leave It!" games, the rest is up to you. Of course, you'll continue to supervise him closely to minimize his access to forbidden objects and redirect his attention when you see him eyeing something he is not allowed to chew. If, however, he does happen to find something he's not supposed to have, odds are he'll bring it to you to exchange for something better. Next time you see your Do-Over dog with Aunt Ida's antique lace doily in his mouth, instead of going into "Omigod the dog has the doily!" panic mode, walk to the refrigerator, take out a bag of his favorite treats, and calmly initiate the Trade Game. You'll be surprised by how easy it is.

Finally, a well-run positive training class can assist in resolving behavior problems, chewing and otherwise, by helping you and your Do-Over Dog learn to communicate more clearly with each other. The better you understand how his mind works, and the better he understands what you expect of him, the stronger the relationship between the two of you. In the end, it's the strength of this relationship that will carry you through the challenges of chewing and other dog caretaking adventures and allow you to experience the joys and rewards of sharing your life with a canine companion.

Digging

Dogs dig. They bark. They chew. They roll in smelly stuff and chase things that move. They eat garbage and they poop and pee. Most owners understand that dogs must poop and pee, and rather than trying to prevent them from doing it at all, they wisely redirect the behavior so that urine and feces are generally deposited in an acceptable location. Your Do-Over Dog may have previously belonged to an owner who failed to understand that dogs must also satisfy their needs to perform other natural dog behaviors, such as digging. It is possible to teach Rowdy to restrict his digging to acceptable locations and objects, just as it's possible to housetrain him.

The pervasive myth of the perfect "Lassie" sets up unsuspecting dog owners to have unreasonable expectations about their dogs' abilities to instinctively know right from wrong and to make ethical judgments about their own actions. Unfortunately for the dogs, normal doggie behaviors like digging, chewing, urinating, defecating, barking, roaming, raiding garbage cans, and even biting, are not considered acceptable behaviors in our human society. Dogs are naturally an opportunistic species. Their philosophy of life is "what's in it for me, right *now?*" If it feels good, they do it, and if it looks or tastes good, they chew it or eat it.

Dusty the digger

Way back in 1990, I was working at the customer service desk of the Marin Humane Society when a familiar fox-like face appeared over the front counter. It was Dusty, an adorable sable-colored 10-month-old, eight-pound Pomeranian pup who had been adopted just a week prior. He was being returned because he was digging holes in his new owner's back yard.

I had fallen in love with Dusty the previous week and was tempted to adopt him immediately myself, but in a world populated by difficult-to-place Do-Over Dogs it didn't seem right for me to take one who appeared highly adoptable. Instead, animal care staff had placed him in the "available for adoption" section of our kennels. As I had suspected would be the case, he was snatched up in no time by a couple who sailed through our adoption screening process with flying colors. Now he was back, returned for doing a perfectly normal dog behavior—digging.

The National Council on Pet Overpopulation conducted a series of studies in the late 1990's, and determined that the generic category of "behavior problems" is the number one reason that dogs are surrendered to animal shelters by their owners (http://www.

petpopulation.org/). Dusty certainly fit the profile—he was surrendered the first time for snapping at toddlers, the second time for digging. The real tragedy is that most of the behaviors that owners perceive as "problems" are, like digging, perfectly normal doggie behaviors.

What's his motivation?

Dogs dig for different reasons. Some breeds of dogs—many of the terriers and scent hounds especially—are genetically programmed to chase small creatures down holes and go digging after them. Others may dig out of boredom or to bury a valuable possession. Still others dig to get cool; there's nothing more refreshing on a hot summer day than digging down a couple of inches to cool earth and resting his bare belly against the dampness.

Your Do-Over Dog may really need to dig. You can help him learn do it in an acceptable spot. Here, Lucy digs after a groundhog.

An ounce of prevention

It's *always* easier to prevent an undesirable habit from developing than it is to change it once it is established. Good management is the key. If you don't want your dog to turn your back yard into a moonscape, don't give him unlimited access to the yard when you're not there to redirect his digging behavior. Gophers and moles may be an irresistible motivator for your dog's digging (and a strong reinforcer, if he ever actually catches one). If you don't want him to rototill the zucchini in your absence, fence off the garden so he doesn't have access to it. Soft garden soil is infinitely tempting to a dog who has an inclination toward excavation.

Manage your dog's access to potential digging spots with the judicious use of crates, baby gates, exercise pens, kennels, dog walkers, leashes, direct supervision, and if necessary, doggie daycare. If he spent the first six to twelve months of his life (or more) learning that digging without restriction is a fun, satisfying, and rewarding behavior, you will struggle with resolving or managing those behavior challenges for a good long time, perhaps for the rest of his life.

A pound of cure

The concept of redirecting digging to an acceptable spot may be a novel idea for some dog owners. Once upon a time, solutions for digging ranged from filling the hole with dog feces to discourage digging there again (or a balloon that would pop when the dog tried to dig), to filling the hole with water and holding the unfortunate dog's head submerged in the hole until he nearly drowned. The first method was relatively ineffective, because a yard has an almost infinite number of places where a dog could dig that he *hasn't* dug before. If anything, it only teaches him not to dig in the same spot twice. The second method was simply abusive.

One of the basic tenets of positive training is that it is much easier to teach a dog what *to* do rather than what *not* to do. If you were to teach your dog "Don't dig here" you would have to teach him in every potential digging spot in the entire yard. If you just teach him "Do dig here," you only have to teach him to dig in one spot. Increasingly, trainers and behaviorists are counseling owners to actually build a digging box or a digging pit and teach their dogs to use it. Eventually, when your dog feels the desire to dig he'll automatically go to his digging box, just as he chews on a Kong when he feels the urge to chew, and goes outside when he feels the need to eliminate.

If your dog is digging to get cool, the digging box may not help, unless it's in a shady spot and/or you dampen the dirt for him. Alternative options include keeping him in the air-conditioned house on hot days, giving him access to a shed or barn with a cool cement floor, or investing in one of the many available "cool" pads, scarves, or jackets. These products are filled with water-absorbing crystals that soften into a gel when wet. The moisture evaporates over time (a period of several days, for the cool pads) and the evaporation action cools the pad and the dog who is lying on it.

If boredom is the culprit, the digging box may help. At the same time, you also need to find ways to engage your dog's mind and body to relieve the boredom. Several daily exercise sessions can help reduce the energy level that contributes to digging. A walk around the block on-leash is probably not sufficient to do the job. Rowdy needs to run in a safe environment, chasing a stick or a ball, squirrels, or whatever, until he flops at your feet, tongue dragging, with a happy grin on his face. A tired dog tends to be a well-behaved dog.

Interactive toys can help here too. Instead of giving him his bowl of food in the morning, fill the Buster Cube or Roll-A-Treat Ball with his kibbles and make him work for his meal by pushing the ball or cube around to make the food fall out. He won't have the time or energy to dig holes if he's out "hunting" for his breakfast!

So what became of Dusty? You didn't really need to ask, did you? Given a second chance, I grabbed the adorable little guy and took him home to join the Miller pack. Over the years, he earned his Companion Dog title in AKC Obedience, worked as a therapy dog in the Marin Humane Society's animal-assisted therapy program, at the age of thirteen, earned his APDT Level 1 Rally Dog title, and was a constant source of joy and companionship to me until we said our sad good-byes when he was fourteen. And no, he never once dug a single hole in our yard. Keeping him indoors as a "house dog" most of the time instead of in the back yard for hours on end was all that was needed to eliminate his digging behavior.

Training your dog to use a digging box

A digging box can be as simple as a designated spot in the yard, dug up and turned over to make it soft and inviting for your canine pal to dig in, or as elaborate as a four-sided wooden structure custom-designed to fit your dog, complete with a roof to protect it from rain and shade it from the sun, and filled with potting soil to allow for maximum digging pleasure. Once you have created your digging box, it's time to teach Rowdy to use it. This is the fun part.

Start by burying some of your dog's favorite toys in the dirt. Treats and stuffed Kongs are good here too. Let him watch you bury the objects, and then encourage him to find them. Tell him "Go dig!" and help him if necessary—the two of you can have a great time digging together!

Gradually give him the "Go dig!" cue from farther and farther away, until you can send him across the yard to his box to dig without your help. When he seems to have the idea, bury objects when he's not looking. Then sometimes tell him to "Go dig!" and sometimes let him discover the buried treasures all on his own. Continue to supervise his yard activities, and if you catch him digging somewhere other than his box, interrupt his activity with a cheerful "Oops, Go dig!" and redirect him to his box. When you are no longer having to redirect his digging to his box, you can start giving him some unsupervised time in the yard—brief periods at first, then longer and longer as he continues to direct all of his digging in the appropriate place. If he lapses, you will need to go back to supervised activity for a period of time. When you are ready to go back to no supervision, start with shorter periods and increase the length of time even more gradually than before.

Remember to address the other areas that motivate his digging, and before long, you should have a dog who can happily "dig it" with the best of them.

Destructive behavior

You arrive home from work, dreading what you are going to find. Your fears are realized as you walk through the door and discover tufts of sofa cushion stuffing scattered in snow-like drifts across your living room floor. Your newly adopted rescue dog grovels at your feet, obviously aware that he's been a very bad dog. You *knew* he was going to get even with you for leaving him home alone all day. Right? Wrong!

Behavior analysis

Do-Over Dogs may be likely to engage in destructive behavior for one or more of several reasons including:

1. **Stress.** Physical activity relieves stress. A stressed human may pace the floor, go jogging, chew her fingernails, tap a pencil on the table, or a foot on the

floor. Chewing, digging, and other destructive behaviors are stress relievers for dogs. Stress-related destructive behavior can be relatively mild, or turn into full-blown catastrophic destruction. Dogs who have lived in several homes and passed through one or more shelters are prime candidates for stress. Change is stressful for all of us.

2. **Teething.** If you adopt a puppy, recognize that when a pup's new teeth are pushing through the gums, and until they are fully set at 18-24 months, a young dog can be in mild to somewhat severe discomfort. Chewing helps relieve teething pain, which is one of the primary reasons puppies and adolescent dogs are such dedicated chewers.
3. **High jinks.** Dogs explore the world with their mouths, and young dogs are particularly driven to explore the world around them, as so much of it is new and exciting. Does this taste good? Does this feel good? Is this fun to play with? In addition, baby dogs and juveniles tend to have high energy levels, and sometimes go on a rampage in a burst of feel-good energy, similar to the teenager who trashes the house when his parents unwisely leave him home alone for a weekend. Poorly-managed puppies and adolescents are at risk for becoming Do-Over Dogs with a strong reinforcement history for engaging in this unsupervised party-destructive behavior.
4. **Boredom.** Your Do-Over Dog may have come from an environment where he was mentally and physically under-stimulated. If, in addition, he's an intelligent, high-energy type of dog, it's especially important that you provide him with ample outlets for his energy. The herding breeds can be workaholics—if you don't give them a job, they'll create one, and it may not be one that meets with your approval. But Herding dogs aren't the only ones. There are plenty of other high-energy dogs who will play destructive games to keep themselves busy in their owners' absence, including the Sporting breeds and some of the Terriers.
5. **Habit.** Many dogs end up in shelters because of poor early management. When you adopt one, you inherit the behavior and the bad habits. You will compound this problem if he continues to be poorly managed and allowed to repeatedly engage in destructive behavior after he arrives at your home. If he is well managed during the honeymoon period, he is unlikely to pick up new destructive behaviors later in life—unless his environment changes drastically and causes him undue stress.

Tame the tornado

It's easy to understand the frustration and anger you feel when you come home after a hard day at work to a house that looks like it's been hit by a tornado. However, any punishment delivered at this point is totally useless and ineffective in altering your dog's behavior. He probably ripped up the sofa cushions hours ago. Dirty looks and stern words may make you feel better in the moment, but will do nothing to change your dog's behavior, other than teaching him to associate your return home with bad stuff. I won't even mention how inappropriate physical punishment is. If you're going to use it, which I *don't* suggest—in fact I strongly recommend *against*—it *must* happen within a *few seconds* of the undesirable behavior in order for the dog to be able to make the connection. You can't do that when the behavior occurred hours earlier.

The solution to your dog's destructive behavior is management, not punishment. Calmly invite your dog into his crate so he's out of harm's way while you clean up the mess and vent your wrath with broom and mop on the unfeeling kitchen floor.

Note that many Do-Over Dogs with separation anxiety cannot tolerate being crated—the confinement causes them to panic, and they may injure themselves in their desperate and sometimes successful attempts to escape. If your dog is easily stressed, be extra careful about not adding to his stress with forceful crating techniques, which can move a moderately stressed dog toward the "full-blown" end of the separation anxiety scale.

Options for destructive Do-Over Dogs who can't be crated include dog-proofing a room or kennel run for him to stay in where he can't do damage; taking him to a doggie daycare center; or leaving him in the custody of a friend, neighbor, or family member who is home all day and willing to dog sit. Some lucky owners are able to take their dogs to work with them. If you are one of these, be sure to supervise your canine closely at work so he doesn't destroy things at the office—or you may lose your dog privileges.

Work it out

Along with management, exercise can be an important element of your destruction reduction program. (Are you seeing a pattern here?) Exercise reduces stress and eliminates one of the primary causes of high jinks behavior—those high energy levels. Even teething and habit-related chewing can be diminished with a good exercise program. A tired dog is a well-behaved dog.

Structured exercise of some kind is best; it keeps your dog focused and minimizes out-of-control arousal. Play fetch with a ball, toy, stick, or Frisbee and require that he sit politely each time before you throw. Play tug of war, and insist that he play by the rules, which include that he give the tug toy to you when requested, and not grabbing it again until invited.

Remember that a walk around the block on leash is not sufficient exercise for any young dog—it's a mere exercise hors d' oeuvre. Try a long hike in the hills—off leash if legal and your dog is under control; on a long line if he's not ready for off-leash hikes yet. As you watch your dog run circles around you, you'll realize why a walk-on-leash barely puts a dent in his energy. My first Kelpie and I would hike to the top of a hill, and I'd throw the ball down the hill for her to retrieve, over and over, taking advantage of the steep incline to give her even more of an exercise benefit.

Mind games

Boredom destruction can often be resolved by giving your dog something to do. Our latest Kelpie, Katie, decided that her house job was to gently herd our youngest cat, Viva. Her attention span was phenomenal. Watching Viva could occupy Katie's brain for hours on end. If Viva was sleeping on the back of the sofa, Katie sat and stared at her. If the cat walked through the house, Katie followed her, nose to tail. Outside, Katie herded Tucker, our Cattle Dog mix, and when we went to the barn she thought she was herding the horses, although truth be told, they mostly ignored her as she trotted behind them.

If your Do-Over dog doesn't obsess on herding all creatures great and small, you can create games that exercise his mind. The Buster Cube and the Roll-A-Treat Ball, available from most pet supply stores and catalogs, are perfect for this. Treats are placed inside the ball or cube and your dog must push the object around the room to make the treats fall out. A whole line of interactive toys produced by Nina Ottosson, in Sweden, are now available in the United States. These Zooactive Toys are puzzles that your dog solves: treats are hidden in the toy and your dog must figure out how to find and access them.

Training is another way to exercise your dog's brain. A good positive training class makes dogs think, and they have to think hard. Dogs generally come home from a training class and sleep like logs—and then you practice at home all week, encouraging him to work that brain every day.

Lucy plays with her favorite Zooactive toy—the Tornado. This, and other wonderful interactive toys, are available at www.pawlickers.com.

"Find it" is another great brain game to play. Before you leave, hide treats all over the house, in reasonably easy-to-reach places. *Don't* hide them under the sofa cushions or in other in places that will encourage your dog to dig or chew—we're trying to make that behavior go away, remember? Your dog can spend hours looking for all the treats! Some dogs make up their own games. I know of at least two Border Collies who will carry a tennis ball to the top of the stairs and push it off, watch it bounce down, and then chase after it and do it all over again. Those obsessive Herding dogs…

A few final tips

If your Do-Over Dog is under the age of two and still doing teething-related chewing, you're wise to keep valuable objects out of his reach, and supply him with plenty of chewable objects. Even mature adult dogs enjoy a good chew now and then, so keep that Kong around—or several, if you have a multi-dog household. A stuffed Kong is our ten-year-old Scottie's favorite chew toy.

If destructive behavior happens while you are *home* with your dog, you need to ratchet up your supervision program so he doesn't have the opportunity to get into things he shouldn't. Crates, leashes, tethers and baby gates are all useful management tools.

Barking

There's a lot of talk these days about the fact that dogs are primarily body language communicators. It's true, they are. But as anyone who's spent time with them knows, dogs also have a pretty well-developed ability to express themselves vocally. Dogs bark.

Some bark more, some bark less, and a few don't bark at all, but most dogs bark at least some of the time. Like chewing and digging, most barking is a normal behavior that's often considered inappropriate, or at least undesirable, by humans.

Why dogs bark

As the owner of five dogs, three of whom are very vocal, with a fourth quite willing to express himself on occasion, I can testify to the domestic dog's ability to speak. Interestingly, while wild *puppies* may be quite vocal, wild *adult* dogs rarely bark, at least not to the degree our canine companions do.

Genetics plays a large role here, of course. Over the millennia that we humans have been selectively breeding dogs, we've purposely selected for some breeds of dogs to be more vocal, others to be quiet.

At the "more" end of the continuum, the Scent Hounds are programmed to give voice to announce the presence of their quarry. Thus Beagles, Coonhounds, Foxhounds, and others in this group are quite vocal—although they do tend to bay rather than yap. Most of the Herding breeds are easily incited to bark. Skilled at telling a recalcitrant sheep or cow to back off, these Type-A workaholic dogs also delight in playing the role of noisy fun police. Many of the Toy breeds also have a well-deserved reputation for barkiness as do the Terriers. Our three *very* barky dogs are two Herding dogs and a Toy. Go figure.

In the "less-barking" category, the Guarding breeds tend to reserve their formidable vocalizing for serious provocation. Sighthounds also lean toward the quiet side, preferring to chase their quarry rather than bark at it. Then, of course, there's the Basenji—a somewhat primitive African breed of dog who doesn't bark—but he sure can scream!

Another reason wild dogs bark less than our own furry family members is that they are less likely to be subjected to environments that encourage frustration or arousal barking, such as fenced yards with potential prey objects (skateboards, joggers, bicycles) speeding tantalizingly past just out of reach; or humans who inadvertently—or intentionally—reinforce barking.

All barks are not alike

Dogs bark for various reasons. If you want to modify your dog's barking behavior (either decrease it or increase it), it's helpful to know what kind of barking your dog is doing, and how the behavior is being reinforced. Different kinds of barks have different tones—learn to recognize the differences in your dog's voice. Here are descriptions of the different kinds of barking, and what to do about them:

Alert/alarm barking. This is the dog who saves his family from a fire, tells us that Timmy's in the well, scares off the rapist, barks at the dogs on Animal Planet, and goes bonkers every time someone walks past on the sidewalk outside the picture window. Alarm barkers can save lives—but sometimes their judgment about what constitutes an alarm-appropriate situation can be a little faulty. A Do-Over Dog who is fearful or anxious may feel the need to sound the alarm or give an alert frequently.

You can manage alarm barking by reducing your dog's exposure to the inciting stimuli. Perhaps you can baby gate him out of the front room, move the sofa away from the windows so he can't jump up and see out, or close the drapes. Outside, you might consider putting slats in the chain link fence to cut down on his visual access to the world surrounding his yard (better yet, install a privacy fence) or put up an interior fence to block his access to the more stimulating parts of the yard. Given that alarm barking will inevitably occur, it's also useful to teach him a positive interrupt—a cue, other than "Shut up!" that you can use to stop him in mid-bark. (See "The Positive Interrupt" below.) However, your dog might be barking because something really *is* wrong. Before you use that positive interrupt, take a moment to see what your dog is barking at. Perhaps your house really *is* on fire.

Demand barking. This behavior is more likely to annoy you than your neighbors, but it's annoying nonetheless. A demand barker has learned that he can get what he wants, usually attention, or treats, by telling you. It often starts as a gentle, adorable little grumble, and can quickly turn into insistent, loud barks—your dog's way of saying, "I want it, *now!"* If he gets it, he will likely try this technique again, especially since you may inadvertently be reinforcing it.

Demand barking is easiest to extinguish early. The longer a dog successfully demands stuff, the more persistent he'll be if you try to ignore him. However, ignoring him is the best answer to this behavior. No treats, no attention—not even eye contact. The instant the demand behavior starts, utter a cheerful "Oops!" and turn your back on your dog. When he's quiet, say, "Quiet, yes!" and return your attention—and treat—to him.

Watch out for extinction bursts. When you're trying to make a behavior go away by ignoring it, your dog may increase the intensity of his behavior—*"I want it now!"* This is an extinction burst. If you succumb, thinking it's not working, you reinforce the more intense behavior, and your dog is likely to get more intense, sooner, the next time. If you stick it out and wait for the barking to stop, you're well on your way to making it go away. You have to be more persistent—and consistent—than your dog.

Frustration/arousal barking. Often confused with anxiety barkers, dogs who have a low tolerance for frustration will bark hysterically when they can't get what they want. Unlike the separation anxiety panic attack, this is simply an *"I want it!"* style temper tantrum similar to demand barking, but with more emotion and directed at the thing he wants, such as a cat strolling by, rather than at you. You can use the positive interrupt to redirect a frenzy of frustration barking. If you consistently offer high value treats in the presence of frustration-causing stimuli, you can counter condition your dog to look to you for treats when the cat strolls by (cat = yummy treats) rather than erupt into a barking fit.

Boredom barking. This is the dog who's left out in the back yard all day, and maybe all night, something many Do-Over Dogs have experienced all too frequently. Dogs are social creatures and the back yard dog is lonely and bored. Boredom barking is often continuous, with a monotonous quality: "Ho hum, nothing else to do, I may as well just bark." This is the kind of barking that's most annoying to neighbors, and most likely to elicit a knock on your door from a friendly Animal Services officer.

The answer here is obvious and relatively easy. Bring the dog inside. Many outdoor barkers are perfectly content to lie quietly around the house all day, wait for you to come home, and sleep peacefully beside your bed at night. If your dog isn't house-safe, use crates, exercise pens, dog walkers, lots of exercise, even doggie daycare to keep him out of trouble, until he earns house privileges. You can also enrich his environment by giving him interactive toys such as food-stuffed Kongs that keep his brain engaged and his mouth busy.

Stress barking. Stress barkers are fearful, anxious, or even panicked about something real or anticipated in the environment, such as the actual approach of a threat or isolation distress/separation anxiety. Given their stress-laden histories, it's not surprising that Do-Over Dogs can manifest stress-related barking, Separation anxiety is manifested in a number of behaviors, including non-stop hysterical barking and sometimes howling. If your dog is barking due to stress, fear or anxiety, consult with a qualified professional behavior counselor who uses positive modification methods and try to manage your dog's environment to minimize his exposure to stressors while you work on a program to counter condition and desensitize him.

Play barking. This is a common behavior for Herding dogs—the cheerleaders and fun police of the canine world. As other dogs—or humans—romp and play, the play-barker runs around the edges, barking, sometimes nipping heels.

If you're in a location where neighbors won't complain and the other dogs tolerate the behavior, you might just leave this one alone. With children, however, the behavior's not appropriate, and the dog should be managed by removing him from the play area, rather than risk a bite to a child.

If you do want to modify play-barking behavior, use *negative punishment*—where the dog's behavior makes the good stuff go away. When the barking starts, use a loss-of-opportunity marker such as "Oops! Too bad!" and gently remove your dog from the playground for one to three minutes. A tab—an old leash cut down to 6-12 inches left attached to his collar—makes this maneuver easier. Then release him to play again. Over time, as he realizes that barking ends his fun, he may start to get the idea. Or he may not—this is a pretty strong genetic behavior, especially with the Herding breeds. You may just resort to finding appropriate times when you allow play-barking to happen.

Uncontrolled barking can be frustrating to humans. I know this all too well, with several vocal dogs in our own personal pack. However, our dogs sometimes have important and interesting things to say. There was the time I was engrossed in writing an article and our dogs were alarm-barking ferociously. Resisting the urge just to tell them to stop, I reluctantly got up to investigate. No, the house wasn't on fire, but I did find our horses running down the driveway toward the road. You want to be able to have some control over your dog's voice, but don't lose sight of the value of his vocal communications—he may be trying to tell you something important. Learn the tones—he is talking to you! If you ignore him you might find your horses on the highway, the house might burn to the ground, or Timmy might really drown in the well.

The positive interrupt

The positive interrupt is a highly reinforced behavior that allows you to redirect your dog's attention when he's doing something inappropriate, like barking. Ideally, you want your dog's response to the "Over here!" cue to be *so* automatic—classically conditioned—that he doesn't stop to think whether what he's doing is more rewarding than turning his attention toward you and running to you for a treat. He doesn't think—he just does it, the way your foot automatically hits the brake of your car when you see taillights flash in front of you on the highway.

Here's how to program a positive interrupt:

1. **Install the cue in a low-distraction environment.** Use a phrase such as "Over here!" or "Quiet please!" as your interrupt cue. Say the phrase in a cheerful tone of voice when your dog is paying attention to you, then immediately feed him a morsel of very high value treat, such as a small shred of chicken. Repeat until you see his eyes light up and his ears perk when you say the phrase.
2. **Practice with the cue in a low-distraction environment.** Wait until your dog is engaged in a low-value activity—wandering around the room, sniffing something mildly interesting—then say your interrupt phrase in the same cheerful tone of voice. You should see an immediate interrupt in his low-value activity, as he dashes to you for his chicken. If he doesn't, return to Step 1.
3. **Practice with the cue in a low-distraction environment—add distractions.** Still in the low-distraction environment so you can control the distraction level, add moderate distractions—one at a time—and practice the interrupt. Gradually move up to major distractions in the low-distraction environment. If you lose his automatic response at any step, return to the previous step.
4. **Move your lessons to an environment with real-life distractions.** Go for a walk around the block with your dog on leash. Use the interrupt when he's sniffing a bush or eyeing garbage in the gutter. Start with mild to moderate real-life distractions if possible, but if a major distraction presents itself, including a stimulus that causes him to bark, give it a try!
5. **Use the positive cue to interrupt barking.** When your dog automatically turns his attention to you in response to your cue when confronted with major real-life distractions, you have a valuable tool for interrupting his barking. Be sure you practice occasionally with mild distractions as well; to keep the cue "tuned up," and remember to thank him and tell him what a wonderful dog he is when he stops barking on your request.

Growling

Growls and grumbling can have several meanings. Some dogs grumble and growl in enjoyment such as when being scratched or massaged in a pleasant manner. However, most growling serves as a warning—"I don't like you" or "Stop what you are doing please." You may not like it when your dog growls, but stop and think about it: a growl really is a good thing, as it serves as a non-violent warning.

Do *not* punish your dog for this invaluable communication! It's the most benign means he has of letting you know that something bothers him. Take away his growl, and a snap or a bite is likely to happen without warning. Rather, when you dog growls in warning, step back to see what is causing him such discomfort, remove the stressor, and figure out how to give him a more positive association with whatever is causing the growling. Meanwhile count your blessing that your dog has the good sense and inhibition to growl his displeasure rather than sink his teeth into nearby human flesh.

Escaping

If your Do-Over Dog was found as a stray, he may have been dumped by his human, but there's at least an equal chance he's good at escaping. Dogs escape because they can. It might be something as simple as a past owner who opened the door to an unfenced yard to allow the dog to relieve himself (which I know *you* won't do) or as challenging as the escape artist who's dedicated to darting out doors and jumping over, digging under, or chewing through fences. Boredom, arousal, and fear are common motives for dogs to escape, as well as the reinforcement they get when they discover how much fun it is to roam the neighborhood, chase bunnies and squirrels, get in garbage, play with other dogs or the kids next door, pursue females in season, and get handouts from dog-loving humans.

Prevention and management are critically important to keeping your dog safe in his new home. The last thing you want to do is leave him home alone in the back yard and come home from work to find him *gone.*

You have the "fresh-start advantage" with your Do-Over Dog. Even though he may have been quite the accomplished escaper in his old life, if you're just bringing him home, he has *never* escaped from yours. Don't let him learn he can escape from his new environment—keep him at home and stop any embryonic escape attempts in their tracks by taking the following prophylactic measures:

1. Provide a safe, secure enclosure. Before your Do-Over guy comes home, make sure your fence is flush to the ground, or even buried a few inches. If the dog can hook his nails in the chain link and climb, trying covering the inside of the fence with a flat, solid surface. Check for rotten spots and crawl behind shrubs and brush to look for holes or loose boards. You *know* your dog will find them if you don't!

2. Go overboard on fence height. Raise the fence to at least five feet for a small dog (perhaps higher for very athletic small dogs like Jack Russell Terriers) and six feet for medium to large dogs. Make sure there are no woodpiles, doghouses, deck railings, or other objects close enough to the fence to provide a convenient launch pad. If necessary, add a "roof" at the top of the fence that comes inward at a 90-degree angle.
3. Teach your dog to "Wait!" at doors until invited through. Use "Wait" at every door to the outside world, every time you open it, whether your dog is going to go through or not.
4. Install dog-proof latches and springs on gates to ensure they always close. There's no point in waiting until after your dog is hit by a car to discover that he can work the latch. In fact, a padlock will prevent accidental release from the outside by a visitor or intruder and at the same time it keeps your dog from practicing his latch-opening skills.
5. Minimize your dog's motivation to roam by neutering at an early age, before he matures, and provide him with ample exercise and companionship at home.
6. Keep your dog indoors when you are not home. Boredom and loneliness are strong escape-motivators and he has plenty of time to plan and execute the great escape when you are not there to interrupt unwanted behaviors such as digging under and chewing through fences.

The fix

What if it's too late for prevention? Maybe you adopted your Do-Over Dog from the shelter after his last adopter inadvertently taught him to jump a too-low fence, taught him to jump higher by gradually raising the fence, and then returned him because he kept escaping. Do you give up on him too? Not at all. There are lots of steps you can take to fortify your defenses and keep your escape artist at home, depending on his proclivities.

Climbers. See points 1 and 2 above to augment your fence arrangement. I recommend fenced yards for just about any dog owner who has a yard.

Jumpers. If your dog gets a good running start and clears the fence with the greatest of ease, you can plant a hedge or place some other obstacle in his takeoff zone, interrupting his stride and making it impossible for him to jump. If you put your last fence extension inward at a 45 to 90-degree angle you may also fool his eye and foil his leap.

Door darters. The dog who bolts out of his house through open doors needs an "airlock"—a system of double doors and gates so that if he makes it through the front door he's still contained on the front porch. Self-closing gate springs will prevent visitors and family members from being careless. A good solid recall—teaching your Do-Over Dog to come when called, is an excellent backup plan for the door darter. Family members also need to remember not to panic and chase him when he slips out—a good game of keep-away just makes door darting more fun for the dog—or frightens a fearful Do-Over dog into heading for parts unknown.

Door-darting Do-Overs may need an "airlock" to keep them safe at home.

Diggers. If you're going to bury the fence for a dedicated digger, bury deep—at least six inches deep, with another 12 inches turned under toward the yard, buried underground. If you bury it two inches, you'll just teach him to dig deeper. You might do better setting the fence in cement or lining your fence trench with large rocks or small boulders. You definitely need a cement pad at the gate, since you can't bury the gate.

Chewers. If your Do-Over Dog has learned to gnaw his way through fences you could be in big trouble. Lining the inside of the fence with heavy-duty wire—like livestock anti-climb fencing or chain link—*may* stop him. It may not, however, and he may break teeth in his attempts to eat his way out. Sheets of FRP (fiberglass reinforced plastic) are good for this also. Cement block walls can be effective, but may not be esthetically pleasing. Ceramic tiles can be glued to the blocks to make them more attractive, but they're not cheap.

In the end, if your Do-Over Dog is committed to escaping despite your best efforts, you'll need to always accompany him outdoors, and supervise to be sure he stays home where he belongs.

Your Do-Over Dog and cats (and other pets)

You've no doubt heard the phrase "fighting like cats and dogs." As well-known as the saying is, it's also an often inaccurate one. Millions of dog-lovers share their hearts and homes with feline family members with nary a scratch between the species. On the other paw, stories of dogs killing cats are fact, not fiction, and many unfortunate Rowdy Rovers have suffered ulcerated corneas, scratched nose leathers, and infected puncture wounds from Tough Tiggers who decided that "fight" was a better strategy than "flight." Many a Do-Over dog has a history of less-than-benevolent experiences with other small companion animals. How do you know if your Do-Over Fido and beloved Fluffy will end up amicably sharing the sofa or if one or both are going to end up at the emergency clinic—or worse?

The media likes to play up stories about personality differences between "cat lovers" and "dog lovers," but many of us are both. We may also fill our lives with one or more small animal companions including rabbits, rats, ferrets, Guinea pigs, iguanas, fish, finches, macaws, and a multitude of other creatures. It's our responsibility and obligation as their guardians to ensure that they have a safe, reasonably low-stress environment in which to live—sometimes a large challenge when we're asking predator and prey species to live in harmony. Whether the multi-species household is one big happy family or not depends on reasonable adoption decisions, careful introductions, good management, training and behavior modification, and a little—or a lot—of luck.

Research compatibility

Chances are if you're bringing home a Do-Over Dog, you have little information about his past history with other animals. To be on the safe side, assume that he'll want to eat your cat, ferret, parrot, or Guinea pig, and take it from there.

When we found our Scottish Terrier running loose in Chattanooga as a stray at age seven months, we were impressed with how well he adapted to our household, including our two geriatric felines: Jackson, age 16 and Gewurztraminer, age 15. However, a year later we brought home an 8-week-old stray kitten. Dubhy came close to committing kitty mayhem when we foolishly assumed he'd be fine with her.

Lulled into a false sense of complacency because Dubhy was so good with our adult cats, I ignored the sound advice I give so often to others about carefully orchestrated introductions, and walked into the house with the foundling kitten in my arms. (See Carefully orchestrate introductions below.) Five dogs charged up to me in greeting, and the kitten did a classic Halloween cat imitation, complete with arched back, bottlebrush tail, and alarmingly loud hissing and spitting. While our other four dogs backed off in awe and respect, this highly arousing stimulus immediately turned on Dubhy's "fierce predator" switch.

Had we introduced Viva to the dogs one at a time, at a distance, with the canine family members carefully restrained, she probably would have reacted much more calmly, and Dubhy might never have "turned on" to her. Once the predatory association was made, however, it was too late to un-ring the bell. We had to work to repair the damage.

To maximize your chances for harmony between species, it's smart to select a Do-Over Dog who has a high likelihood for compatibility with whatever other pets you have (or visa-versa). Since most Terriers were originally bred to rid barns, homes, and fields of unwanted rodent pests, it may be unwise to bring one home if you have a cat—or a pet rat—*unless* you are prepared to do a significant amount of very careful management and conditioning. Similarly, Sighthounds (such as Greyhounds, Borzois, Wolfhounds) have a strong genetic predisposition to chase—and kill—small animals that run.

It's also smart to select younger, rather than older. If you want a Do-Over Dog who will be trustworthy around other small animal species, you're generally better off starting with a pup and raising him to know *only* appropriate behavior around other animals. It's much more challenging to *change* inappropriate behaviors and associations in an adult dog than it is to *create* them initially in a young one. Alternatively, to keep life simple, you can choose to adopt a dog who has a known history of living peacefully with other types of animals—but that's often not an option when you're opening your home and your heart to a Do-Over Dog.

Carefully orchestrate introductions

Your chances of a successful multi-species relationship are best if you plan your introductions carefully. It's rarely wise, although it sometimes works, to simply march in with a new family member and, in essence, "throw her to the wolves." Far better to have both (or all) non-human family members safely restrained and have the introduction be a positive classical conditioning experience (or counter-conditioning if one or more of the participants have some prior association with the other's species).

Here's an example of a well-orchestrated introduction in the case of where a Do-Over Dog is brought to a home with a cat. For other species, substitute "other" for "cat" and figure out how to alter the process as appropriate. (For example, "snake in tank" rather than carrier, and at some point a human would hold snake, rather than releasing snake to roam around freely.) Depending on the participants, the processes described could take several weeks or conditioning could occur all in one session:

- Have cat in carrier—one person stays with the cat.
- Place carrier on the floor on the far side of the room.
- Second person enters with the dog on leash.
- Do classical conditioning with both dog and cat at sub-threshold distance, feeding high-value treats until both the dog and the cat are looking happily to their humans for treats in the presence of the other (conditioned emotional response, or CER).
- Gradually decrease the distance between dog and cat and repeat the process to obtain CERs at each new distance.
- When both are comfortable in close proximity to each other, return to original distance and remove the cat from her crate (but keep her restrained, ideally on harness and leash).
- Repeat conditioning process until the dog and cat are comfortable in close proximity, both restrained.
- Return to original distance and release cat (dog is still restrained). Continue conditioning until the behavior of both is appropriate.

You will find that some species are more difficult to incorporate in the process as anything more than a silent presence. Because of their feeding habits, for example, it would be difficult to do both counter-conditioning and desensitization with the snake as the dog enters the room and approaches his tank. In this case, you may just have to settle for desensitization (becoming accustomed to the increasing intensity of the stimulus—the dog) without the classical conditioning (association) part.

Good management

Good management requires effective barriers (doors, baby gates), sturdy containment units (crates, pens), restraint (leashes, tethers), and unwavering supervision (your eyeballs and awareness). However, all of your management tools are only as good as your ability to ensure their use. A moment's lapse can result in a lifeless pile of fur instead of a warm, purring cat.

If your children (or roommates) aren't good at heeding your warnings to keep doors closed, or if your talented canine can open doors, then you might need to add self-closing springs, child-proof latches, and/or padlocks to your list of management tools. You're likely to be more successful in the long run commingling species if you combine a foolproof management plan with an effective program of training and behavior modification.

Good management *and* good training

If you combine management, basic good manners training and a program of counter-conditioning and desensitization you're even further ahead. The better you and your dog can communicate to each other, the more effectively you'll be able to control his behavior when the need arises. Lucy, our Cardigan Corgi, is fond of chasing cats, albeit from the Herding dog "wheeeeeeee, it's fun to chase and round up things that move" perspective rather from the Terrier *"kill!!!"* motivation. Although her motive is gentler, she can still make their lives miserable. Counter conditioning worked for her as well, but while our Scottish Terrier, Dubhy, has completely given up any "kill" association with our cat Viva, Lucy still yearns to chase our cats when they move. Her well-practiced "leave-it," "come," and "down" cues give us an added layer of insulation against inappropriate cat tormenting.

Rehoming

There may come a time when you decide that it's in the best interests of all concerned to remove one or more incompatible species from your household. This is a painful decision for any animal lover—and a very selfless one. It's not easy to put the welfare of your cat, hamster, or cockatiel above your own emotional connection and feelings of commitment and responsibility. You may feel guilty that you perhaps haven't done as much to make the situation work as you could—or should—have. However, someone's life is at risk, and there are times when rehoming really is the best choice, giving the at-risk pet a better chance for a long and happy life, and removing much stress from your own home, thereby improving the quality of life for all your remaining family members, including yourself.

There are millions of successful multi-species households, so chances are good that, if you put your mind to it, you can make it work for yours. Take time to make wise adoption choices, orchestrate careful introductions, implement good management and training programs, and you're likely to succeed in your desire to turn your home into a peaceable kingdom, where lions lie down with lambs—or at least cats and dogs can live peacefully with canaries, rabbits, and boa constrictors.

Chapter 8

A Do-Over Repair Manual

Part II: High Risk Behaviors

President Franklin D. Roosevelt, speaking about the Great Depression, said, "We have nothing to fear but fear itself." If only it were that simple when dealing with dog behavior instead of failing economies. Fear-related behaviors can be debilitating to the inappropriately fearful dog. They are heartbreaking, frustrating, even sometimes dangerous for the human trying to deal with her dog's strong emotional responses, and for the dog who may injure himself or others in his desperate efforts to escape or protect himself from the fear-causing stimulus. Because so many Do-Over Dogs are under-socialized, fearful behaviors—fears, phobias, and anxieties—are among the most common *high-risk* behavior challenges adopters may have to deal with, behaviors that if not modified can lead to tragic results. Under-socialization and fear are often accompanied by aggression and other difficult-to-live-with, stress-related behaviors. While the behaviors in this chapter may be more challenging to modify, they are not set in cement—you *can* help make life better for your Do-Over Dog.

After a discussion of fear and counter-conditioning techniques, the high risk behaviors I will review and offer solution for in this chapter include:

- Sensitivity to touch and restraint
- Counter-conditioning and desensitization to touch
- Resource guarding
- Isolation distress/separation anxiety
- Obsessive compulsive disorders
- Aggression

Three faces of fear

The complex of fear-related behaviors includes: 1) fears; 2) anxieties; and 3) phobias. While they are closely related emotional responses, they differ significantly in several ways, including the presence or absence of a physical trigger, the intensity of the dog's response, and the ease with which the emotional response and related behaviors can be modified. In general, these three faces of fear can be among the most difficult of behavioral problems to treat.

There is a strong genetic component to fear-related behaviors. Whereas once we tended to place a lot of the blame on owners for their perceived role in creating fearful dogs, today it is generally recognized that a genetic *propensity* toward fearfulness is a significant factor in the actual manifestation of fear-related behaviors. While environment—especially lack of early socialization—can play a critically important role in bringing these behaviors to fruition, genes explain why two dogs with similar upbringing and socialization can react so differently in the presence of a potentially fear-causing stimulus, and why even a well-socialized dog can suddenly develop phobic behaviors.

Fear

Fear is defined as a feeling of apprehension associated with the *presence or proximity* of an object, individual, or social situation. It's a valuable, adaptive emotion, necessary for survival, and appropriate in many situations. It's good to be afraid of grizzly bears, tornados, and semi-trucks skidding out of control on icy highways. Your dog is wise to fear the flashing heels of a galloping horse, strong waves crashing on an ocean beach, the spinning wheels of a passing car. People and animals who feel no fear are destined to live short lives.

Of course, overly fearful dogs may lead short lives as well. Fear-related aggression is a significant risk to a dog's long and happy life. A fearful dog's first choice is usually to escape, but he may bite defensively if cornered or trapped and dogs who bite are often euthanized. In addition, a constant emotional state of fear makes for a poor quality of life for a dog and for humans who are stressed by their fearful dog's behavior.

Debates about anthropomorphism aside, most biologists agree that human and non-human mammals experience fear similarly. Recall one of your own heart-stopping, adrenalin-pumping life experiences. Perhaps you were approached by a menacing stranger in an alley on a dark night, threatened by a large predator on a camping trip, charged by a free-roaming aggressive dog as you walked in your neighborhood, cornered by an angry bull in a pasture, or just missed rear-ending a car in front of you when a moment of inattention caused you to miss the warning flash of taillights. Remember how helpless, vulnerable, and terrified you felt? You can empathize with your dog when you see him trembling in the presence of a stimulus that elicits a similar response in his canine brain and body.

Anxiety

Anxiety is the distress or uneasiness of mind caused by apprehensive *anticipation of future* danger or misfortune, real or imagined. Anxious dogs appear tense, braced for a threat they can't adequately predict sometimes one that doesn't actually exist. Anxiety can be a chronic condition, one that significantly impairs a dog's (and his human's) quality of life, and one that can be more challenging to modify than the fear of a real and present danger. Separation distress is perhaps the most widely discussed anxiety-related behavior in dogs, but owner absence is not the only cause for canine apprehension. Many dogs are anxious on car rides—anticipating, perhaps, a visit to the vet's office, or some other "bad" place. A dog who has been attacked by a loose dog while walking on leash may become anxious about going for walks—constantly stressed, scanning the neighborhood for another potential attacker.

Again, human anxieties are similar to canine. If you've been mugged in a dark alley, you are likely to experience some degree of stress anytime you find yourself walking down an alley at night. Some people experience extreme anxiety over taking exams, even when their past successes show that they pass tests with flying colors. Barabra Streisand, successful singer that she is, suffers from extreme performance anxiety, still becoming physically ill every time she's about to walk on stage. The danger or misfortune may be imagined, but the anxiety is very real.

Phobias

Phobias are persistent, extreme, inappropriate fear or anxiety responses, far out of proportion to the level or nature of threat presented. They are stubbornly resistant to modification through habituation or desensitization—repeated low-level exposure to the stimulus that causes the extreme response. While inappropriate in degree, a phobic response is not totally irrational—it is often directed toward something that *could* be harmful. Common human phobias are related to snakes, spiders, high places, flying—all things which have *potential* to be life threatening. In reality, the majority of snakes and spiders are relatively harmless, it's rare for humans to accidentally nosedive off a skyscraper, and only a tiny percentage of airplanes ever crash. Common canine phobias include extreme reactions to thunderstorms and other sounds, fear of humans, and neophobia—an inappropriate fear response to novel stimuli (anything new and different).

Counter-conditioning and desensitization

Whether you're working with fears, anxieties or phobias, the solution to an inappropriate emotional response is *counter-conditioning and desensitization* (CC&D) to *change* your dog's emotional response to the stimulus or situation. In *The Cautious Canine,* author and behaviorist Dr. Patricia McConnell calls counter-conditioning a "universally effective treatment for fear-based behavior problems." Think of it as training your dog's emotions rather than training his actions. Behavior change will follow emotional change.

Counter-conditioning and desensitization involves changing your dog's association with a scary stimulus from negative to positive. The easiest way to give most dogs a positive association is with very high-value, really yummy treats. I like to use chicken—canned, baked, boiled, or freeze-dried since most dogs love chicken and its a low fat, low calorie food.

Perhaps your dog is afraid of your vacuum cleaner. Here's how the CC&D process could work:

1. Determine the distance (X) at which your dog can look at the non-running, stationary vacuum cleaner and be alert and wary, but not extremely fearful. This is called the *threshold distance.*
2. With you holding your dog on leash, have a helper present the non-running vacuum at threshold distance X. The instant your dog sees the vacuum, start feeding pea-sized bits of chicken, non-stop.

3. After several seconds, have the helper remove the vacuum and stop feeding chicken.
4. Keep repeating Steps 1-3 until the presentation of the vacuum at that distance consistently causes your dog to look at you with a happy smile and a "Yay! Where's my chicken?" expression. This is a *conditioned emotional response* (CER)—your dog's association with a non-running vacuum at threshold distance X is now positive instead of negative.
5. Now you need to increase the intensity of the stimulus. You can do that by decreasing distance slightly, by increasing movement of the vacuum at distance X, or by turning the vacuum on. I'd suggest decreasing distance first in small increments by moving the dog closer to the location where the vacuum will appear, achieving your CER at each new distance, until your dog is happy to be right next to the non-running, non-moving vacuum, perhaps even sniffing or targeting to it.
6. Then return to distance X and add movement of your non-running vacuum, gradually decreasing distance and attaining CERs along the way, until your dog is delighted to have the non-running, moving vacuum in close proximity.
7. Now, back to distance X, with no movement, have your helper turn the vacuum on briefly, feed treats the instant it's on, then turn it off and stop the treats.
8. Repeat until you have the CER, then gradually increase the length of time you leave the vacuum running, until he's happy to have it on continuously.
9. Begin decreasing distance in small increments, moving the dog closer to the vacuum, obtaining your CER consistently at each new distance.
10. When your dog is happy to have the running, stationary vacuum close to him, you're ready for the final phase. Return to distance X and obtain your CER there, with a running, moving vacuum. Then gradually decrease distance until your dog is happy to be in the presence of your running, moving vacuum cleaner. He now thinks the vacuum is a *very good* thing, as a reliable predictor of very yummy treats.

This example concerns a fairly simple fear behavior. The more complex the stimulus and the more intense the response, the more challenging the behavior is to modify. Anxieties and phobias generally require a greater commitment to a longer term and more in-depth modification program, and often beg the intervention of a good, positive behavior professional.

A personal experience

It's vitally important that you recognize and respect your dog's fear, and respond appropriately. I learned this the hard way, through personal experience. A few years ago I made the mistake of underestimating the extent of my dog's fear, and my error has had a lifelong impact on her behavior.

We adopted Lucy, our Cardigan Welsh Corgi, from the shelter in June of 2004, when she was about six months old. She was bright, energetic, outgoing, and confident. That October, I had her in the downtown Halloween parade. She was having a grand time, tail wagging, eyes bright…until our float met up with the marching band and the drums sent her into a meltdown. I thought I could use high value treats to counter-condition her through the experience. Not so. She was way over threshold; she wouldn't eat treats, and the experiences *sensitized* her to loud sounds, including thunder, our horses banging in their stalls, and even applause. Five years later we are still working to repair the damage.

Because I failed to recognize the extent of Lucy's fear at the time, I subjected her to a much greater intensity of the noise stimulus than she could handle, *sensitized* her to the noise, triggering an intense sound phobia. Given the genetic component of fear behavior, there's a good chance that some future event might have triggered the same intensity of fear for her, but I still feel horribly guilty that I was the one who did it to her.

It would have been hard to miss the signs of Lucy's fear. Often, however, people do miss or misread more subtle signs of fear, inadvertently subjecting their dogs to social situations where the dog becomes defensively aggressive. It's important that you are able to recognize the subtle signs of fear in your Do-Over Dog, so you can help him out of difficult situations rather than forcing him to accept the attentions of someone who is making him uncomfortable and who might get bitten as a result. Dogs who bite people tend to have short lives.

Recognizing fear

Most people, even non-dog owners, can identify a dog who is in abject fear—trembling, drooling, crouched low, tail tucked, pupils dilated, perhaps even losing control of bladder and bowels. It's much easier to miss the more subtle early-warning signs indicating the early onset of fear. Yet, as with all undesirable behaviors, fear is easier to deal with sooner, rather than later, so there is real value in being able to determine when a dog is slightly fearful and take prompt steps to alleviate the fear—either by removing the fear-causing stimulus and/or implementing a program of counter-conditioning and desensitization.

Ignorance of subtle fear signals is one of the primary reasons a purportedly "child-friendly" dog mauls the unsuspecting toddler. Because the dog never exhibited overt aggression to the child—growling, lunging, snapping—the owner assumed the dog was kid-friendly. Instead, the dog may have always felt threatened by the presence of children—their high-pitched voices, sudden movements, and sometimes inappropriate behaviors toward the dog. Misinterpretation of fear-signals can also be the cause of inappropriate owner behavior—punishing the dog or forcing the dog to confront the threat—both of which can worsen a dog's fears and trigger an aggressive response. To avoid exacerbating your dog's fear, or perhaps turning a fear into a phobia, watch for the following early warning signs and be prepared to protect your dog from the perceived threat:

- Makes an effort to leave
- Hides behind you

- Averts eyes
- Panting—increase in respiratory rate
- Sweaty paws—leaving footprints on cement
- Reluctance to take/eat treats
- Ducking the head
- Licking, yawning, blinking

An excellent resource to help you better understand your dog's body language signals is the DVD *The Language of Dogs* by Sarah Kalnajs available at www.dogwise.com.

Sensitivity to touch and restraint

Sensitivity to touch and restraint is sometimes, but not always, a fear-related behavior (it could simply be a medical problem, for example), annoyance at being disturbed, or low tolerance for frustration. It is however, a high risk behavior. The modification approach is the same: to change your dog's association with touch and restraint from negative to positive. It's not uncommon to find under-socialized Do-Over Dogs who are sensitive to touch and restraint and especially to having their feet held and handled. While the counter-conditioning program described below is for a dog who is sensitive to paw touching, it's also appropriate for dogs who are uncomfortable with touch or restraint of any part of their body; just apply the procedure to the appropriate body parts or the entire body.

You can see Mo's stressed reaction—whale eye, ears back—as his owner, Danielle Dersch, works on counter-conditioning him to touch.

Counter-conditioning and desensitization to touch

1. Determine the location of touch your dog is aware of and can handle without reacting fearfully or aggressively (his stimulus threshold). Perhaps it's his shoulder, perhaps his elbow, or maybe his knee. He should be a little worried, but not growl or try to move away.
2. With your dog on leash, touch him briefly and gently at the threshold location. The instant your dog notices the touch, start feeding bits of chicken, non-stop.
3. After a second or two, remove your touch, and stop feeding chicken.
4. Keep repeating Steps 1-3 until touching at that location for one to two seconds consistently causes your dog to look at you with a happy smile and a "Yay! Where's my chicken?" expression. This is the conditioned emotional response you should be seeking—your dog's association with the brief touch at that location is now positive instead of negative.
5. Now, increase the intensity of the stimulus by increasing the length of time you touch him at that same location, a second at a time, obtaining a new CER at each new time period before increasing the time again. For example, several repetitions at two seconds, until you get consistent "Yay!" looks, then several repetitions at three seconds, then several at four seconds, etc., working to get that consistent CER at each new duration of your touch.
6. When you can touch him at that spot for any length of time with him in "Yay" mode, begin to increase the intensity of stimulus again, this time by moving your hand to a new location, one to two inches lower than your initial threshold. Start at your initial touch location and slide your hand to the new spot, rather than just touching the new spot without warning. Continue with repetitions until you get consistent CERs at the new location.
7. Continue gradually working your way down to your dog's paw, a half-inch or so at a time, getting solid CERs at each spot before you move closer to the paw.
8. When you get below the knee, also add a gentle grasp and a little pressure to the procedure—making each of these a separate step in the CC&D process. Be sure to get the "Yay!" response with touch before you add the grasp, and with the grasp, before you add more pressure. Continue working down the leg, all the way to the paw.
9. When you can touch, grasp, and put pressure on the paw, add lifting the paw.
10. If your goal is happy nail trimming, start the process over, this time with the nail clipper in your hand. Show him the nail clipper or grinder you plan to use, feed a treat, and repeat, until the appearance of the clipper or grinder elicits a "Yay!" response. Then do CC&D with the clipper or grinder action—eventually working up to squeezing the clipper or turning on the grinder to make the sound and motion it would make if you were actually clipping or grinding nails. Go through the whole touch sequence again, this time with the clippers in your hand, also touching him with the clipper or grinder, then again while you squeeze the clipper or have the grinder turned on. Remember that you are still feeding yummy treats and obtaining CERs alone the way, throughout the whole process. When you can hold his paw and make the clipper/grinder action

right next to the nail with a happy CER response, clip or grind *one* nail, feed lots of treats, and stop. Do a nail a day until he's happy with that, then advance to two nails at a time, then three, until you can do all his nails in one setting.

We encountered nail-trimming procedure sensitivity with several of our dogs in the last few years. I resolved Bonnie and Dubhy's discomfort using the above procedure, and switching from a clipper to a grinder. They both have black nails, and it was too easy to misjudge and hit the nail quick by accident, which is guaranteed to reinforce a very negative association with the procedure. In addition, it required considerable pressure to cut through the hard denseness of their Scottie-ish nails, which I'm sure was uncomfortable for them. Switching to the nail grinder in conjunction with the counter-conditioning program has made all the difference in the world for them.

Resource guarding

Many animals, including humans, naturally guard valuable resources. We put locks on our doors and install burglar alarms; some people even keep a shotgun by the door. Dogs use their teeth to guard what they think of as valuable resources such as food, toys, beds, even you! When you think about it, resource guarding makes a lot of sense. Animal in the wild who don't stake some claim to their food are more likely to starve to death. Although our dogs are long-domesticated, this is one of those behaviors that has stuck with them despite the often-plentiful supply of food and other important life-sustaining resources.

While resource guarding is one of the behaviors that may cause shelter and rescue dogs to fail their assessments, it's not always the most difficult presentation of canine aggression to manage, live with, or even modify despite the risks involved. Several of my own dogs guard selected resources in various circumstances.

Some degree of *dog-dog* guarding is not unexpected or inappropriate if you live in a multi-dog household. It's perfectly appropriate for one dog to say to another, "This is mine, and you can't have it." An ideal dog-dog resource guarding encounter would look like this:

1. Dog A has possession of high-value (to him) resource.
2. Dog B approaches with a "Hey, watcha doin'?" attitude.
3. Dog A looks up and glares "Chewing on this cow hoof. *My* cow hoof. Go 'way."
4. Dog B says, "Oh, sorry dude!" and moves away.

In the not-so-ideal encounters, one of three things usually happens:

1. Dog A overreacts to Dog B's approach and launches ferociously at Dog B rather than giving fair warning,
2. Dog A gives fair warning but rather than deferring, Dog B reacts violently in return, or
3. Dog A gives fair warning, and Dog B bumbles forward anyway, not intentionally being offensive, but still not heeding the warning; a fight ensues.

Any of these responses requires the owner to install immediate management protocols (don't give dogs high value objects unless they are safely separated), and either manage the behavior for the life of the dog(s), or manage while modification efforts are implemented.

Guardable resources can include food, water, chew objects, toys, humans, space, and the randomly-dropped piece of paper, crumpled paper towel, sock, or anything else a dog decides to claim. Dogs seem to have at least *some* respect for the "possession is nine-tenths" rule; often a smaller, less assertive dog can quite successfully guard his resources from a larger, more assertive one. Just because it's a natural canine behavior, however, doesn't mean it's an appropriate one, especially when a dog fiercely guards resources from his human. It's generally not acceptable for dogs to bite their humans—it tends to damage the relationship.

You can *prevent* resource guarding by convincing your dog you're not a threat to his possessions. Teach your dog to trade good stuff for better stuff—then give him the original good stuff back again. Win-win! He'll *want* you to approach!

The trade game part two

We have already reviewed the "trade game" back in Chapter 7 in terms of chewing problems. For that case, the idea is to have the dog give up "forbidden items." The same technique can be applied to resource guarding where the dog is "guarding" something he is not allowed to have—a favorite toy or his food bowl, for example. To teach "Trade," give your dog a favorite toy. When he's happily playing, say "Trade" and offer a treat. When he drops the toy to take the treat, click your clicker or say "Yes!" and feed him the treat, letting him nibble it slowly from one hand off to one side while you pick up the toy with the other. Then toss the toy for him to play with again.

You can also do this with higher value items—stuffed Kongs, chew-hooves, and pig ears—as long as you can find a valuable-enough treat to trade for and you know he won't resource guard. You may need to work up to the high-value items slowly.

A resource guarding modification program

If your dog already guards his food bowl, you can modify the behavior by implementing the Ten-Step program that follows. Your role as benevolent distributor of valuable resources is the foundation of your behavior modification program. *Note: following the program outlined below does not guarantee that a bite will not occur.*

1. **Manage** the environment until the behavior has been modified. Identify/remove all potential guarding triggers. Food bowls, even empty ones, should not be left on the floor. Put away stuffed Kongs, favorite toys, pillows—anything that triggers even a mild possession response. Give them to your dog only in very controlled circumstances—when he's crated or when there are no humans in the home who might unknowingly trigger your dog's guarding response.

2. **Relocate** your dog's feeding area to a low traffic area: a little-used room that visitors are not likely to stumble into, such as the basement office, or the pantry.
3. **Spend** two to four weeks pre-conditioning your dog. Feed two to three times a day. Confine him away from the feeding area. Place his bowl in the feeding room, bring him to the room, leave and close the door until he's finished eating, or until 30 minutes have passed. Don't feed more than he will eat in one meal.
4. **Attend** a positive training class using desirable food treats as rewards. (Do not do this if your dog lunges aggressively for food in your hand). Be sure to let the trainer know that your dog guards resources.
5. **Implement** a "Say Please" program. Have him sit or lie down in order to get anything he wants, including food, toys, and going outside to play.
6. **Exercise** him more. A tired dog is a well-behaved dog. Endorphins released during aerobic exercise help to regulate mood.
7. **Identify** and avoid situations that trigger aggression.
8. **Teach** your dog to trade on cue and *always* trade instead of trying to take something away from him.
9. **Avoid** punishing your dog if a food guarding or other aggressive incident occurs.
10. **Implement** the following Food Bowl Desensitization program after two to four weeks of the pre-conditioning program.

A food bowl desensitization program

It can take four to eight *months* (or longer) to rehabilitate a serious food-guarder. Even then, your dog may never become completely trustworthy. If you are fearful or feel inadequate to deal with your dog, call a qualified positive behavior professional. This program should be implemented only by an adult. Don't move to the next phase before the minimum time indicated, or before your dog's demeanor is perfectly calm at the previous phase.

Phase 1: No bowl (one to two weeks)

Place your dog's meal in a bowl on a counter or shelf in his feeding room. Include some high-value treats as part of the meal. Schedule several feeding sessions throughout the day. Feed one-quarter to one-tenth of his day's ration in each session, a piece at a time, by hand. If he lunges aggressively at your hand while feeding, tether him and feed him, a piece at a time, by tossing them from just out of lunging reach. Wait until he's sitting quietly each time to toss him another piece.

Phase 2: Empty bowl, single pieces (two to four weeks)

Schedule several feeding sessions throughout the day. Place your dog's meal in a bowl on a counter in his feeding room. Place his empty bowl on the ground at your feet. Alternate between feeding him several pieces from your hand, *a piece at a time,* and dropping several pieces of food, *a piece at a time,* into his food bowl from waist height. If you drop them from a lower position he may aggress toward your hand. Wait until he finishes each piece before dropping the next.

Phase 3: Empty bowl, multiple pieces (two to four weeks)
During several feeding sessions throughout the day, place your dog's daily meal in a bowl on a counter in his feeding room. Place his empty bowl on the ground at your feet. Drop *several* pieces of food into his bowl from waist height and wait until he has finished them. Then feed him *several* pieces, one at a time, from your hand. Now drop several more pieces into his bowl. While he's eating those, drop more pieces, one at a time, into his bowl from waist height.

Phase 4: Two partial bowls (two to four weeks)
Schedule several feedings throughout the day and place your dog's meal in a bowl on a counter in his feeding room. Put a handful of food in each of two bowls and place one bowl on the floor. Put lower-value food into the bowls; save higher-value food for treat dropping. If you cannot safely put down the bowl in your dog's presence, tether him, put him on a sit-stay, or shut him out of the room while you put the bowl down. While he's eating from the first bowl, place the second on the floor a safe distance away. "Safe" will depend on your dog, and could be as much as 10-15 feet or more. Err on the side of caution. Return to the first bowl and drop treats into it as he continues to eat.

When he has finished the first bowl, stop dropping treats and direct him to the second bowl. While he's eating from the second bowl, return to the first bowl and pick it up. Continue to drop treats into the bowl from which he's eating.

Over the two to four weeks of this phase, very gradually—a few inches at a time—place the bowls closer together. Watch for signs of tension or aggression. If you see any, you have decreased distance too quickly; increase distance between bowls to where he was relaxed and work there for several days before decreasing the distance again.

Phase 5: Several partial bowls (two to four weeks)
Repeat Phase 4 using several bowls (up to six). Prepare all the bowls and set them on the counter, but place them on the floor one at a time, while he's eating from the first bowl. Continue to drop treats into the bowl he's eating from, and occasionally pick up an empty one that is a safe distance from the dog. During this phase, reduce the number of meals to two or three. Also, look for opportunities outside of feeding time to drop treats near your dog when he's in possession of other reasonably valuable items.

Phase 6: Calling the dog (two to four weeks)
Repeat Phase 5, except try to call your dog to you from a distance of six to eight feet just as he finishes the food in a bowl. Have the other bowls set out so he must pass you to go to another bowl. Be sure to give him a *very high value treat* when he comes to you. Gradually start asking him to come to you *before* he finishes the food in the bowl—first, when he's almost done, then when there is more and more left. As long as he stays relaxed, gradually move closer to the food bowl he's eating from before you call him.

Practice this phase for at least one full week before moving closer to him. Also, look for opportunities outside of feeding time to call him to you to feed him high value treats when he's in possession of other reasonably valuable items.

Phase 7: Adding people (two to six weeks)
Starting back at Phase 1, have a second person repeat the exercises. This should be another person who is close to the dog, not a child, not a stranger. Have the person move through the phases, spending up to a week at each phase or longer if necessary. If he's doing well with a second person, do the program with a third, then a fourth. Be sure to use people who are well-educated as to their training duties and able to follow directions.

Phase 8: Coming out of the closet (two to six weeks, for the rest of the dog's life)
Starting back at Phase 1, move the exercises out of the dog's feeding room into other areas of the house: the kitchen, the dining room, etc. Assuming the training has been progressing well, you should be able to move through the phases relatively quickly. Look for other real-life resource-relevant opportunities to reinforce the message that your presence means more good stuff. Remember that, depending on the success of your desensitization program, your resource-guarding dog may never be totally reliable in the presence of valuable items. For the rest of your dog's life, always be aware of the environment and be prepared to intervene if there is a potential risk.

Isolation distress/separation anxiety

The term "Separation Anxiety" is a pretty mild-sounding label for a devastating and destructive behavior that can result in human frustration, anger, sometimes even the euthanasia of an offending dog when a despairing owner reaches her wits' end. If you've ever had the misfortune of walking into your house to find overturned furniture, inches-deep claw gouges on door frames, blood-stained tooth marks on window sills, and countless messages on your answering machine from neighbors complaining about your dog barking and howling for hours on end in your absence, you're probably familiar with the term. Thirty years ago the phrase was relatively uncommon in dog training circles. Today it's a rare dog owner who hasn't heard of separation anxiety, experienced it with a personal dog, or at least had a dog-owning friend whose canine companion reportedly suffered from this difficult disorder.

Unfortunately Do-Over Dogs seem to suffer from isolation and separation distress and anxiety at a markedly higher rate than the general dog population. Whether this is because dogs with these difficult behaviors are more likely to be abandoned and surrendered by owners, or because the stress of a shelter environment and abrupt relocation triggers the behavior is up for debate. I'd argue that it's probably a combination of the two. At any rate, your Do-Over Dog may well have some isolation/separation behaviors in his repertoire of tricks.

In her excellent book *Clinical Behavioral Medicine for Small Animals,* Dr. Karen Overall defines separation anxiety as, "A condition in which animals exhibit symptoms of anxiety or excessive distress when they are left alone." Common signs of the condition include:

- Destructive behavior.
- Housesoiling.
- Excessive vocalization.

Many dogs with this challenging behavior also:

- Refuse to eat or drink when left alone.
- Don't tolerate crating.
- Pant and salivate excessively when distressed.
- Will go to great lengths to try to escape from confinement, with apparent total disregard for injury to themselves or damage to their surroundings.

It's natural for young mammals to experience anxiety when separated from their mothers and siblings; it's an adaptive survival mechanism. A pup who gets separated from his family cries in distress, enabling Mom to easily find him and rescue him. In the wild, even an adult canine who is left alone is more likely to die—either from starvation, since he has no pack to hunt with, or from attack, since he has no pack mates for mutual protection. Given the vital importance of a dog's canine companions, it speaks volumes about their adaptability as a species that we can condition them to accept being left alone at all! We're lucky we don't have far more problems than we do, especially in today's world, where few households have someone at home regularly during the day to keep the dog company.

There was a time in our society when fewer dogs were left home alone—Mom stayed home while Dad went off to work every day—so dogs had less exposure to the kind of daily isolation that contributes to separation anxiety behavior. Some behavior scientists theorize that experiencing a fear-causing event when a young dog is already mildly stressed about being alone can trigger more intense "home alone" anxiety behaviors. In today's world, there are a significant number of dogs who are afflicted with some degree of separation distress. Fortunately, many dog owners these days are willing to seek solutions to behavior problems rather than just "get rid of" the dog. As a result, behavior professionals are likely to see canine clients with separation distress disorders.

Differential diagnoses

Another reason separation anxiety *seems* so prevalent these days, at least compared to a few decades ago, is that it is misdiagnosed with some frequency. With an increased awareness of the condition has come an increase in misidentification of behaviors that resemble separation distress behaviors, but really aren't.

For example, housesoiling *can* be related to anxiety, but the cause could also be incomplete housetraining, lack of access to appropriate elimination areas with unreasonable owner expectations (expecting the dog to "hold it" for 10 hours or more), fear, excitement, marking, submissive elimination, or physical incontinence. Destructive behavior may be a result of separation anxiety or it could be normal puppy behavior, play, reaction to outside stimuli, and/or an outlet for excess energy. Separation distress could be the cause of excessive barking and howling, or the dog could be stimulated to bark by street sounds (traffic, people talking), trespassers (i.e., mail carrier, intruder, Girls Scouts selling cookies), social facilitation (other dogs barking), play, aggression, or fear.

It's critically important that a problem behavior be correctly identified prior to the implementation of a behavior modification program. It does no good to try to modify separation anxiety if that's not really the problem.

If elimination accidents occur when the owner is home as well as when the dog is left alone, it's more likely a housetraining problem than a separation issue. Separation-related destruction is usually directed toward escape efforts—chewing or clawing at or through doorframes, windowsills, and walls. If the destruction is more generalized throughout the house, it points toward one or more of the other possible causes, rather than an isolation issue. A strategically located video camera or sound-activated tape recorder can help identify possible outside stimuli, such as visitors to the home or unusual noises, that might trigger what otherwise may appear to be separation-related behaviors.

Case study: Misdiagnosis

Lexi was a five-year-old spayed female Husky/Greyhound mix rescue, presented by the foster mom as having separation anxiety that manifested as destructive behavior. Lexi had been in several prior foster homes, none of which reported destructive behavior.

As we discussed Lexi's behavior during her behavior consultation, the dog paced almost constantly, and displayed numerous other signs of general stress, including whining, attention-seeking, and exploring doorways, even though her current human was sitting quietly in a chair in the center of the room. This was the first clue that her stress behavior might not be separation related. Her behavior did not change significantly when her human left the room. This was the second big clue. The foster parent mentioned that she had noted a heightened anxiety when Lexi heard "mystery electronic beeping" in the house—probably from a watch hidden in a drawer that the owners were unable to locate. She also reportedly reacted badly to the beeps of other watches, cameras, and other electronic devices.

I concluded that while Lexi did, indeed, have anxiety problems, they were not separation related, but rather a more generalized anxiety. While we have no way of knowing for sure, I surmised that at some point she may have been contained in an underground shock fence and the beeping sounds that caused her heightened anxiety were similar to the warning beep of the fence. For a dog who has been trained to such a fence, the sound of the beep, through association with the shock, can be every bit as aversive and stress-causing as the shock itself.

We implemented a behavior modification program for generalized anxiety that included partnering with a veterinarian for the administration of anti-anxiety medication, and the foster parent made sure not to leave Lexi alone with access to the room where the mystery beeping occurred (the kitchen). Lexi was eventually adopted and is doing well in her new home, where her owners are continuing her behavior modification program.

A continuum

Distress over being left alone is not always a full-blown separation anxiety problem. A dog may suffer from mild to severe *isolation* distress or anxiety or mild to severe *separation* distress or anxiety.

The difference between distress and anxiety is a matter of degree on a continuum. "Distress" indicates a lower intensity of stress behaviors when the dog is alone, while "anxiety" is an extreme panic attack. The distinction between "isolation" and "separation" is equally important. Isolation distress means the dog doesn't want to be left alone—any ol' human will do for company and sometimes even another dog or some other species will fill the bill. True separation distress or anxiety means the dog is hyper bonded to one specific person and continues to show stress behaviors if that person is absent, even if other humans are present.

Our Cardigan Welsh Corgi, Lucy, suffers from moderate isolation distress—she doesn't like to be left alone outdoors. Before we realized the significance of her behavior, she managed to injure herself badly, falling off a stone wall onto cement steps eight feet below, in her persistent attempts to reach us through a window. Indoors, her isolation distress is milder. She may bark briefly if we leave her alone downstairs, but quickly calms and settles.

Missy, on the other hand, demonstrates true *separation* distress. The eight-year-old Australian Shepherd had been in at least four different homes prior to joining our family in the Fall of 2007. As is sometimes the case with dogs who have been rehomed numerous times, she attached herself to one of her new humans (me) completely and almost instantly. If we are out cleaning the barn, it matters not to Missy that my husband is still there—if I go back to the house for some reason she becomes hyper vigilant, watching anxiously for me to return, ignoring Paul's attempts to reassure her or engage in other activities. Fortunately for us, her stress level is mild—other than some scratches inflicted to our kitchen door on Day Two of her addition to our family, she's done nothing destructive—her level of stress over my absence is low, and tolerable, and consists primarily of pacing and whining. But it may explain why we're at least her fifth (and final!) home.

You couldn't tell from Missy's innocent expression that she suffers from isolation distress!

Preventing isolation distress and separation anxiety

The most important ingredient in a successful separation anxiety prevention program is to set your dog up for success. When you bring a new dog or puppy home, implement a program to help him be comfortable with being alone for gradually increasing periods. This will help to assure him that it's not necessary to panic—you haven't abandoned him; you always come back. Be sure to exercise him well before you practice—a tired dog is a much-better candidate for relaxation than one who's "full of it."

Here are the ten steps of a program to create a dog who is comfortable being left alone:

1. Bring your dog home at a time when someone can spend a few days with him to ease the stress of the transition.
2. Prepare a quiet, safe space in advance such as a playpen or puppy pen, or a dog-proofed room such as a laundry room.
3. When you bring your dog home, give him a chance to relieve himself outdoors, and spend 10-15 minutes with him in the house under close supervision. Then put him in his pen and stay in the room with him.
4. Stay close at first. Read a book. If he fusses, ignore him. When he's quiet, greet him calmly, take one step away, and then return before he has a chance to get upset. Speak to him calmly, then go back to reading. You're teaching him that if you leave, you will return. Other family members should make themselves scarce during this time—your dog needs to learn to be *alone.*
5. Continue to occasionally step away, gradually increasing the distance and varying the length of time that you stay away, so that eventually you can wander around the room without upsetting your dog. Each time you return, greet him *calmly.* Every once in a while say "Yes!" in a calm but cheerful voice before you return to him, then walk back to the pen and feed him a treat.
6. After an hour or so, give him a break. Take him outside to potty and play. Hang out for a while. Then go back inside and resume his pen exercises.
7. Begin again, staying near the pen until he settles. More quickly this time, move along steps 4 and 5 until you can wander around the room without generating alarm. Now step into another room very briefly, and return before your dog has time to get upset. Gradually increase the length of time you stay out of the room, interspersing it with wandering around the room, sitting near him reading a book, and sitting across the room, reading a book. If he starts to fuss, wait until he stops fussing to move back toward him. Teach him that calm behavior makes you return, fussing keeps you away.
8. Occasionally, step outside of the house. Your goal for day one is to get your dog to be comfortable with you being away from him for 15 to 20 minutes. (It's usually the first 20 minutes of separation that are most difficult.) Vary the times, so he doesn't start getting antsy in anticipation of your return. Remember to give him plenty of potty and play breaks: every hour for a young pup, every one to two hours for an older dog.
9. On day two, quickly go through the warm-up steps again, until you can step outside for 15-20 minutes at a time, interspersed with shorter separations. On

one of your outdoor excursions, hop into your car and drive around the block. Return in 5-10 minutes, and calmly re-enter the house just as you have been during the rest of the exercises. Hang out for a while, then go outside and drive away again, for a half-hour this time.

10. Now it's time for Sunday brunch. Be sure your dog gets a thorough potty break and play time, then give him fifteen minutes to relax after the stimulation of play. Put his favorite stuffed Kong into his pen, round up the family, and calmly exit the house for an outing of a couple of hours' duration. When you arrive home to a calm and happy dog, drink an orange juice toast to your graduation from separation anxiety prevention school.

If you are modifying an already existing distress or anxiety condition, you will need to work through the steps of the program much more slowly. Plan on weeks or even months, rather than a few days. In the meantime, the better you are at managing your dog's environment so he doesn't experience repeated high-stress incidents, the more quickly your program will be effective. Try to utilize family, friends, neighbors, understanding employers, commercial daycare options, and even paid help if necessary to minimize the times your dog must be alone.

Again, if your efforts to modify his isolation/separation behavior don't improve reasonably quickly, consult a qualified, positive behavior professional. This is one behavior for which intervention with behavior drugs can be appropriate almost immediately in a program. If your dog's destructive or injurious behavior is so severe that you can't manage it safely while you work to modify, you will need to consult with a behavior-knowledgeable veterinarian or a veterinary behaviorist to be sure you're getting the most appropriate, most effective drug for his anxiety.

Graduate school

It's unfair to ask a young dog to stay home alone for eight to ten hours—he needs to get out to relieve himself midway through the day. If you force him to soil the house, at best you may create housetraining problems, at worst you can cause stress-related behaviors. Options may include taking him to work with you, having you or other family members come home on their lunch hour, arranging for stay-at-home neighbors to take him out, hiring a pet walker to walk him and play with him, or sending him to a well-run doggie daycare environment. *(Note: the daycare option is not appropriate for a very young pup.)*

If you set up a routine to help your dog succeed, he'll someday earn his Master's Degree in Home Alone, and be trusted with full house freedom. It may be too late for some dog owners to say they've never had had a dog with separation anxiety, but it's never too late to say "never again."

Behavior modification

There are a number of steps you can take to resolve your dog's isolation or separation anxiety behavior. the "Preventing separation anxiety program" can also be used to modify an existing isolation/separation condition. However, you will progress much more slowly through the steps of the program with a dog who already suffers from separation-related behaviors; your dog's strong emotional response to being left alone will make this a much more challenging proposition.

Here are some other avenues to explore, to complement your modification work:

- Exercise your dog well before you leave. A tired dog has less energy with which to be anxious and destructive. Be sure to end your exercise session 20 to 30 minutes before you go, so he has time to settle down.
- Five minutes before you leave, give him a well-stuffed Kong to take his mind off your imminent departure.
- Make your departures and returns completely calm and emotionless. No huggy/kissy "Mummy loves you" scenes. If he gets excited and jumps all over you when you return, ignore him. Turn your back and walk away. When he finally settles down, say hello and greet him very calmly.
- Defuse the pieces of your departure routine by also doing them when you are *not* leaving. Pick up your car keys and sit down on the sofa to watch TV. Dress in your business suit and then cook dinner. Set your alarm for 5:00 a.m. on a Saturday, then roll over and go back to sleep.
- Mix up the pieces of your departure routine when you *are* leaving, so his anxiety doesn't build to a fever pitch as he recognizes your departure cues. We are creatures of habit too, so this is hard to do, but can pay off in big dividends. Eat breakfast before you shower instead of after. Pick up your keys and put them in your pocket before you take your dog out for his final potty break. Put your briefcase in the car while you are still in your bathrobe. Make the morning ritual as unpredictable as possible.
- Use a "safe" cue such as "I'll be back," *only* when you know you'll return within the time period your dog can tolerate. As suggested in Patricia McConnell's wonderful booklet on separation anxiety titled *I'll Be Home Soon!,* this helps your dog relax, knowing he can trust you to return.
- Explore alternative dog-keeping situations to minimize the occasions when you do have to leave him alone—doggie daycare may be suitable for some dogs, but not for others. You may be able to find a neighbor or relative who is housebound and might appreciate some canine companionship during the day.
- If you are considering adoption of a second dog, try borrowing a calm, stable, compatible dog from a friend, to see if that helps to relieve your dog's distress. If so, you know it's an isolation problem, not a separation one, and could consider providing him with a canine companion to mitigate his stress over being left alone.
- Use Comfort Zone (DAP) plug-ins and sprays in his environment to help ease his anxiety, available at pet supply stores and online websites.
- Condition your dog to enjoy the *Through A Dog's Ear* soothing CD of bio-acoustically engineered classical piano music while you are home and then set it on "repeat" on your CD player to help keep him calm in your absence.
- Remove as many other stressors from your dog's world as possible to help him maintain his equilibrium in your absence. No choke chains, shock collars, physical or harsh verbal punishment (especially in connection to his anxiety behaviors).

- Consider working with a behavior professional to be sure you're on the right path. A good behavior professional can also help you explore the possibilities of using anti-anxiety medications to maximize the effectiveness of your modification efforts.

Fixing separation anxiety is hard work. It's all too easy to get frustrated with your dog's destructive behavior. Remember that he's not choosing to do it out of spite or malice—he is panicked about his own survival without you (his pack) there to protect him. It's not fun for him either—he lives in the moment, and the moments that you are gone are long and terrifying. If you make the commitment to modify his behavior and succeed in helping him be brave about being alone, you'll not only save your home from destruction, you will enhance the quality of your dog's life immensely, as well as your own, and perhaps save him from destruction too.

Obsessive compulsive disorders

You've probably heard about people who wash their hands repeatedly until the skin wears off, who pull out their hair until they're bald, or return home, time after time after time, to make sure the stove is turned off. These are obsessive compulsive disorders and they can constitute a high risk behavior for a dog if not treated.

An obsessive compulsive disorder is defined by MedicineNet.com as:

> A psychiatric disorder characterized by obsessive thoughts and compulsive actions, such as cleaning, checking, counting, or hoarding. Obsessive-compulsive disorder (OCD), one of the anxiety disorders, is a potentially disabling condition that can persist throughout a person's life. The individual who suffers from OCD becomes trapped in a pattern of repetitive thoughts and behaviors that are senseless and distressing but extremely difficult to overcome. OCD occurs in a spectrum from mild to severe, but if severe and left untreated, can destroy a person's capacity to function at work, at school, or even in the home.

Sad to say, OCD behaviors aren't confined to humans—dogs get them too. They can be high-risk behaviors if not treated, and have a significant impact on your dog's quality of life—and yours. Oh, you won't see your dog worrying about whether the stove was left on, nor will you catch him washing his paws repeatedly in the sink. Dogs have a whole set of potential OCDs all their own, specific to canine behavior. Canine OCDs are just as capable of destroying a dog's ability to function as human OCDs are capable of affecting human lives. Dogs who have been housed in a stressful kennel environment for long periods of time, as is the case with many shelter, rescue, puppy mill, and hoarder dogs, are at especially high risk for developing OCDs.

The last thing you want is for your dog to develop one of these debilitating behaviors. The more you know about them, the better armed you are to prevent them, and the better able to recognize and take action sooner rather than later—a critically important element of a successful behavior modification program for OCDs. If your newly adopted Do-Over Dog has an OCD already, you'll do well to seek professional help sooner, rather than later.

Noted veterinary behaviorist Dr. Karen Overall suggests that as much as two to three percent of our canine population may be afflicted with OCD. She also identifies it as one of the most difficult canine behavioral disorders to successfully treat, and emphasizes that genetic, environmental, and neurochemical/neurophysiological elements all come into play.

Certain breeds have a clear genetic propensity for specific OCDs. Cavalier King Charles Spaniels are prone to fly snapping, shadow and light chasing; Doberman Pinschers tend to flank-suck and self mutilate from licking; a high percentage of Golden and Labrador Retrievers seem to suffer from pica (eating inappropriate objects); and several of the Herding breeds are likely to engage in spinning and tail chasing behaviors. It's a good idea to research your own breed thoroughly, so you can be especially watchful for telltale signs of any that may plague your breed.

In addition to the genetic component of OCD behavior, environment plays a significant role. The behaviors most often emerge in young dogs, between 6 to 12 months, in dogs who have a genetic predisposition to the behavior, or when subjected to environmental stressors that trigger the onset of the behavior. Dogs who may be genetically prone to a behavior *may* dodge the OCD bullet if they avoid being significantly stressed during this period. Or maybe not.

Early signs

The early sign of any OCD is the *occasional* performance of a behavior out of context. It's normal for a dog to chase a real fly. It's not normal for him to start snapping at things in the air that you can't see. Because well-practiced OCDs are heartbreakingly difficult to modify, and destructive to quality of life for the dog and his human, it's critically important to identify and modify OCD behavior in its early stages.

Our own Lucy, exhibited tail chasing behavior in the shelter before we adopted her, both in her kennel, and during the assessment process. Note that tail-chasing and spinning are seen disproportionately in the Herding breeds. Fortunately for us and for her, Lucy was young when we adopted her (six months). Simply removing her from the stressful shelter environment and providing her with large daily doses of physical exercise resolved her behavior. Ben, a four-month-old Golden Retriever client in Monterey, was also treated successfully, simply by having his owners remove all reinforcement (getting up and leaving the room) the instant the pup started to chase his tail. His embryonic spinning behavior ceased within a month. The Standard Poodle client I worked with in Santa Cruz was not so fortunate. At age three, Giselle's spinning behavior was well-established; her owners couldn't even walk her on leash because of her non-stop spinning anytime she was the least bit stimulated. She required extensive pharmaceutical intervention.

Here are some common OCD behaviors:

Lick granuloma. Also known as Acral Lick Dermatitis or ALD, this disorder presents as repetitive licking of the front or hind legs, ultimately causing a bare spot, then an open sore, sometimes causing systemic infection. In extreme cases, a limb may need to be amputated.

Light chasing (shadow chasing). Likely related to predatory behavior, light chasing is characterized by staring, biting at, chasing or barking at lights and shadows. This behavior is sometimes triggered by an owner playing with the dog with flashlights or laser lights—something I strongly recommend against doing, for obvious reasons.

Tail chasing/spinning. Also, perhaps a displaced predatory behavior, tail chasing often starts as an apparently innocuous, "cute" behavior that is reinforced by owner attention. Only when it attains obsessive proportions do many owners realize the harm in reinforcing this behavior.

Flank sucking. A self-explanatory term, flank sucking behavior is likely a displaced nursing behavior. Similarly, some dogs may suck on blankets or soft toys—behaviors that can be equally obsessive, but are less self-destructive.

Fly snapping. No, this one doesn't refer to dogs who chase real flies—that's a normal behavior. The OCD version of fly-snapping involves snapping at what appear to us to be *imaginary* flies. Dogs who exhibit this behavior may appear anxious, apparently unable to escape their imaginary tormentors. While some fly-snapping may be seizure-related, a significant percentage of sufferers don't demonstrate behaviors typical of seizure activity and those episodes are characterized as true OCD behaviors.

Pica. While many dogs are happy to eat object that humans consider inappropriate, dogs with pica do so obsessively. Pica induces some dogs to obsessively eat and swallow small objects such as stones, acorns and twigs, while others ingest large amounts of paper, leather or other substances. Pica can cause life-threatening bowel obstruction that requires emergency surgery.

This Pomeranian is stressed in a shelter kennel and sucking his blanket—a relatively innocuous obsessive compulsive behavior.

It's also important to note that dogs who are prone to one obsessive compulsive behavior can easily adopt another. I firmly prohibited my husband from playing with Lucy with a laser light, or water from the hose, knowing full well she'd delight in these activities. We didn't need light chasing on top of tail chasing! Ben, the tail-chasing Golden pup, had a more serious OCD problem—he was obsessive about eating pebbles, small sticks, and acorns. At the tender age of four months, he had already undergone one emergency surgery for intestinal blockage and had to wear a muzzle when he was outside, on leash or off, to prevent a recurrence.

For this reason, simply suppressing the behavior through punishment is a dangerously inappropriate approach. Not only does the punishment *add* stress to a behavior already triggered and exacerbated by stress, it heightens the risk of having the dog transfer to a new OCD. You'll do far better to approach an OCD modification program more scientifically.

Modifying OCD behavior

There are five key components to most successful OCD modification programs:

- Increase exercise
- Reduce stress
- Remove reinforcement
- Reinforce an incompatible behavior
- Explore behavior modification drugs if/when appropriate

Let's look at each of these more closely.

Increase exercise. A useful part of almost *any* behavior modification program, exercise relieves stress and tires your dog so he has less energy to practice his OCD behavior. While physical exercise is hugely important, don't overlook the value of mental exercise for relieving stress and tiring a dog mentally.

Reduce stress. This is an important and obvious step, given that OCDs are triggered and exacerbated by stress. You will need to identify as many stressors as possible in your dog's life. Have the whole family participate in making a list of all the things you can identify that cause stress for your dog—not just the one(s) that appear to trigger the obsessive behavior. Then go down the list identifying any you can simply eliminate (i.e.: shock collar for that evil underground shock fence) and commit to removing those from his environment. Next, mark those that might be appropriate for counter-conditioning—changing his opinion of them from "Ooooooo, scary/stressful" to "Yay! Good thing!" Finally, try to manage his environment to at least reduce his exposure to those that can't be eliminated or modified.

Remove reinforcement. All too often, owners mistakenly think obsessive behaviors are cute or funny. They reinforce the behavior with laughter and attention and may even trigger the behavior deliberately, unaware of the harm they're doing. When the behavior becomes so persistent that it's annoying, the dog may be reinforced with "negative attention" when the owner yells at him to stop doing it. As in the case of Ben, the Golden pup, removing reinforcement by having all humans leave the room can work well to help extinguish an OCD in its early stages.

Reinforce an incompatible behavior. this was also an effective part of Ben's modification program. When the puppy *wasn't* chasing his tail, his owners used a high rate of reinforcement for calm behavior, especially for lying quietly on his bed. Also, look for other calm behaviors to reinforce during otherwise potentially stimulating moments, such as sitting quietly at the door for his leash rather than leaping about in excitement over the pending walk.

Consider drugs. With persistent and well-practiced OCDs, referral to a qualified veterinary behaviorist for consideration of pharmaceutical intervention is nearly always imperative. The selection, prescription, and monitoring of the strong, potentially harmful psychotropic drugs used for modification of difficult behaviors requires the education and skill of a licensed veterinary professional. You can find veterinary behavior professionals at: www.avsabonline.org or at www.veterinarybehaviorists.org. Alternatively, virtually every veterinary behaviorist is more than willing to provide free phone consultation services with your own veterinarian.

Obsessive compulsive disorders and breed predispositions

Certain obsessive compulsive disorders are known to be strongly associated with particular breeds of dogs. This doesn't mean that every dog of that breed will display the behavior, nor does it mean that dogs of other breeds won't—just that there's a higher than normal appearance of the disorder in that breed. Here are some:

Lick granuloma. Breeds most commonly affected are Dobermans, German Shepherds, Great Danes, and Labrador Retrievers.

Light chasing (shadow chasing). Breeds prone to light chasing include Wire Haired Fox Terriers, Old English Sheepdogs, Schnauzers, Rottweilers, and Golden Retrievers.

Tail chasing/spinning. Tail chasing is seen disproportionately in Herding and Terrier breeds, especially German Shepherds and Bull Terriers.

Flank sucking. Doberman Pinschers are most likely to engage in flank-sucking.

Fly-snapping. Breeds that suffer from fly-snapping may include Cavalier King Charles Spaniels, English Springer Spaniels, Dobermans, Bernese Mountain Dogs, Labrador Retrievers, German Shepherds, and a variety of Terrier breeds.

Pica. Most common in Retriever-type dogs who are highly reinforced by putting objects in their mouths.

If some of this information has alarmed you, good. Obsessive compulsive disorders are alarming. If your dog, or a friend's, is showing early signs of OCD behavior, I want you to take it seriously, and intervene immediately, in order to prevent the behavior from developing into a debilitating disorder. Dogs like Lucy, Ben, and Leo can lead full and happy lives because steps were taken early to prevent their behaviors from becoming extreme.

If your Do-Over Dog already has a severe obsessive compulsive behavior, do something about it now. Dogs can lead quality lives because their owners care enough to find solutions for difficult behaviors. Make the commitment to find the help you need so you and your dog can have a full and happy life together.

Aggression

The word "aggressive" strikes fear in a dog owner's heart, and rightfully so. The term covers a hugely broad range of behaviors—everything from a hard stare, stiffly wagging tail, and piloerection (raised hackles) to the two or three dozen tragic dog-related human fatalities that occur every year in this country. Obviously aggression is a high risk behavior and must be treated. This is a case where seeking professional help is often prudent.

It makes sense that a percentage of Do-Over Dogs include aggression in their repertoire of behaviors. The stresses that many of them have endured through multiple life changes alone, not to mention abuse, neglect, fear and the opportunity to learn that aggression makes people—and other dogs—leave them alone, are all factors that explain why your Do-Over Dog *might* come with some aggressive baggage.

In Volume Two, *Etiology and Assessment of Behavior Problems,* of the excellent three-book series, *Applied Dog Behavior and Training,* dog behavior consultant, trainer and author Steve Lindsay describes aggression as, "...an adaptive effort to establish control over some vital resource or situation that cannot be effectively controlled through other means." Veterinary Behaviorist Dr. Karen Overall, in her book *Clinical Behavioral Medicine for Small Animals,* defines it as, "...an appropriate or inappropriate threat or challenge that is ultimately resolved by combat or deference."

Overall points out that aggression can be appropriate or inappropriate and suggests that while some might argue that a dog should *never* bite, it might be unreasonable to expect a dog *not* to bite in self-defense, to save its own life. And, if one accepts that premise, how does one determine when a dog feels that its life is at risk?

The appropriateness or inappropriateness of aggressive behavior and presence of *provocation,* or lack thereof, is often the subject of heated debate in dangerous dog hearings around the country. Most of the news articles with sensationalist *"Dog Mauls Toddler!"* headlines include the notation that the bite was "unprovoked." However, a bite is rarely, truly unprovoked. Provocation from the dog's perspective is often radically different from provocation from the human's perspective. When someone says "unprovoked" they usually mean "not justified from the human perspective." From the dog's perspective, if he wasn't provoked, he wouldn't have bitten.

Tying a dog up where he can be approached by someone who makes him uncomfortable can be adequate provocation for aggression—from the dog's perspective.

Those same articles almost always include a quote from a bereaved family member that "the dog was always good with kids" and "we just don't understand how this happened." This is most often a function of the owners' failure to correctly interpret their dog's communication signals. Dogs who merely *tolerate* the presence of children are often misperceived as liking them when in fact they're just putting up with them. When the child does something inappropriate or worrisome to the dog who truly *adores* children, the behavior is often accepted by the dog, while the dog who merely tolerates the child may take offense and bite.

Definitions aside, an in-depth examination of aggression in all of its various presentations is far too ambitious for the scope of this book. Aggressive behaviors carry with them a significant risk of injury to others, ultimate euthanasia of the dog, and legal liability for the owner—costs too high to rely on do-it-yourself advice garnered from a book. I can't emphasize enough the importance of seeking hands-on help from a qualified positive behavior professional if your dog has significant aggressive behaviors. I will, however, explore some of the broader aspects of aggression, and hopefully help to point you in the right direction if you are facing any of these difficult high-risk behaviors with your Do-Over Dog.

Classifications of aggression

While some behavior professionals argue that putting labels on aggression does little to actually help modify the behavior, there is value in understanding aggressive behaviors based on function and context, in order to assist both with management and modification. Besides, having a name for your dog's behavior will help you withstand the advice of those who insist on labeling almost every presentation of aggression as "dominance aggression." (Note that I don't even include that label in my list.) While there is no widespread agreement regarding classification, those presented here are some that are accepted by many behavior professionals.

Regardless of the classification(s) of aggression your Do-Over Dog may be exhibiting, many steps of the process are similar; it's often just fine details of the protocols that differ.

1. First and most important on the list is to *manage* your dog's environment so he doesn't successfully practice the behavior. The longer your dog practices the behavior, the harder it is to change it. In addition, if he actually bites someone, his chances of long-term survival decline. I've said it before, and I'll say it again: dogs who bite people (and in some jurisdictions, other dogs, cats, and other domesticated animals) have short lives.
2. Identify stressors and determine which long-term strategy to apply with each stressor on the list to reduce your dog's stress load as much as possible. Strategies include management, changing associations, training a new behavior, getting rid of the stressor, or deciding the dog can live with it (low level stressors only).
3. Implement as many general stress-reduction programs as possible, including increasing exercise, evaluating your dog's diet, calming music, massage, and more.
4. Determine which of the stressors identified as candidates for counter-conditioning you want to work with first and create a step-by-step protocol to start changing your dog's association with that stimulus—or stimuli, if you choose to address more than one at a time.
5. Remember that the use of force is *never* appropriate when modifying aggressive behavior. Techniques like alpha-rolls, pinning, shocking, hanging, and helicoptering are dangerous, can injure or kill your dog, and can elicit more intense aggression back at you. The only time force is appropriate when dealing with an aggressive dog is if it's necessary to protect yourself or someone else. A properly implemented protocol should not put you or anyone else at risk. If someone tries to convince you to use force as part of an aggression-modification protocol, politely but firmly decline.
6. Keep a journal to track your progress. Be prepared to consult with a qualified positive behavior professional if you aren't seeing the progress you'd hoped.

It's not my intent to try to offer detailed modification protocols for all the various aggression presentation possibilities. There are simply too many variables in each case to create a cookie-cutter protocol. Observation skills—and the ability to interpret observations—are critically important to success, to know whether it's appropriate to continue with a protocol or if it's necessary to make changes to help the dog succeed. If your Do-Over Dog is offering significant aggressive behavior, I urge you to seek the help of a qualified positive behavior professional, to give your dog the best chance for a long and happy life with you.

That said, here is a brief discussion of each of the classifications offered here:

Fear-related aggression. The dog attempts to move away from fear-causing stimuli and can become dangerous if cornered. He may shake and tremble and he may bite from behind and then run away. This type of aggression can be associated with lack of socialization, painful medical treatment, or abuse. It is common in Do-Over Dogs who come from puppy mills, hoarders, and other environments prone to lack of socialization. Manage the fear-aggressive dog's environment scrupulously by protecting him from the unwelcome advances of strangers. Know that at first your fearful Do-Over Dog may be afraid of you and other family members. Expect to invest a lot of time and energy in counter-conditioning to convince him that his world is good and safe. Do not make the common mistake of having scary strangers feed him treats. The counter-conditioning "good stuff" needs to come from *you* until he's quite comfortable with strangers. Then have them drop treats as they walk by, very slowly working up to the point where he can actually take treats from strangers. Some dogs with fear-related aggression adjust to their world and become normal or reasonably normal. Many must be carefully managed for life and are never able to take treats from strangers.

Idiopathic aggression. "Idiopathic" means "we don't know what causes it." This is a rare form of aggression with *no* identifiable context. At one time, it was called "rage syndrome," "Cocker rage," or "Springer rage," but most dogs who are alleged to have this type of aggression are misdiagnosed. If the aggression is at all predictable or in any way can be deliberately triggered, it is *not* idiopathic aggression. Dogs who truly suffer from this are thankfully few. They are unpredictable and dangerous and are usually euthanized.

Interdog aggression. Related to social hierarchies, this form of aggression may start as low-level challenges—stares, bumps, body-blocking—and escalate over time. It's often presented as same-sex aggression and may be generalized or situation-specific. An older/weaker dog may be a target. This type of aggression usually happens because neither dog is willing to defer to the other and tension escalates as incidents repeatedly occur. An elderly dog whose faculties are failing often doesn't notice the other dog's "go away" signals and fails to respond, thereby triggering the aggression, or notices but is physically unable to defer quickly enough. Manage these dogs to prevent tension through multiple incidents of aggression. Teach operant responses to cues for deference behaviors (look away) to help defuse tension. Use classical conditioning to convince both dogs that being in each others' presence makes good things happen.

Maternal aggression. A mother dog may naturally protect her pups, her den area, and possessions in that area, although not all mother dogs do. The aggressive behavior can also occur with false pregnancies. It often passes when hormones eventually subside after pups have left the nest, but not if aggressive behavior has been mishandled with punishment during this time. Pups can also learn aggressive behavior through *social facilitation*—watching their mother be aggressive with humans and practicing the behavior along with her. Because propensity for aggression can be both heritable and learned, dogs with known history of aggression should not be bred, and mothers-to-be should be well-socialized. Whelping pens need to be located in a quiet, low-traffic area to reduce stress and interactions with humans carefully supervised. If signs of aggression are noted, keep visitors to a minimum (while still providing ample socialization for the pups away from mom's influence) and do counter-conditioning to help give mom-dog a positive association with the presence of visitors. When pups are ready to be adopted or sold, it may be necessary to remove mom from the room when prospective new owners are present.

Pain-related aggression. This form of aggression is also understandable—we are all grumpy and snappy when we hurt. When injuries are obvious—broken bones or wounds—this type of aggression is often excused. Less obvious are internal aches and pains such as arthritis and other pain-causing conditions. A bite often occurs in response to painful handling or anticipation of painful handling—a dog can become conditioned to *expect* pain and offer aggressive behavior to prevent contact. When touched or handled, the dog may grab hands with his teeth in an attempt to stop the pain. This can be in response to rough play from humans or other dogs, especially if arthritis or other painful conditions are present. It can also morph into fear-related aggression if the dog comes to anticipate being hurt. The simple answer here is to alleviate the pain. While some of the very effective non-steroidal anti-inflammatory drugs used for pain-relief have some potential to cause liver damage, careful monitoring can forestall significant complications. Even if a dog's life is shortened somewhat by the drugs, a pain-free quality of life is important—and his life will be shortened for sure if he bites people. Once the pain issue is resolved, you may still need to do counter-conditioning to change his now pain-related association with dogs and humans.

Play aggression. This can start out with aroused play and change to serious aggression in response to rough play—either with other dogs or with humans. Often, two dogs are playing roughly together and one tries to signal the other to stop—that he's not comfortable with that level of arousal. When the play-aggressive dog fails to heed the signal, the other now unwilling playmate may be compelled to snap to try to stop the play and at that point the fight occurs. Often the dog who wanted to stop the play is blamed for the fight, since he's the one who may snap first—but in reality it's the rougher dog's failure to heed the "please stop" signals that causes the aggression. You can avoid this form of aggression by making sure canine playmates have compatible play styles, and by supervising play and cheerfully interrupting the fun when it starts to escalate to dangerous levels. After a brief time out to reduce arousal levels (length of time depending on the dogs involved), play can resume.

Possession aggression (resource guarding). A dog who guards resources will bite if he perceives a threat (real or imagined) to food or other valuable objects, including toys, humans, and preferred space, such as a crate or dog bed. While some resource guarding is very mild and manageable, with serious guarders, aggression can be elicited at very long approach distances, and can be extremely fierce and dangerous. (See previous section in this chapter for in-depth discussion of resource guarding.)

Predatory aggression. A dog who exhibits this form of aggression may stalk or stare at small animals, infants, bicyclists, skateboarders. It is not considered a true "social" aggression, but rather is part of the food-acquisition behavior complex—although the result to victim may be the same. If a CAT-scan were done of this dog's brain during a predatory attack, the results would be very different from those of a dog attacking an intruder; significantly different areas of the brain would light up. Many "dog mauls infant" cases are believed to be predatory behavior, hence the universal advice from dog trainers to *never* leave dogs alone with small children, even dogs who appear quite friendly with small children. Many dogs who are predatory toward small animals respond well to counter-conditioning to give a new association other than "fun—chase!" and can also be taught operant responses to cues to interrupt predatory chase/kill behavior.

Protection aggression. This is the dog who protects people or other members of his social group from dogs, other people, and any other perceived threats. He stands forward, between the person being protected and the threat. Aggression can be stimulated by quick movement, hugs, or touching. While protective behavior is sometimes taught, many dogs are protective of their own accord, without intentional training. One way to differentiate this from other classifications of aggression is that protection aggression doesn't occur in the absence of the person(s) being protected, even if the same stimulus is present. While the dog who guards resources stays close to his person and may be saying, "this person is mine and I am not willing to share him," the dog who is protectively aggressive moves forward toward the threat and says "this person is part of my social group and I won't let you hurt him." This behavior can be modified through a combination of counter-conditioning to change the protective dog's opinion of the perceived threat and operant conditioning to teach the dog a new behavior when his person is approached.

Redirected aggression. A redirected bite occurs when the dog's intentions are thwarted by a person or other animal. The victim of the bite was not part of the original social interaction; a bite occurs as the person or animal intervenes to interrupt the behavior. It's a not uncommon occurrence when an owner attempts to intervene in dog-dog aggression, and often occurs when two dogs are fence-fighting; another dog runs up to see what the fuss is about and his packmate turns on him instead. This is primarily a management situation. Avoid direct intervention when a dog is highly aroused for any reason—use means other than your hands to intervene. Then evaluate the reason for the dog's arousal and determine if you need to manage or modify *that* behavior or environment.

Status-related aggression. As could be expected by the name, this type of aggression arises around control of resources within a social group. Conflict develops from the failure of one member to defer to another. Like many types of aggression, it worsens with punishment, as the use of force or violence only adds tension to an already tense relationship. There was a time when the behavioral recommendation was to "support the higher ranking dog" in status disputes. Now that we have more information about canine social groups and we understand that hierarchies are fluid rather than static, the recommendation is to reinforce appropriate behavior. As always, manage the environment to minimize incidents of conflict, but if they do occur, the dog or dogs who are inappropriate get a cheerful time out, and dog or dogs who are appropriate get reinforced. In multi-dog households, going out doorways can be a high-arousal activity where conflict is likely to occur. You can manage this by training all dogs to "wait" or "stay," and then inviting them through the door one at a time, with the dog most likely to be aggressive waiting until last to be released through the doorway.

Territorial aggression. The territorial dog protects property—his yard, his house, his car, his crate...and, if he's allowed to run loose, the entire neighborhood. The aggressive behavior can be exacerbated by fences or confinement that defines the boundaries of his territory. In many cases, it doesn't take long for the dog to define new territory; if he visits your office on "Take Your Dog to Work Day" he may soon be snapping at your secretary or your boss when they dare to trespass. This calls for management—don't leave him in places where he'll feel compelled to guard territory from unaware approachers—and counter-conditioning, to convince him that having someone approach his territory makes good stuff happen. As always, the management piece is critically important, so he doesn't bite, risk losing his home and his life, and so you don't get sued.

At this point, we have scratched the surface as far as identifying and modifying problem behaviors, aggression or otherwise. Hopefully, after reading this litany of potential problems, you're thankful that your Do-Over Dog engages in only a few of them, and that they are ones you can live with and work with. It matters little whether you inherited your dog's behaviors from his previous owners or now recognize that in some way you may have contributed to reinforcing inappropriate behaviors and creating negative associations, like I did with Lucy. What's important is that you're committed to giving your Do-Over Dog the fullest life possible, for the rest of his time on this earth.

In the final chapter of this book, you will read stories of exceptional dog owners who have done exactly that for their various Do-Over companions. I trust you'll find them as inspiring as I do.

Chapter 9
Happy Endings

When I put out a call for Do-Over Dog stories with happy endings, I didn't expect to get the tsunami of responses that I did. It was difficult to choose just a few from the many, many wonderful stories. It's gratifying, encouraging, and humbling to realize how many humans there are out there who are truly committed to helping their dogs enjoy the absolute best quality of life possible. I hope you're as touched by these stories as I am.

Gracie

Gracie

Gracie is an eight-year-old, 60-pound, spayed female Golden Retriever. She shares her life with Barbara and Wayne Davis of Corona, California. Barbara is the President of the Golden Retriever Club of Greater Los Angeles Rescue, and operates her own training and behavior business, BAD-Dogs, Inc.

In Barbara's own words:

Gracie originally turned up in an Orange County, California animal shelter as an eight-month-old stray. Her physical condition was so poor that she was almost unrecognizable as a Golden Retriever. A shelter scout pulled her at the last minute, saving her from euthanasia. She went into Golden Retriever rescue, where she bounced around several foster homes for being too active and escaping from the yard. She was adopted out to one family and returned about a week later for being "hyper." So of course, I wanted her desperately. She's been with us ever since, more than seven years now.

My connection with Gracie was instantaneous; just from a photo on the rescue web site. I didn't even find her particularly attractive, but something drew me to her. When we went to see her, she was really a mess, but it didn't really make any difference. Initially we were told she was "very active," but of course that's the rescue version of "out of control." We were told about her high energy level by the rescue, but all of her other challenging behaviors came to us during our journey of discovery.

The journey

Gracie housetrained instantly, but everything else was an uphill battle. She was almost continually in motion, hardly ever sleeping. She was hyperactive (clinically, I believe), hyper-vigilant, noise sensitive, dog-aggressive, touch-sensitive (you could see and feel her skin ripple and 'pop' when you touched her), and neo-phobic. She had multiple compulsive behaviors, including grooming herself and others, pacing, and circling. She was severely anxious and she spent hours tethered to a table leg, hyperventilating/chuffing, unable to eat or interact in any way.

Fortunately, her dog-related aggression was limited to dogs of a certain profile: those that resembled Huskies or German Shepherds. Unfortunately, one of our dogs was an aging Siberian Husky, and she hated him intensely. Every time he came into her line of sight, she immediately launched into a full-blown offensive display, lunging, barking, and snarling. Because of this, she had to be crated, tethered, or sequestered somewhere in the house and monitored constantly to make sure there was no contact.

Right after we adopted her, she was thoroughly checked out at the vet's, including blood work, urinalysis, and radiographs. The vet said she was suffering from malnutrition, but otherwise had no diagnosable medical conditions. The vet suspects that dietary deficits in her early life may have resulted in some neurological deficits in her development that may be at the heart of the problems she's had, still has, and always will have.

Gracie was diagnosed as hypothyroid at age five and has been taking thyroid supplements ever since. I believe this medical issue caused some minor changes in her behavior, but these resolved with the meds and some behavior modification. In the scheme of things, this was a mere blip on her behavioral radar!

Speaking of behavior modification, we did lots. And lots. Initially, we weren't getting anywhere because her anxiety was so profound it was impossible to find a threshold level under which we could work. Her stress was so intense, the slightest stimulation would send her racing. For instance, if someone sniffed, she might startle. The type of trainers we had out here to work with were useless, old-school obedience types, and behavior consultants really were not available. Veterinary behaviorist help was far outside our budget, especially after all Gracie's vet bills for diagnostics. We did find a few people who were able to give us some good advice on a piecemeal basis, but that was mixed in with a lot of junk. We spent months calling, emailing, and reading to figure out what to do.

Our vet helped us by being willing to try out anxiolytics (anti-anxiety medications). We were having conversations almost weekly about whether or not to euthanize Gracie; her problems were so profound, and I felt that she was suffering. When clomipramine didn't work, we went to amitriptyline (at dosages enough to paralyze a pony and it didn't even take the edge off!), and then finally found fluoxetine (Prozac). After three weeks on Prozac, there was a huge change in her overall behavior. She could sleep through the night, eat regular meals, learn things (previously she didn't have enough focus to even learn simple behaviors like "sit" and "down") and play. She still didn't care for our Husky, and although that was manageable, we still had to keep them separated.

For the next two years, Gracie went to every positive-reinforcement dog class I could find, just for the experience of having a good time in new places, in the presence of other people and dogs. Two of the instructors were so moved by Gracie's problems, they invited us to repeat classes at no charge, just so she'd get the exposure. I got a little folding camp chair with a carry sack integrated into the seat which I filled with water bottles, cheese, sausage, bacon, and cold cuts, and we'd sit in strip mall parking lots, school yards, parks, and other places for hours looking for things that bugged Gracie and do counter-conditioning exercise until the bad moment passed.

As her anxiety declined, her confidence grew, and so did her attention-span. Gracie learned a few tricks, but her ability to practice is limited to about five to eight repetitions, so things tend to go more slowly than we'd like sometimes. She also seems to get so excited by just participating in the training exercise that she can get over-aroused and we have to abort and just get silly for awhile.

Gracie has been on and off fluoxetine over the past seven years, and is doing really well. She's learned a few tricks and turned into a social butterfly. She's very friendly with people, enjoys having company at home, and is a rescue greeter dog at the annual Pet Expo, where she works the crowd and meets thousands of people and other pets. She's learned to get along with other dogs and avoids the ones who make her uncomfortable. She accompanies me on "career day" presentations at the local high school where she gets to meet class pets of all species.

Present and future

We understand we have a lifetime of work and management. Gracie is still subject to little panic attacks and we find her resting on a sofa or off in a corner somewhere, hyperventilating/chuffing, almost as though she's trying to compose herself. If she's having a less intense episode, she may crawl up on my husband's lap so he can hold onto her until the moment passes. I still occasionally encounter things she seems concerned about, so we work on positive training or counter-conditioning to deal with those. She is prone to bursts of explosive behavior. Door-darting is still one of her weaknesses; she will wait calmly at the door about 90% of the time now, but occasionally bolts (she runs like the wind) and can be half a block away before her right mind returns.

Our biggest challenge is gates and doorways to the outside. Although the bolting issue is largely under control, when she has a notion to run, she's gone. She's also still on the anxiety medication, and probably will be for life. Considering where she started, some extra vigilance, and the daily meds seems a small price to pay for the quality of life she has now.

Gracie's problems frequently seemed like a curse, but as with many trainers, Gracie's and our "baptism of fire" turned out to be a long-term blessing for me in my work. Without having this first-hand experience, I probably wouldn't have the skill and experience to work effectively with folks whose dogs have similar problems. I certainly wouldn't have the hope or the patience and the empathy factor is huge also. Gracie is so far opposite today from where she started out, the change is almost unbelievable. Wayne and I find ourselves watching her playing with toys, playing with the other dogs, making up games, learning behaviors, playing pranks on us and the other dogs, solving problems and it's difficult to process the concept that she was withdrawn, terrified, anxious, and almost completely non-functional when she first arrived.

Had someone with a crystal ball told us the extent of the issues we'd be facing with Gracie prior to adoption, we wouldn't have taken her. Wayne was very concerned about going the rescue route because he didn't feel like he wanted to take on someone else's "baggage." Little did we know we'd get enough baggage to take us on a life-long world cruise! I was working a fulltime corporate job, traveling, and trying to get my business started; had we known this adoptee would have caused so much disruption and taken so much time and resources, we would have likely passed. Once she stepped foot into our lives, though, she was part of the family and we were committed to whatever was to come. We'd had the conversation many times about how to proceed if we couldn't get things under control, and we both agreed we'd find a way to make things work; Gracie was, is, and always will be, part of the family.

Roda

Roda is a three-year-old, spayed female Pitbull mix who weighs in at 50 lbs. A year-and-a-half ago, Jessica Westermann and her partner, Jessica Rooney, adopted Roda from the Animal Care and Control shelter in Brooklyn, New York, where she ended up because she had been found abandoned, tied to a fence.

Roda

In Jessica's own words:

Roda had clearly just given birth, but her puppies were never located. We had originally gone to the shelter hoping to adopt a seven-year-old Flat Coated Retriever we had seen posted on Petfinder.com. By the time we got there, he (and every other non-pit) had been cherry-picked by a rescue organization and we found ourselves in the middle of Pitbull death row. We decided, before we went home, to "just say hello" to a few of the dogs. Roda was curled up in the back of her cage looking very depressed, but when the shelter employee opened the door, she lit up, climbed right into my lap and covered me with kisses. There was really no turning back after that. In the cab home, she threw up on us.

The journey

Once home, we discovered a long list of difficult behaviors. She did compulsive mouthing—she could not keep her teeth off of us when she was excited, anxious, bored, or annoyed, and she had not much in the way of bite inhibition, so she left pretty serious bruises up and down our arms. Her behavior was very difficult to live with. In addition, we discovered the following challenges:

- High energy—ridiculous zoomies that sent her flying around the apartment, leaping over furniture, knocking over lamps, taking us out at the knees.
- Constant trouble-making—stealing shoes, chewing at furniture, taking tissues out of the garbage, counter-surfing. We could not watch movies, have a peaceful dinner, sit and talk to each other, or otherwise act like normal adults. Instead we spent all of our free time monitoring her like she was a toddler.
- Sock swallowing—she ingested socks whole, resulting in two very expensive late-night trips to the emergency vet.
- Crippling fear of wind—if it was at all breezy, she would collapse to the ground and refuse to move. On several occasions, I had to carry her home, stopping every block to rest.
- Aggression towards cleaning products—we could not sweep in her presence. She would attack the broom, steal it, catch a crazy case of the zoomies, and whirl around, knocking things over.
- Night-time hysteria—screaming in her crate; not cool in an apartment building. We had many, many sleepless nights in the beginning. We once both had to call in sick to work because she kept us awake all night.
- Peeing in her crate.

We knew nothing about any of these behaviors when we adopted her. She also had numerous medical issues, including:

- Infected uterus, from giving birth (treated)
- Bladder infection (treated)
- Infected salivary glands (treated)
- Patchy, scaly, rashy skin (ongoing battle)
- Recurring gastritis (ongoing vigilance)
- Structurally weird hind quarters (ignoring)
- Violent car sickness

When we realized the extent of Roda's challenges, we enlisted the help of professional behavior consultant Jolanta Benal, because we knew we could not keep Roda much longer if it didn't get easier to live with her. The major things Jolanta taught us to do were:

- Tons of physical and mental exercise—long runs and walks, obedience class, fetch, tug, clicker training. This has been huge.
- Tether training—for management, and time outs for egregiously bad behavior, like mouthing. Also huge.
- Structure and routine.
- Working for food—freezing meals in Kongs.
- Lots of outlets for positive chewing—marrow bones, bully sticks, frozen Kongs.

Present and future

Eighteen months later, Roda is now 90% a great dog to live with. She still requires a ton of exercise and will still find trouble if she gets bored, but we can now sleep at night, eat meals without too much interruption, watch movies, have friends over, etc. She still destroys the occasional shoe and will get mouthy when she wants to engage us in play, but these things have become pretty manageable. She has a reliable "give" when she does steal a shoe.

We continue to implement management strategies:

- Rigorous exercise: 3-5 mile runs, 6 mile walks on weekends and in summer.
- Dog-proofing: we keep shoes off the ground and keep her out of certain tempting areas of the apartment.
- Keeping socks out of her reach at all times.
- Preempting zoomies with structured games of fetch and tug.
- Continued frozen meals out of Kongs.

If we had known what Roda was like, we would not have adopted her. She definitely ruined four or five months of our life and cost us a lot of money that, being teachers, we didn't have. That said, we are now very happy to have her. I think the one thing that kept us committed to Roda was her temperament. She was hell to live with, but she always fundamentally liked people and other dogs. She never lunged or growled, she was reliably friendly on walks and in crowds. That always seemed like good raw material worth working with. She is funny, sweet, and a great exercise partner. We made it this far—we have every intention of keeping her for the rest of her life.

Kona and Lhotse'

Kona and Lhotse' are both Beagles. Kona was a 30-pound spayed female, who was born in January of 1990, purchased at a pet store (before they new better) at age six weeks by trainer/behavior consultant Laura Dorfman and her partner Alison Oakes. Kona died in 2000. Lhotse' is a five-year-old, 17-pound, spayed female Beagle, still living with Laura and Alison.

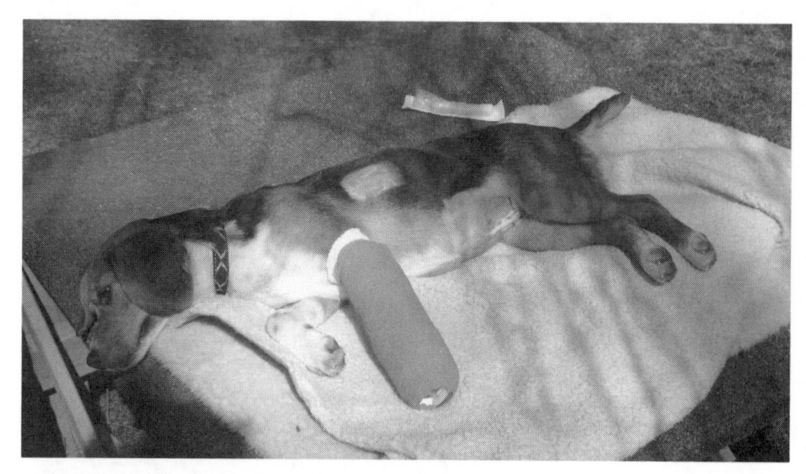

Lhotse'

Kona

In Laura's own words:

Kona was purchased at a pet store and it's likely she was from a puppy mill in Iowa. She was a first sight /first love dog from the moment I saw her in the store. The feeling was "we're finally together again," as if somehow, somewhere, we'd known each other before. I don't think I could have separated from her if I wanted to.

She was the devil dog from hell; she bit us, she ate everything in the house, (books, albums, pictures, clothes, furniture), she growled at visitors, she chased us up the stairs and bit our ankles, she guarded everything furiously (food, places, us), and she scared our other dog when he arrived a year later. We were new dog owners and we thought we had a cute innocent little Beagle. She was only six weeks old, and already difficult.

She came to us with an upper respiratory infection and severe dietary and environmental allergies to food. We treated the allergies all through her life and eventually deleted beef from her diet. Her aggressive behavior changed dramatically for the better as soon as we took her off beef and transitioned her to a natural raw diet. She still seriously resource guarded, but her general "mean streak" diminished.

Lhotse' was found with another Beagle, walking down a path very close to a puppy mill. She was picked up by animal control and taken to the shelter. The night before she was to be euthanized, Beagle Rescue came and took six Beagles, including Lhotse'. She was delivered to my niece, who works with the rescue. She was an exact duplicate of Kona, my heart dog, and when my niece brought her over, I almost fainted. Lhotse' had some relationship difficulties with my niece's dog and then accidentally broke her leg in my backyard. I kept the little Beagle here for rehabilitation and three years later she is still here.

The journey—Kona

We hired a professional and trained the old-fashioned way with Kona. We didn't know any better. It made matters worse immediately. She not only was scared, but now she didn't trust us and we were hurting her. Things just kept getting worse. It was a disaster. Finally, we stopped training her and used management for the rest of her life. We did positive training, just by being nice to her and rewarding her, but we didn't know what we were doing. We just didn't want to hurt her anymore. We had a nice unwritten, unspoken agreement that we would keep her safe and we would love her, and she would try to be calm and gentle with us. As she reached adulthood and we became more dog savvy, her behavior improved greatly and we had a wonderful, full life together.

We managed Kona her whole life and we didn't even know it at the time. We made sure she didn't eat the plumber. She destroyed many things in our house, for a very long time. She had a crate, she loved it, and we didn't have a clue how to use it for management. Despite her challenges, there's no way I would ever have given up this dog. I knew that if we sent her to a shelter, she would have been adopted and returned until she bit someone badly enough that she would have been euthanized.

The journey—Lhotse'

Lhotse' has been perhaps even more challenging than Kona. She jumped up on tables, she screamed like a maniac at all hours, she ran out of doors, she badgered the other dogs in the house, she had to be first always, she was shy and fearless at the same time and she was reactive to everything and anything. She also had minor resource guarding issues from the other dogs, not from humans.

She also came with many health issues in addition to the broken leg. Her health issues are ongoing and have been treated since she first got here. She had a few seizures when she first arrived, and we have been treating them for three years. She has some brain injury issues, either from an injury or poor breeding, or a form of epilepsy. She's smaller than most Beagles, causing concern about genetic anomalies. Her health when she got here was very poor, and she'd been over-vaccinated, then spayed, then broke her leg, all in a few days. She is much better now with everything except her brain. I think her brain issues affect her life every day. They do affect her behavior and they also affect how we treat her. If she doesn't seem right, we manage. If she's alert and all there, we train. We try not to overwhelm her with too intense training sessions.

Present and future

We initiated many management protocols and a gentle, positive training program when Lhotse' first came here. She must be evaluated every day, and sometimes throughout the day, to determine her learning ability that day. In the house, we have "house rules" and she handles them well. We are very consistent with her and it helps with the every day training. We have her sit before eating, she sits for treats, sits at the door before going out, and sometimes we practice more complicated cues if she's up for it. We use "wait" a lot. Sometimes she still disregards the cue, but not very often, and not when it matters for her safety. We make sure she is in her crate when the front door is being used. She still has some issues with screaming/barking at inappropriate times, but we do our best to manage the barking. We're very happy with her progress in these last three years and we are always still working. We will continue training for her lifetime. Her reactivity is much diminished and she is both a challenge and a pleasure to live with.

We will always use management and training hand-in-hand with her. In fact, we use it with all of our dogs. Management is even more critical with her because of her neurological issues, and always will be. I am fine with long term management to keep her safe.

The similarities between these two Beagles are astounding. Kona didn't get the benefits of "official positive training" and she would have loved it and thrived. She had the best "down" I have ever seen, but it came at a huge price. I didn't use it much when I realized what it was doing to her, but in an emergency if I needed her to stop, I could yell "down" and she would drop every time and not move. She was and still is the only Beagle I've ever seen that could be safely off leash. The differences in their training are night and day. I often think if I knew positive training with Kona, our lives would have been entirely different. And if I had used traditional on Lhotse', I believe she would not have survived. As it is, I would adopt her again in a heartbeat. She will be a treasured member of our family for the rest of her life.

Chance

Owned and loved by retired trainer Mardi Richmond and her partner Melanee Barash of Santa Cruz, California, Chance is a three-year-old, 40 pound, spayed female Queensland Heeler mix. Mardi says, "Her name is 'Chance of a Lifetime' because when we were fostering her, a good friend of mine said, 'You can't let this one go… this is a once in a lifetime dog.' And she is."

Chance

In Mardi's own words:

Chance came from the Navajo Nation near the town of Kayenta, Arizona. She was living in the desert near a gas station/rest area where there were 20 to 30 dogs that had to compete for food from the tourists. From the information I was given, her and her sister were paired up and were pretty much inseparable. The two sisters, along with several other dogs from this group, were all picked up and taken into rescue because they were not faring well. We were told she was getting attacked by the older dogs. She was certainly hungry and tick infested. An acquaintance of mine who helps with spay/neuter clinics on the reservation brought the group of dogs back to Santa Cruz.

The two adolescent sisters went into rescue through Harbor Vet Hospital and my friend called and asked if I would come to help work with the dogs and get them ready for adoption. I have to admit, from the moment I met her, I was smitten. When I first went into the yard where they were kenneled, the two dogs hid in the crate inside their run. But very quickly, within a few minutes, they had come out and were climbing all over me, mouthing, jumping, and generally being unruly. Chance was the bolder of the two—very social and affiliative. One of my first tasks was to teach them to wear a collar and leash, because at that point, they would panic, bolt, and buck with a collar just around their necks. But they were incredibly food motivated (as any dog that hasn't had enough to eat would be) and within a few minutes they were comfortable with me wrapping the collar around their necks. In a few short sessions, they could handle a leash and sit on cue.

The journey

Chance's sister got adopted after several weeks in rescue, leaving Chance alone in a kennel run—probably alone for the first time in her life. We didn't want to leave her by herself for the weekend, so I took her home as a foster. For the next month, she came home with me at night, and went back to the hospital in the day in hopes that someone would come to see her and adopt her. During that month, however, I grew more attached, and my two elderly dogs started to accept her into our family. In fact, my older heeler mix seemed to more than accept her; she fell in love with the pup…I knew adopting an adolescent feral dog when I had two 14 year old dogs in failing health was not a good idea—but my heart overrode my good judgment, and we decided to have her live with us.

I want to emphasize that I would not consider her a "broken" dog, by any stretch of the imagination. Even calling her a Do-Over Dog is tricky. I do consider her "differently socialized." Her experience in life was not the same as she would have had if she had lived in a home. But her experiences were very rich. She had to learn to negotiate the world from dealing with other dogs, to finding food, to negotiating roads, people, wild animals, weather—you get the idea. These experiences gave her a whole slew of survival skills and behaviors to draw on. From day one, she truly seems to understand that I would keep her safe and give her food and other rewards. For example, she was an expert at a slightly submissive grovel, though she is not truly submissive at all! I think this is a very different beginning than a lot of dogs who are considered under-socialized.

On the other hand, she was not well socialized to much of what we typically need our dogs to be socialized to.

Because I was working with her first in rescue, and later fostering her before adoption, I was aware of some of the behavior challenges when I adopted her—but certainly not all of them. There were a few surprises along the way.

In the beginning: She didn't know much of anything about living with people—from walking on a leash (and I don't mean not pulling, I mean not panicking), to walking through doorways, down stairs, negotiating small rooms in houses, to riding in cars, to being touched, and restrained. The biggest challenge was her lack of experience and socialization to people and our city life. Yet her overall make-up is a rather confident dog—so she showed various levels of concern, fear, and suspicion, but generally she got past her fears quickly and showed a great deal of flexibility. Much of the fear-type behavior she showed was not unusual for adolescent dogs—spooking at things they don't know, etc.—except that she pretty much didn't know anything about our life—so everything was potentially scary. It was really the sheer volume of things that she didn't know about that made this a challenge. Unfamiliar things included:

- Strangers of any sort—adults, children, etc. In particular, she would spook at strangers who came into her space too quickly. This manifested in a variety of behaviors on her part, from hyper-greetings, to urinating, to bolting and hiding, to occasionally barking.
- People (even familiar people) doing various things, from biking to gardening to playing soccer to climbing ladders.
- Any new place.
- Big spaces like parks, the beach, and parking lots.
- Cars and car rides (she threw up on every car ride for about a year, despite careful and slow conditioning).
- Objects like garbage cans, piles of soccer balls at the park, etc.
- Plus all the typical adolescent things like hats, sunglasses, strollers, backpacks, etc.

Other challenges included:

- Strange dogs. While she has overall good social skills with dogs, she was not comfortable with meeting strange dogs everywhere, all the time, as we do in our neighborhood.
- She was very independent and would make her own decisions (a mixed blessing…).
- Extreme mouthing. In social arousal—with people or dogs—she became uncontrollably mouthy. She has a soft mouth and never left a mark or bruise, but she would constantly put her mouth on people and the more excited she was, the more uncontrollable she became.
- Extreme excitability with social contact from people or new dogs (she is otherwise a fairly calm and even dog).
- She ate everything—and I do mean everything she could get to—for example all toys, beds, blankets, dirt, plants and fruit from the garden, foxtails, anything on the sidewalk, anything left on any surface in the house—chewed and swallowed. So extreme that management was nearly impossible.
- She had a very hard time with space issues—like when people (including us) would step into her space. She would react as if we were seriously threatening her—sometimes by running away and hiding, sometimes by rolling over and urinating, occasionally by barking.
- When we first walked her, as long as we had another dog along, she could walk down the street on the sidewalk, but if we took her out without another dog, she would often freeze or try to bolt for home.

She does have a few other behavior challenges that we do not consider part of her early experiences. For example, she has very strong predatory behaviors and is pretty bossy, both of which are typical of her breed type and personality. When we first started working with her, she was hungry and covered in ticks. She was treated for tick disease (Ehrlichia) because her sister was very sick from it, but Chance did not have overt symptoms. She was very weak at first. She would get tired very, very fast and it took a year or more for her stamina to build up.

We started working with her by simply creating a consistent and safe place. We tried to give her a safe routine and set up positive experiences. For example, since she was overwhelmed going out on walks, we kept them very short and easy, taking the same routes and incorporating treats and easy training exercises that she enjoyed. We would exercise her at home and we would have other young dogs that she became friends with come over for play dates while she was learning to walk in the world.

We took everything very, very slowly and let her set the pace for getting to know new places, people, and things. For example, at our local park, we stood on the edge quite a few times and let her just look before she was ready to walk through on the grass. We discovered that if we rushed her or pushed her, it would backfire and something or someone that she might have needed a few minutes or a couple of meetings to get to know, would become a big, bad, scary thing that took weeks or months to get over.

She would take her cues from other dogs a lot, so we would use our other dogs and her doggy friends to help her learn about the world. The first time we took her to the beach, for example, she froze, and then became very agitated. So when we tried it the next time, we took our Border Collie and some balls with us. She saw our BC having a blast, and within a few short minutes, she'd loosened up and decided it was a great place to be. For about the first year, when we would take her somewhere new, we would try to do so with a dog she knew. We went to training classes with a friend, on hikes and walks with friends, etc.

We also did traditional classical conditioning, pairing great food with anything that was scary. We still do that all the time, always carrying treats on walks and adventures.

We focused our training on building confidence and reinforcing calm focused behaviors. At first, we kept it to just a few simple behaviors that she could get really, really good at—sit, down, eye contact, and stay. These became so ingrained that they are what she would do when she didn't know what else to do or when she was overwhelmed. As part of this, we used the Dr. Karen Overall relaxation protocol. It really seemed to be a good fit for her needs.

We also spent a lot of our training time learning to play together. Because she was nervous about us stepping into her space and she didn't know how to retrieve or tug with people, I spent several months gently working on play with people. She now loves to play with us!

We did clicker training and trick training, but really it took a long time, over a year, I'd guess, before she started enjoying training and offering behaviors. She was very reserved in training, and tried to figure out what we wanted before she did it, rather than experimenting. And still, she has a hard time learning a new behavior away from home; she can "work" easily away from home now, but it is still hard for her to "learn" although we are seeing some glimmers of change in this now.

I did some things that some people might see as sort of backwards with her. One thing, for example, was I started leash work with her by teaching her to pull and counter conditioning her to like the restraint. I did this before I taught her to walk on a loose leash. I thought that at some point, she would get spooked when on leash and that if she suddenly hit the end of the leash, it could make her concern worse. It paid off the first time a dog barked and scared her on a walk, she jumped and started to run, but when she hit the end of the leash, she just turned back to me for a treat. Of course this did make teaching loose leash walking a little harder…

I also sought help from other trainers. I had a trainer who worked with aggressive dogs do some "pushing" with her to make sure she was going to be safe with strangers. She showed so many warning signals when she was afraid that I could not judge on my own how much to push her. I also got help from a T-Touch practitioner. She was so squirmy and over-stimulated with touch of any kind that we needed more ideas on how to help her get used to it. I took her, and continue to take her, to group training classes and practice groups so that we could expose her to new people, places, and things in a controlled manner.

Present and future

Our efforts have been very successful. She now enjoys walks, going on vacation with us, going to stores and other places. She is nervous in some new places, but is overall well-behaved and is getting more and more confident all the time. She recently passed her CGC test. The handling exercises and leaving her with a stranger were the hardest for her to do and we worked for about six months specifically on these before she was ready.

She is almost always calm around new people now, sometimes enjoys meeting and greeting, sometimes choosing not to, but she seldom spooks. She is comfortable being handled by a variety of people now, even some strangers. She is still uncertain about children touching her, but she can walk through parks and playing kids without getting stressed.

She is still nervous about strangers coming to the house, and we will continue to work on that. And she is still nervous about meeting new dogs. She is not reactive, just aroused and untrusting.

She has almost completely stopped chewing and eating things besides her meals and appropriate bones and toys. In fact, she doesn't even eat the fruit in the garden anymore, preferring her kibble and other food from the refrigerator.

Her mouthing is 99 percent better with us and about 50 percent better with other people. This is one area that we have not been as successful as we would like. We will continue to work on it.

We are comfortable with long-term management of some of her behaviors if needed—and we may always need some with strangers in our home. Some of the things we still do are to go for a walk with a new person before they come into to the house, or if we are having someone come to work on the house we will simply take her away or put her in her crate.

We do use management for her mouthing by asking her to hold a toy when she is interacting with people. We would like to be able to fade the toy out over time, but so far have not been able to keep her from mouthing when she becomes very excited socially—which happens very easily.

We do have to introduce her slowly to any new people or dogs if we want her to accept and become comfortable with them. But as long as we take it slowly, she has not yet met someone she didn't like. The few times we rushed her, she went over threshold and we could not backtrack—it became a problem to be undone.

Chance is the first dog I have lived with that I'm pretty sure did not imprint on people as a puppy. She is not like a wild animal at all—she is most certainly a domestic dog. But she is not quite like any other domestic dog I have lived with or known before, either.

We had to spend a lot of time earning her trust, and I don't think it totally clicked until she'd been with us for close to 18 months. But when it did click in—there was a dramatic change in how she was at home and in the world.

I think her close and intense relationship with her sister early on really helped her. I think it taught her to form close relationships and gave her that inclination. Her connection and trust of other dogs really served her as she transitioned to living with people. If another dog was okay with a person, she was much more likely to be okay with them too.

For a long while, I wasn't sure she would ever be really happy—she seemed content, but always serious and pensive. But today, she is playful, socially engaged, and spends much of her time in happy, joyous clowning. She smiles a lot! And that is why I consider her transition from un-owned desert pup to city dog to be a success.

I probably would have adopted her, even knowing all of the challenges. She snuck in and grabbed my heart; my brain did not make the decision. We would absolutely not give her up for anything.

Bella Roo

Roo is a three-year-old spayed female Doberman, approximately 70 pounds. MJ and Dale Williams of Hagerstown, Maryland, adopted her from Doberman Rescue when she was six months old. Roo's first owners dumped her at a shelter in Colonial Heights, Virginia, claiming she was "too dumb to housetrain."

In MJ's own words:

We had been working with (Doberman Rescue) DAR&E for several months. We wanted a young female, and because we had six cats we thought it would be best for all if our new addition was young. I was interested in one young girl, but her write-up said "no small children," and our 18-month-old grandson spends a considerable amount of time with us.

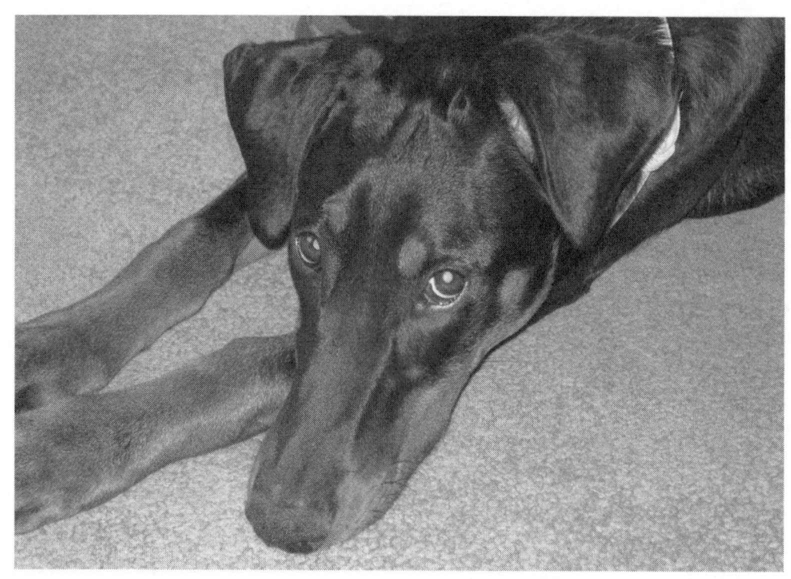

Bella Roo

A few weeks later I got a call from Roo's foster home, asking if I'd be interested in the same dog. I explained the child problem, and she said she had included that caution because she didn't *know* if Roo would be good with kids. She had since had the dog interact with her own two-year-old son, and Roo was fine with him.

I fell in love with our little Dobiegirl from the moment I saw her picture. She stole my heart. I decided we would take her even though we hadn't met her yet. It might have been an emotional decision, but I knew we could make it work.

The journey

Roo had not been socialized as a young pup. She had been abused both emotionally and physically at a very young age. We knew her previous owners had mistreated her—probably something to do with her housetraining. We were aware that she was frightened and shy when we brought her home.

When we went to see her at her foster home, we found a beautiful girl with sparkling eyes, and a shiny, healthy coat. A few short weeks in foster care had done wonders for her. She was even starting to learn that not all humans were cruel.

She made up to us very slowly. This was new for me—our other Dobermans had always been affectionate and never let us out of their sight. This pup was curious but hesitant and I could see fear in her eyes. I knew we would have a lot of work to do.

One of the conditions of adoption with DAR&E is that you enroll your newly adopted dog in a training class within one month of adoption. We signed her up for the Good Manners class at Peaceable Paws. We weren't expecting her to be petrified the first night of class! She was afraid to enter the building and not the least bit interested in a treat to motivate her. We continued for over a year in classes, even repeating classes to enhance socialization. We knew we were working with positive professionals who understood our dog's inability to trust, and have had continued contact with them as necessary since that time.

We continue to manage Roo's shyness and fear, realizing she will never be a "social butterfly." We adopted another female Doberman so Roo would have a sister to share her life with and they are good friends. Her sister, Jaden, is a year younger, pretty much bomb-proof and has "never met a stranger," so she's a good role model for Roo.

The future

Knowing what we now know about Roo, we still would have adopted her. She is loyal, at ease, and loving in her own home. We continue to include her in as many activities as we think she can handle. We will not expose her or force her into any situation that we think will trigger fear and we realize this is just who she is. Are we okay with it? Of course we are. We would never consider doing anything but trying to give her the best, happiest life possible.

Manray

Manray is a large mixed breed, probably some kind of Lab/Pointer mix, although at the time of his adoption Nancy Fitzgerald was told he was Chocolate Lab and Vizsla. He was neutered by the shelter prior to adoption and weighs about 70 lbs.

Manray

In Nancy's own words:

The story we were given was kind of convoluted. Apparently this dog wound up in the care of a local rescue group for reasons unknown. He was placed in a foster home, where he promptly proceeded to get into trouble. He reportedly pinned the foster mother against the wall with her arm in his mouth, growling, in the middle of the night. She panicked and called animal control to have the animal removed from her home. Manray (then called Hershey) wound up at the local SPCA, where he would have likely been euthanized. The director of the local humane association had previously worked for the rescue organization that had placed him in foster care and she insisted that the humane association staff immediately retrieve the dog from the SPCA. The humane association trainer, of course, had concerns about Manray suitability for rehabilitation and rehoming, appropriate ones given the reports of aggressive behavior, but she had her orders.

So the dog came to Delaware Humane, where I was working part-time. I was handed his leash in the parking lot and told he was "my project." He seemed nice enough at first, but one by one we all got a taste of what the foster mother had reported. When he didn't want to cooperate with something, even something innocuous such as putting on a new collar or coming in from a field, he would turn into an obnoxious, pushy dog who thought nothing of tossing his weight around, knocking or pinning people down, or mouthing them, hard. If you tried to get him off of you, he would respond with a more aggressive display, but it was almost as if he was laughing—he seemed to enjoy being a bully.

I adopted him in July of 2002 after working with him at the shelter for about eight months. He knew a lot of "stuff" (in terms of basic manners) for a shelter dog by then, but he was only good for me. If you took him out to show to a potential adopter, sooner or later he would revert to his bully mode and terrorize them. I took him because no one else was going to—plus I had gotten attached to him by then. There were a lot of personnel changes going on at the shelter at the time, and I wasn't sure how much longer I would be able to work there. Thinking that I might have to leave my job at the shelter in a hurry, and knowing that I couldn't leave Manray behind, I started introducing him to my two dogs at home, and finally adopted him about a month later, after multiple dog meetings and home visits.

The journey

Manray came to me with a number of issues:

- He had significant handling and restraint issues. No vet had been able to successfully examine him without him either being first muzzled or being sedated heavily. Even muzzled he would fight the technicians when they tried to restrain him. Ordinary things like ear cleaning were problematic; forget clipping his toenails! You couldn't take his collar to lead him somewhere without being met with resistance, sometimes in the form of a warning growl, other times avoidance and attempts to bite.
- He would guard resources, even lower value items, with growling, snarling and moving away with the item. Higher value items were worth biting humans to hold onto, especially dangerous items like chicken bones picked up off of the city sidewalks.
- He seemed to dislike most dogs he saw in the neighborhood, and would launch into a lunging, barking display when he would see them. That was bad enough, but when prevented from being able to get at the other dog, he would whirl and redirect a bite to his handler, up high, usually upwards towards the face. Most of the time he would get my forearm as I tried to protect my face with my arm.
- He was completely inappropriate in play with people, mouthing them, hard, whenever he got excited or aroused.
- There was some initial separation distress, largely in the form of vocalization, but this dissipated fairly quickly after the first month or so.

- Manray is always the opportunist—so he would counter-surf if we weren't attentive, steal your dinner from your plate if you weren't paying attention, and raid the garbage—until we bought a Manray-proof trash can.
- He darted out the door and ran away three times before we added a slide bolt to the screen door to stop him if he made it to the front porch and taught him a rock-solid "wait" that we would cue when we were leaving. He's wickedly smart—which was probably his biggest problem in the first place!

We never found any medical issues we felt might have contributed to his behavior. He just was who he was. The handling and husbandry issues improved as Manray grew to trust me more and more over the years. For awhile, we had an agreement with regard to his toenails—he would let me trim the front ones, and he would take care of the back ones. He would, literally, chew on his back nails when they got too long. We had that arrangement for years. More recently we've actually done some counter-conditioning with regard to handling his back feet, and I can usually trim all of his nails now without an aggressive response. He likes human handling now, and will often solicit petting from people once he's been introduced.

Present and future

Manray is the dog who turned me into a trainer, trying to learn how to handle his multitude of problems. We traded for lower value resource items, working up to easily giving up stuffed Kongs. We still manage behavior with regard to extremely high value items—he is not as quick to bite as before, you are much more likely to get long growls and snarls, but the meaning is clear, and you are risking a bite if you insist. He won't trade for treats when he's found items like discarded bones on the sidewalk. But these incidents are rare now, and we manage by trying to keep an eye out so that we see temptation before he does. We pick our battles if we fail to spot the item in time.

We still use a Gentle Leader head halter on walks, which we originally introduced to help with the lunging and redirected biting. I'm not sure he really needs it now, but we are both comfortable with it and so haven't really had a compelling reason to change equipment.

He's one of my best dogs now with regard to other dogs, ignoring most dogs he sees in the neighborhood. He's one of the first dogs I introduce to anyone new that might be joining our pack, as he rarely initiates a problem. In fact, he is often the dog that everyone else picks on (mounts or harasses). I always thought it was interesting that the dog that was the pushiest with the humans turned out to be the most submissive with regard to other dogs!

He's wonderful in the house now. He's had maybe two accidents in the entire time we've had him. He tries to counter-surf sometimes, but gets off right away when you ask. He's very responsive to positive reinforcement training, and reliable on almost everything I first taught him when we were training together seven years ago at the shelter. Because we did a "no free lunch" type program with him, he is extremely polite, always sitting or laying down, waiting patiently for just about everything. Most of the time he just lays around the house—pretty low maintenance!

We continue to use the Gentle Leader when out of the house, more out of convenience than necessity. Our vet can examine him now without a muzzle for most of the visit—we only need to muzzle him to draw blood, but the technicians can get the muzzle on him now. I still usually put him away initially when new people come into the house, but he can often come out pretty soon after without much of a problem. I expect we will always manage him in some way, as he can be problematic every now and then, but it is so much less often.

Because I had worked with him for so long at the shelter before adopting him, I had a pretty good idea what I was getting into with Manray. I did probably expect him to bite me less than he did in the beginning, but I would have taken him anyway, even if I had known, because by then I loved him.

He has found his forever home with us. I'd never give him up now—he's finally good!

Daisy

Do-Over Dogs can come in all sizes. Our final happy ending is a three-year-old spayed female Yorkshire Terrier, a mere ten pounds. Originally a breeder-dog at a puppy mill, Daisy moved into Sybil Schiffman's Hagerstown, Maryland home with her fair share of Do-Over problems.

Daisy

In Sybil's own words:

Daisy was a brood bitch at a puppy mill where the average number of dogs was 300 at any one time. She was turned in to a rescue shelter at age two by the owner. She was fostered by the shelter's owner in her own home for about three months, where she was with children and other dogs her size. The shelter is in Missouri, but is affiliated with one in West Virginia. About a year prior to adopting Daisy I had decided that I wanted to adopt an adult small dog. I spent months researching shelters on the internet and interviewing people who had adopted dogs. I learned a lot about puppy mill dogs and their potential problems. I saw several dogs online and submitted my application.

This particular shelter had called and we spent quite a long time on the phone interviewing each other before talking about the three possible dogs they had. I had my criteria and they were very up front about theirs, which I appreciated. I placed my deposit. Afterwards there were several more conversations and I felt that my questions were adequately answered. I have now had Daisy for a little over six months and she is a wonderful companion.

I learned that her feet had never touched the ground until she came to the shelter and that she had been fed and watered with automatic feeders and waterers. She also had three or four litters before she came to me; her teats were hanging low. I can conjecture why she was turned in to the shelter. She has tested positive for brucella which means that she probably aborted her last litter and was not useful for breeding any more.

The journey

Daisy conquered her first big fear a day our two after she came to live with me. She laid down near my feet and I knew she was here to stay. Keeping Daisy safe from her own fears and anxieties has been a challenge.

- At first she was afraid of everything; sounds, especially loud ones; cars when we took a walk; people, including me; she ran around confused when she was scared, sometimes hitting her head on the wall or on a chair.
- Although Daisy now knows to pee and poop outside, she does not know how to tell me that she needs to go outside, so keeping up with training can be frustrating. Daisy is schedule trained, but in between she will often wet the carpet. Using a lot of paper towels and catching her if she seems to want to go out helps.
- When Daisy found her voice after having been here for two months, she used it all time. Teaching her to use it appropriately is an ongoing challenge. We'll think we have it for a while and then she reverts back and we start again.
- Daisy came with no habits—no good ones and no bad ones, but eager to learn. Teaching her takes a great deal of patience and consistency.
- Daisy doesn't trust people. She would bolt and panic when anyone would make an overture to her, including myself. If on the leash, she would run to the end of the leash and fly into the air. I do not use a collar on her for fear she will hurt herself. I always use a harness.

Daisy came with a number of medical issues which didn't make it any easier to transition to life in the real world. She had some skin problems that good professional grooming and a healthy diet cleared up. Her teeth were in really bad shape. She had her teeth cleaned and five of them had to be pulled. The major problem that she had was an eye issue (anterior uveitis) which we thought may have come from a blow to the head. Blood testing was done to rule out several infections, then a couple of months after it was cleared up it recurred. I took her to an ophthalmologist about 60 miles away and we treated it aggressively. We tested her for more things and found that she tested positive for brucella canis, a sexually transmitted disease, a symptom of which can be uveitis. We now have to take certain precautions which preclude interactions with other dogs, especially dogs who might be used for breeding.

Present and future

Daisy has come such a long way. She is bonded to me now. She's still a bit fearful of people, but she doesn't panic anymore. Sometimes she still barks at the dust in the air. She's learning to play—she completely missed her puppyhood. Not too long ago we had a major play breakthrough: she initiated an interaction with me one morning when she touched my knee and I patted her head. Then she did it again and again.

She was playing! We play her game every day now. She hunkers down and runs and runs when I tease her and she squeaks as if she laughing. She's also learning to play with her stuffed elephant—I hide chicken under it and she finds it, then I hide the chicken and the elephant.

I've learned that Daisy needs a safe place to call her own. I made a "room" for her near my kitchen with a bed, her water and food. It has a gate. When I'm home, she has the run of the house. When I am not home she's gated in her room. At night she sleeps in her closed crate in my bedroom. The rest of the time, Daisy can come and go as she wishes.

At first, she always was leashed until she learned not to run from me. For the first couple of months I literally held her leash all the time, then she dragged the leash and I could step on it. Now she's learned several cues and doesn't need the leash indoors any more. She has learned "Go to your room", "Let's go for a walk", "Dinner", "Come", "Treat", "Daisy", and "Thank you for telling me" (when she barks at the door or door bell).

Daisy and I work with Pat Miller at Peaceable Paws. Pat has helped me understand these wonderful dogs. Perhaps the one most powerful thing I've learned is that in the past, Daisy's world always controlled her. Now she is learning to have some control in her world.

We have a long way to go. My dream for Daisy is that some day she'll become a therapy dog. Meanwhile, management is all the time. I think Daisy has made the progress she has *because* everyone who is with her has been consistent, including my grand-children and the pet sitter who comes once a week. We may be able to progress with some things faster than others, but if something gets frustrating to either of us we slow down and work at a pace that works for us.

- I never raise my voice to Daisy.
- I am consistent.
- She has her safe place.
- She knows the schedule and yet has some flexibility.

I went into this having done my homework. Daisy's temperament was as it had been described to me, so my eyes were wide open. I had turned down a couple of puppy mill dogs because I knew from their descriptions they would probably never fit my lifestyle, nor would I have had the patience to give them what they needed.

This is a wonderful and exciting journey. People have often asked me why I chose this breed. My answer is that I did not choose the breed, I chose the dog. Daisy has given me a wonderful gift and a wonderful opportunity to be part of her growth. There is a puppy inside her, and we're finding it. After her bath, she runs and rolls and we take that opportunity to play. When she finally wagged her tail for the first time it was a great breakthrough. And when I come in the back door and yell "Hey, Squeaky" and she jumps up and down and squeaks and squeaks, so happy to see me, I know we're together for the long haul. What a great journey this is!

For every dog, a home

Scooter, our Pomeranian you met in the first chapter is, of course, doing just fine. His coat has grown out, he's gained confidence in the year he's been with us, and we've modified some behaviors while managing others. Like all of the dogs we adopt, he will be with us for the rest of his life.

Fluffy and happy, Scooter has found his forever home.

I am constantly amazed and inspired by the example set by dog owners like Barb, Jessica, Laura, Mardi, MJ, Nancy, and Sybil. These compassionate humans—and others like them, take on dogs they know will be challenges, or discover challenges after-the-fact and, undaunted, fulfill the commitment they made to their dogs when they welcomed them into their lives, their homes and their hearts. Their dogs have found their forever homes.

What's even more inspiring is the willingness of true dog lovers like these, who, as they strive to help their Do-Over Dogs be as happy and well-adjusted as possible, also accept their dogs for who they are. Like a good marriage, the best dog owners enter into a relationship with some expectations about their new canine partners and if the journey of discovery reveals a different path, adjust accordingly and still fulfill the social contract they made to love them "until death do us part". These are the humans who know how to love their dogs enough. Every dog should be blessed with at least one, for the rest of his life.

Appendix 1
TREATS

Be creative with your dog's treats. While there are many good, high-value commercially produced treats, you can also make your own and/or use "human food" for treats. With a few exceptions (grapes/raisins, onions, chocolate), food that's healthier for us is healthier for our dogs. Food that's less healthy may still be high value, and you may choose to use them—just use them more sparingly. Remember to use small, pea-size pieces for treats to avoid overfeeding.

Commercially produced

- Bellyrubs Dog Treats: meyercountryfarms.com
- Carnivore Crunch: stellaandchewys.com
- Etta Says! Meaty Treats: ettasays.com
- Wet Noses Little Stars Training Treats: wet-noses.com
- Liv-A-Littles: halopets.com
- Liver Biscotti: premier.com
- Natural Balance Dog Food Rolls: naturalbalanceinc.com
- Nothing But Natural: evangersdogfood.com
- Nothing But…Treats: aplaceforpaws.com
- Primal Dry Roasted Treats: primalpetfoods.com
- Pet Botanics Training Reward Rolls: cardinalpet.com/pet_botanics.html
- Real Meat Treats: petfooddirect.com
- Wellness Pure Rewards and Wellbites: wellpet.com
- Zukes: zukes.com

"People" food

- Cheerios
- Popcorn
- Rice cakes
- Baby carrots
- Hot dogs
- Cheese cubes
- Cheese tortellini
- Vienna Sausage
- Liverwurst
- Baby food
- Frozen Italian meatballs (thawed in microwave)
- Canned chicken, rinsed and drained
- Boiled chicken
- Roast beef

Appendix 2

Tools and Techniques for Breaking Up a Fight

I hope you will never need these! Still, if you plan to do any dog-dog introductions, it doesn't hurt to have some of them on hand. Please note—these work because they are aversive, and are only to be used in a crisis. I am not *in any way* recommending them as regular training tools or methods.

Hands-off intervention

- Blasting dogs with water from a nearby hose may work—assuming a hose happens to be nearby with a powerful enough spray. A good tool to keep in your arsenal for the right time and place—not particularly useful, however, when there's no hose handy!
- One of the easily portable aversive sprays, such as Spray Shield (citronella) or Halt! (pepper spray) might be an effective alternative to the hose. Of the two, Spray Shield, available from Premier (premier.com), is the safer choice, since pepper spray products are more corrosive and the spray can drift and affect innocent bystanders—humans as well as dogs. There are laws in some jurisdictions requiring that users of pepper spray products complete a training course and carry a permit.
- In a pinch, even a fire extinguisher might just happen to be a handy and effective aversive tool.
- Some doggie daycare providers swear by air horns. Available at boating supply stores, air horns can be effective at warding off attacking dogs, but your own dog has to be desensitized to the cacophony, or you are likely to lose him as well. You also risk damage to eardrums, both canine and human, and take a chance of frightening your own dog beyond repair.

Physical intervention with objects

- Attach a couple of handles to a sheet of plywood so you can lower it between two sparring dogs.

- Dogfighters—and some Pit Bull owners who don't fight their dogs but know the breed's potential—always carry a "parting stick" or "breaking stick" with them. This is usually a carved hammer handle, tapered to a rounded point at one end. When two dogs are locked in combat, the parting stick can be forced between a dog's teeth and turned sideways to pry open the jaws. Parting sticks can break a dog's teeth, and a dog whose jaws have just been "parted" may turn on the person doing the parting. Like many other techniques offered here, this method should only be considered for dire emergencies. Breaking sticks can be found online at: pbrc.net/shop/bsticks.html.
- A blanket can also be useful. Tossed over the fighters, one over each, blankets muffle outside stimuli, reducing arousal. This also allows the humans to physically separate the combatants by picking up the wrapped pooches with less risk of a serious bite—the blanket will cushion the effect of teeth on skin if the dog does whirl and bite.
- When a dog's life and limb are at stake, extreme measures may be called for. You can wrap a leash round the aggressor's neck or get hold of a collar and twist to cut off the dog's airflow, until he lets go to try to get a breath of air, then pull the dogs apart. This could be more difficult than it sounds. It might be difficult to get a leash around the neck of a dog who is "attached" by the mouth to another dog without getting your hands in harm's way; grabbing a collar to twist also puts hands in close proximity to teeth.

Physical intervention by humans

- One method I heard about recently is a rather drastic technique observed at a dog show 20 years ago. Two dogs got into it and were going to cause major damage. The elderly judge was a tiny woman and she had the handlers both grab their dogs and hold on *tight.* Then she went up and took the dog on top by the tail and jammed her thumb up his rectum. He let go in an instant and whirled around to see what was happening. The judge excused the two dogs, calmly washed her hands, and continued her classes without a hitch—just as if it happened every day.
- Another approach could be difficult if the aggressor is a 150-pound St. Bernard, but may be worth trying with a smaller dog in a one-on-one fight. It is not recommended for a multi-dog brawl. Lift the rear of the clearly identified aggressor so that he is suspended with his forefeet barely touching the ground. The dog lets go and the target can scoot free. Supposedly, in this position the dog is not able to turn on the human suspending him, although I'm not giving any guarantees.

Armed and ready

Now, all you need to do is stuff a canister of Spray Shield in your pocket, attach a parting stick to your belt, carry a blanket over your arm, balance a sheet of plywood on your head, wear an air horn around your neck, be sure you have at least two friends with you to hold dogs while you put your thumb in private places, and you're ready for anything.

Seriously, if and when that fight happens, take a deep breath, resist your instincts to yell or leap in the middle of the fray, quickly review your available options, and choose the one—or ones—that are most likely to work in that place and time. When the fight is over and no one is being rushed to the hospital in an ambulance, remember to take a moment to relax and breathe, and then congratulate yourself for your quick thinking.

Appendix 3

Secondary Reinforcers

Secondary reinforcers: things that take on value for your dog through association with a primary reinforcer. Secondary reinforcers are valuable in your training and behavior modification program because they allow you to reinforce your dog without always having to use food. Although there is nothing wrong with using food, it's nice to have options. This is by no means a complete list, nor are the things listed here necessarily reinforcing for all dogs. Think of the things your dog loves! Make your own list of secondary reinforcers—and add to the list as you create new reinforcers by associating new things with good stuff for your dog.

- Ball
- Frisbee
- Tug toy
- Kong
- Stick
- Training games
- Going for a walk
- Riding in the car
- Scratch under the chin
- Tummy rub
- Verbal praise
- Go sniff
- Go swim
- Get out of the car
- Return to play with another dog
- Go greet a person

- Go fetch a toy
- Play tug
- Go play in the grass
- Move forward
- Exit the house
- Come up on the sofa
- Jump up on the bed

Appendix 4

A Dozen Tricks to Teach Your Do-Over Dog

There's a bunch of tricks here—don't try to teach them all at once! Start with the ones your Do-Over Dog is most likely to love and learn easily; save the harder ones for down the road, when the two of you know each other better. For more challenging fun try *shaping* some of these behaviors instead of luring or targeting.

1. **Take a Bow**. While your dog is standing, lure (or target) his front end down while he keeps his hind end raised.
2. **Roll Over**. Have your dog lie down, then use a lure or target to encourage her to roll on her back, then over. (Move the food slowly so she can follow it.)
3. **Crawl**. Have your dog lie down, then move the lure or target forward slowly, close to the ground, to get him to follow it without getting up.
4. **Weave**. Hold the lure or target between your legs and move it away from your dog to get her to walk back-and-forth between your legs as you walk.
5. **"Bang!" (Play Dead)**. Point your index finger at your dog with your thumb "cocked," say "Bang!" and lure him to his side.
6. **Jump Over (or through) My Arm(s)**. Kneel facing a wall, 2 feet away, with your dog on your left side. Touch the fingers of your left hand to the wall, arm low. Use the lure or target in your right hand to encourage her to jump over your arm. With the dog on your right side, switch arms and do it again, the opposite direction.
7. **Spin/Twirl**. Move the lure or target in a slow circle at your dog's nose level, so he can follow. Use different words for left and right hand circles.
8. **Side Pass**. With the dog standing in front of you, use a lure or target to keep her nose centered in front of you and slowly step sideways.
9. **Sit Nice (beg)**. Hold the lure or target just above your dog's head to get him to raise his front paws off the ground. If he jumps up, you are probably holding it too high. Reward small attempts to lift front paws off the ground.

10. **Dance**. Hold the lure or target the height of your dog's body length off the ground. When the dog stands on her hind legs, move the lure/target as if asking for a spin.
11. **Walk (on hind legs)**. Hold the lure/target the height of your dog's body length off the ground. When he stands, step backwards and encourage him to follow you.
12. **Shake (Give Paw, "High Five")**. Close a food lure in your fist and hold it in front of your dog's nose. If she gets frustrated and paws at it to get it, say "Yes!" and reward. If not, hold the treat over her nose slightly off to one side and mark and reward for small paw lifts at first, gradually for higher ones. Use a different cue for each foot.

RESOURCES

Books and DVDs

Am I Safe? DVD, by Sarah Kalnajs, 2006, Blue Dog Training and Behavior.

The Bark Stops Here, Terry Ryan, 2000, Legacy Canine & Behavior.

Basic Good Manners; A Seven-Week Course DVD, Pat Miller, 2009, Peaceable Paws.

Bonding With Your Dog, Victoria Schade, 2009, Howell Books.

Canine Body Language, Brenda Aloff, 2005, distributed by Dogwise Publishing.

Cautious Canine, 2nd Edition, Patricia McConnell, 2005, McConnell Publishing Limited.

Circles of Compassion, edited by Elaine Sichel, 1995, Voice and Vision Publishing.

Clinical Behavioral Medicine for Small Animals, Karen Overall, 1997, Mosby.

The Culture Clash, Jean Donaldson, 2005, James & Kenneth Publishing.

Dogs Are From Neptune, 2nd Edition, Jean Donaldson, 2009, Dogwise Publishing.

Dogs Being Dogs; Digging Barking and Chewing, Pat Miller, 2001, Peaceable Paws.

Don't Shoot the Dog, 2nd Edition, Karen Pryor, 1999, Bantam Books.

Dog Language, Roger Abrantes, 1997, distributed by Dogwise Publishing.

Family Friendly Dog Training, Patricia McConnell and Aimee Moore, 2007, McConnell Publishing Limited.

Feisty Fido, Patricia McConnell, 2009, McConnell Publishing Limited (leash reactivity).

Fight! A Practical Guide to Dog-Dog Aggression, Jean Donaldson, 2004, McConnell Publishing Limited.

For the Love of a Dog, Patricia McConnell, 2007, Ballantine Books.

Help For Your Fearful Dog, by Nicole Wilde, 2006, Phantom Publishing.

Help! I'm Barking and I Can't Be Quiet, Suzanne Hetts, 2006, Island Dog Press.

How Dogs Learn, March Burch and Jon Bailey, 1999, Howell Book House.

I'll Be Home Soon!, Patricia McConnell, 2009, McConnell Publishing Limited (separation anxiety).

The Language of Dogs DVD, Sarah Kalnajs, 2006, Blue Dog Training and Behavior.

Living With Kids and Dogs Without Losing Your Mind, Colleen Pelar, 2007, C&R Publishing, LLC.

Management Magic, Leslie Nelson and Gail Pivar, 1997, Tails-U-Win.

Mine! A Guide to Resource Guarding in Dogs, Jean Donaldson, 2002, distributed by Dogwise Publishing.

Oh Behave!, Jean Donaldson, 2008, Dogwise Publishing.

The Other End of the Leash, Patricia McConnell, 2002, Ballantine Books.

Peaceable Paws Good Manners Class Book, Pat Miller, 2008, Peaceable Paws.

Play Together, Stay Together, Patricia McConnell, 2008, McConnell Publishing Limited.

Play With Your Dog, Pat Miller, 2008, Dogwise Publishing.

Positive Perspectives, Pat Miller, 2004, Dogwise Publishing.

Positive Perspectives 2, Pat Miller, 2008, Dogwise Publishing.

The Power of Positive Dog Training, 2nd Edition, Pat Miller, 2008, Howell Book House.

Reaching the Animal Mind, Karen Pryor, 2009, Scribner Book Company.

Reality Bites, Pat Miller, 2001, Peaceable Paws.

Really Reliable Recall DVD, Leslie Nelson, 2004, Healthy Dog Productions.

Rescue Me!, Bardi McLennan, 2007, Kennel Club Books.

Successful Dog Adoption, Sue Sternberg, 2003, Howell Book House.

Tales of Two Species; Essays on Loving and Living With Dogs, Patricia McConnell, 2008, Dogwise Publishing.

The Thinking Dog; Crossover to Clicker Training, Gail Fisher, 2009, Dogwise Publishing.

Way to Go!; How to Housetrain a Dog of Any Age, Patricia McConnell, 2003, McConnell Publishing Limited.

When Pigs Fly; Training Success With Impossible Dogs, Jane Killion, 2007, Dogwise Publishing.

The Whole Dog Journal Handbook of Dog and Puppy Care and Training, edited by Nancy Kerns, 2008, Belvoir.

Internet

Animal abuse and neglect: pet-abuse.com/pages/home.php

Animal abuse and neglect: aspca.org/fight-animal-cruelty

Animal hoarding: tufts.edu/vet/cfa/hoarding

Animal hoarding: animalhoarding.com

American Humane: americanhumane.org

American Society for the Prevention of Cruelty to Animals: aspca.org

American Veterinary Society of Animal Behavior: avsabonline.org

Congenital and heritable disorders in dogs: hsvma.org/pdf/guide-to-congenital-and-heritable-disorders.pdf

Humane Society of the United States: hsus.org

Puppy mills: prisonersofgreed.org

Puppy mills: aspca.org/fight-animal-cruelty/puppy-mills

Puppy mills: unitedagainstpuppymills.org

Puppy mills: missiondog.com

Puppy socialization: avsabonline.org/avsabonline/images/stories/Position_Statements/puppysocialization.pdf

Shelters and rescues: animalshelter.org

Shelters and rescues: petfinder.com

Shelters and rescues: petango.com

Shelters and rescues: akc.org/breeds/rescue.cfm

Sue Sternberg's website: suesternberg.com

American Veterinary Society of Animal Behavior: avsabonline.org/avsabonline/images/stories/Position_Statements/dominance statement.pdf

America Veterinary Society of Animal Behavior: avsabonline.org/avsabonline/images/stories/Position_Statements/dominance statement.pdf

The Dog Trainer/Jolanta Benal: dogtrainer.quickanddirtytips.com

Karen Pryor: clickertraining.com

Animal Behavior Resources Institute: abrionline.org

Dr. Ian Dunbar: dogstardaily.com

Kathy Sdao's website: kathysdao.com

Patricia McConnell: patriciamcconnell.com

Periodicals

Animal Sheltering Magazine—animalsheltering.org/publications

The Whole Dog Journal—whole-dog-journal.com

Programs

"Assess-A-Pet," Sue Sternberg: suesternberg.com/00assess.html

"Safer/Meet Your Match," Dr. Emily Weiss: emilyweiss.com/safer.html

Trainers

Find a trainer/behavior professional; remember to screen carefully—not all members of all these organizations are positive:

- Pat Miller/Peaceable Paws—trainer referral page: peaceablepaws.com/referrals.php
- Certification Council for Professional Dog Trainers: ccpdt.org
- Truly Dog Friendly: trulydogfriendly.com
- Association of Pet Dog Trainers: apdt.com
- International Association of Animal Behavior Consultants: iaabc.org
- American Veterinary Society of Animal Behavior: avsabonline.org
- Animal Behavior Society: animalbehavior.org

About the Author

Pat Miller is internationally known for her leadership in the field of force-free, positive dog training, following a 20-year career in animal protection at the Marin Humane Society in Novato, California. Pat is a certified dog behavior consultant and certified professional dog trainer, past president of APDT (the world's largest professional dog training organization), and operates her own 80-acre training facility in Fairplay, Maryland. She is also training editor for the *Whole Dog Journal;* a popular columnist for *Your Dog* and *Popular Dogs;* and is the author of *Positive Perspectives, Love Your Dog, Train Your Dog; Positive Perspectives 2, Know Your Dog, Train Your Dog; Play With Your Dog* and *The Power of Positive Dog Training.* Pat's five dogs of various breeds and sizes were all either shelter adoptees or found strays. Pat also shares her life and home with her husband Paul, who is the Executive Director of the Humane Society of Washington County, three cats, five horses, a donkey, and a pot bellied pig.

INDEX

C

D

E

F

Q

R

S

Dogwise
Publishing

The Dog Trainer's Resource. The APDT Chronicle of the Dog Collection. Mychelle Blake (*ed*)
The Dog Trainer's Resource 2. The APDT Chronicle of the Dog Collection. Mychelle Blake (*ed*)
The Thinking Dog. Crossover to Clicker Training. Gail Fisher
Therapy Dogs. Training Your Dog To Reach Others. Kathy Diamond Davis
Training Dogs. A Manual (reprint). Konrad Most
Training the Disaster Search Dog. Shirley Hammond
Try Tracking. The Puppy Tracking Primer. Carolyn Krause
Visiting the Dog Park, Having Fun, and Staying Safe. Cheryl S. Smith
When Pigs Fly. Train Your Impossible Dog. Jane Killion
Winning Team. A Guidebook for Junior Showmanship. Gail Haynes
Working Dogs (reprint). Elliot Humphrey & Lucien Warner

HEALTH & ANATOMY, SHOWING
An Eye for a Dog. Illustrated Guide to Judging Purebred Dogs. Robert Cole
Annie On Dogs! Ann Rogers Clark
Another Piece of the Puzzle. Pat Hastings
Canine Cineradiography DVD. Rachel Page Elliott
Canine Massage. A Complete Reference Manual. Jean-Pierre Hourdebaigt
Canine Terminology (reprint). Harold Spira
Breeders Professional Secrets. Ethical Breeding Practices. Sylvia Smart
Dog In Action (reprint). Macdowell Lyon
Dog Show Judging. The Good, the Bad, and the Ugly. Chris Walkowicz
Dogsteps DVD. Rachel Page Elliott
The Healthy Way to Stretch Your Dog. A Physical Theraphy Approach. Sasha Foster and Ashley Foster
The History and Management of the Mastiff. Elizabeth Baxter & Pat Hoffman
Performance Dog Nutrition. Optimize Performance With Nutrition. Jocelynn Jacobs
Positive Training for Show Dogs. Building a Relationship for Success Vicki Ronchette
Puppy Intensive Care. A Breeder's Guide To Care Of Newborn Puppies. Myra Savant Harris
Raw Dog Food. Make It Easy for You and Your Dog. Carina MacDonald
Raw Meaty Bones. Tom Lonsdale
Shock to the System. The Facts About Animal Vaccination... Catherine O'Driscoll
Tricks of the Trade. From Best of Intentions to Best in Show, Rev. Ed. Pat Hastings
Work Wonders. Feed Your Dog Raw Meaty Bones. Tom Lonsdale
Whelping Healthy Puppies, DVD. Sylvia Smart